# Words of Re-enchantment

Anthony Nanson is a member of the storytelling company Fire Springs – with whom he co-produced the ecobardic epics *Arthur's Dream, Robin of the Wildwood*, and *Return to Arcadia* – and the founder of Bath Storytelling Circle. He was educated in natural sciences at Cambridge and creative writing at Bath Spa University, where he now teaches creative writing. He is the author of *Storytelling and Ecology* (2005), *Exotic Excursions* (2008), and *Gloucestershire Folk Tales* (forthcoming in 2012) and co-author of *An Ecobardic Manifesto* (2008). He's been involved in the Tales to Sustain network since its inception and has worked as a storyteller in many different contexts, including WWF's One Planet Leaders programme in Switzerland. He was previously a science teacher in Kenya, manager of a peace studies initiative, and editor of the arts magazine *Artyfact.*

# Words of Re-enchantment

writings on storytelling, myth, and ecological desire

Anthony Nanson

AWEN  Stroud

Published by Awen Publications 2011
78 Daisybank, Bisley Road, Stroud, GL5 1HG, England
www.awenpublications.co.uk

ISBN 978-1-906900-15-1

Cover photograph by Kirsty Hartsiotis

Production by Wordsmith Communication
Printed in England by CPI Antony Rowe

To Kevan, David, Kirsty, and Richard

and in memory of Mary Palmer

# Contents

## Ecobardic

# Foreword

There's no doubt about it. Modern technology is miraculous. With my handheld mobile I speak and send messages to people worldwide; take high-res pics and videos; look at a map or satellite photo that tells me where I am and how to get elsewhere; play music, record sounds, and connect up to the World Wide Web. In hospital, scans peer into my body in alarming detail, tiny probes travel through my tubes to snip and mend and save my life. A plane can pick me up in one place and drop me off almost anywhere on the earth in a matter of hours. These transforming technologies, which have all happened so recently, are truly a source of wonder, though we quickly become used to them. How would we manage now without broadband, email, and holes-in-the-wall? We soon learn to depend on the ingenious inventions designed to make us free. And, despite all our time-saving devices, we have less time and are busier than ever.

There is a bigger cost to all of this. Our insatiable hunger to consume is driving us to devour the earth. Once plentiful 'resources' are becoming scarce. As our rubbish piles up, exhaust fumes from burnt oil fill the atmosphere and warm the world. And as the human population pushes ever outwards, the natural world shrinks. Technology, we're often assured, will solve these problems. One day, this view implies, there'll be an app or update that will help us restrain our desires, limit our consumption, and reduce our carbon footprint. But such thinking ignores the fact that it's science and our capacity to manipulate external reality that led to these troubles in the first place. As Einstein reputedly put it: 'One cannot alter a condition with the same mindset that created it in the first place.' So we need to be looking for something more than technological fixes. We need another mindset, something that changes our internal reality, that touches our hearts and helps us see beauty and meaning in our world.

That's where 'stories and re-enchantment' come in. It may seem quaintly retro to be fascinated by this, yet paradoxically our spiritual salvation may lie here. Since learning to speak we humans have always mediated our experience through story. Stories enchant an otherwise dull existence, adding depth and meaning to our lives. And meaning, some say, is what we seek above wealth, power, knowledge, and even love. Stories passed down over centuries, embellished by the fertile imagination of generations of tellers, expressed timeless truths. Gradually these tales evolved into legend and myth, providing the bedrock of meaning to a culture. Contained within them was guidance on how to live. For example the story of the hero's journey, found in a thousand cultures, gave us courage to respond to the call to adventure and face dangers on the road of trials; prepared us to take heed of helpers and to fall into the depths of ourselves; inspired us to discover a boon and to bring it back to our people. Such stories gave resolve to our hearts, wisdom to our minds, and strength to our arms. Many of these ancient tales still speak to us today, to a human condition that, despite the shifts wrought by technology and postmodernity, is at core unchanged.

Maybe that's one reason why there's been a renewal of interest in storytelling over the last thirty years. And not just in the old tales. People are discovering that listening to a good live storyteller is exhilarating. It's edgy, intimate, and interactive. The audience emerges from the story as from a journey, drenched in image and emotion. It's like theatre but more personal; like cinema but responsive, small-scale, and always different. But despite its impact on audiences the mainstream media have largely ignored this growing interest in storytelling. And although its value has now been discovered by academia and business (usually under the more respectable name of 'narrative'), except in a few magazines not much has been written about the 'storytelling revival'.

*Words of Re-Enchantment* changes that. In this book Anthony Nanson makes visible and validates a dimension of culture that has not, so far, received such thoughtful attention. These essays, written over ten years for various publications, dovetail perfectly together and show Anthony to be an incisive critic and a tireless chronicler of the growing storytelling movement in Britain. He has a rare combination of talents and interests. He's an accomplished writer of fiction and non-fiction, and a teacher of creative writing. But he's also an exemplar of the art of oral storytelling. He has a penchant for traditional tales, which has led him to delve deeply into the significance of mythic themes that have long underpinned our culture. But he's also keen to find and shape new stories, especially ones that speak of humanity's troubled relationship with the Earth and that offer hope for a better future.

The book begins with an enjoyable personal account of a journey exploring the mythic landscapes of Greece and seeking the archetypal vision of Arcadia. The author moves on to a critique of myth in contemporary culture, ranging with ease and insight from *The Lord of the Rings*, *Star Wars*, and James Bond to imaginary worlds, lost islands, dreams of paradise, and the great Arthurian cycle. In the second part Anthony reviews several storytelling performances, then goes on to tackle some of the knotty questions that preoccupy storytellers. What's the difference between amateur and professional? Should storytellers be accredited? What stories do we have the right to tell? Can storytelling catalyse change? His answers are sensitive and illuminating.

In the final part of the book he reaches his most cutting-edge theme: how storytelling can be used to raise environmental awareness and to inspire action on behalf of the planet. He fully acknowledges that there's 'a tension between … making great art and applying art to the purpose of social transformation' but firmly believes we should creatively embrace that paradox. Art is a fundamental part of the fullness of life *and* can serve a sense of responsibility. With his colleagues in Fire Springs he has produced an Ecobardic Manifesto which challenges storytellers (and other artists) not only to value diverse cultural roots and to cultivate 'the appreciation of beauty by means of well-wrought craft', but also to take a stand and offer critical leadership, helping to distinguish between what matters and what doesn't, and to suggest ways of life that will enhance the future well-being of all who share the planet. The manifesto is not a prescriptive programme but a set of provocative principles, inviting artists to 'consider how their work might respond, with integrity, to the needs of our age of ecological crisis'.

A storyteller's choice of story is inevitably affected by the values he or she holds. So a well-chosen story can promote the values of 'sustainability' without ever mentioning the word. But Anthony goes further. He gives examples of what might be considered 'ecobardic tales'. There's the savage Greek story of 'Erysichthon', which shows us the source of our insatiable hunger. And there are the true eco-historical stories he's researched and shaped for telling, such as the immensely sad tales of 'The Passenger Pigeon' and 'The Golden Toad' and the hopeful story of 'Père David's Deer'. He's noticed that there's a new gravity of attention in an audience when they realise the story is about something that really happened, and encourages us to find and make such tales. He shows how we might tell the story of our two-million-year relationship with the Earth with two possible endings: a 'business as usual' dystopia and a positive, visionary emergence. He also describes how a storyteller working with parties in conflict could, 'if thoroughly acquainted with its complexities', be able to 'advance the situation into the future in a positive way' by telling a transformational story. At the very least this would 'seed our imaginative culture with reconciliatory story patterns'.

Anthony Nanson has written a richly wise and provocative book. He encourages us, instead of indulging our biological instincts to populate and consume, to 'sit still in our deep selves and dream good things for humanity' (Ben Okri). His words are threaded through with a passionate faith that well-chosen, well-told stories, spoken directly to the ear of the listener, can lift us from the mundane and help us see and feel what is truly valuable in life. Such storytelling, he believes, can re-enchant the world and help us 'live with joy in the face of a deepening crisis'.

**Eric Maddern**

# Introduction: the impetus of desire

One thing in the title of this book that may invite explanation is the word 'desire'. Well, it's a sexy-sounding word. Barry Lopez deployed it in the title of his remarkable book *Arctic Dreams: Imagination and Desire in a Northern Landscape.* In an elegant blend of travel memoir, natural history, ethnography, and the history of exploration, Lopez examines how different groups of people project on to the natural environment different kinds of desire: to survive, to make money, to understand, to seek communion with nature. The implication is that there's a profound linkage between the way we use our imagination and the way we live in the world, and therefore that much may be at stake when we tell stories.

Stories are animated by desire – good stories anyway, that have a strong forward momentum that keeps the audience engaged. It's the protagonist's impetus to pursue some desire that propels the story forwards: the desire of Odysseus to get home to Ithaca; Frodo's desire to destroy the Ring to nullify the power of Sauron; Lancelot and Guinevere's desire for each other; Sir John Franklin's desire to find a way through the ice of the Northwest Passage. Some of the desires that characters have are much like the desires, or instincts, that animate the ecosystem: the desire for resources, like food, water, territory, so that one may survive; the desire for a mate so that one may reproduce. It's the pattern of significance imparted by the sequence of events resulting from particular characters' pursuit of particular desires that distinguishes a story, whether based on real events or not, from the inchoate mass of experience and information that makes up life.

But what about the storyteller, or story-writer? What desire do they pursue in telling the particular stories they choose to tell? Is it merely to entertain the audience or to make a living from doing something they enjoy? Some would say so. But stories inevitably mediate particular values, promote particular desires, even if the author claims to have no agenda. Lots of Hollywood action movies, whose intention is merely to be exciting and thereby make lots of money, do by default promote violence as something admirable. But for many storymakers the choice of which stories to tell – and which stories to imbibe – is influenced by deeper desires, which may be conscious and deliberate, or may operate unconsciously. These desires of the storymaker will interact in complex ways with the desires of the characters in the stories: sometimes converging with them, other times questioning them.

Years ago, in a writers group I attended, someone nosily asked each of us what was the core theme of our creative work. I'd never before asked myself that question, but I realised at once that the answer for me was the longing for earthly paradise. There are aspects of that desire that you might call spiritual or otherworldly. There are no doubt aspects that concern my personal psychopathology. But this desire has since then connected with my longstanding love of the natural world, my ever-growing concern about the impact of human activities on nature, and thereby with the politics of the environment.

Much of the discourse of human ecology and sustainability is couched in terms of necessity: we must do this, this, and this in order to preserve the viability of the ecosystem in order that civilisation may continue and much suffering be averted. That is one, eminently justified, kind of 'ecological desire'. But I think it's useful to distinguish from this pragmatic, imperative desire another kind of ecological desire, which concerns not so much necessity as the kind of world we wish to inhabit and to pass on to future generations. It may be, for example, that many of the species of plants and animals we're driving into extinction are not absolutely vital to the functioning of the ecosystem and will never be of economic value to human beings. It may be that the global ecosystem together with human ingenuity could sustain gigantic conurbations that I would regard as a cyberpunk nightmare but which other people might regard as exciting and appealing. So there's a competition, a debate, between different priorities of desire, different kinds of world we might wish to inhabit; a debate that's not purely pragmatic but concerns sophisticated moral, aesthetic, and spiritual choices.

Many of the essays in this collection are, like the stories I write and tell, motivated by conscious desires of these kinds. They were written for a panoply of different publications and occasions, and so vary greatly in approach. Some are journalistic, some more scholarly, others more personal. All of them, I hope, have relevance to the art of live storytelling; but modern storytelling exists in relationship with other narrative arts, like literature, film, and theatre, and so the scope of many of the essays extends into the wider cultural ecosystem.

The first section, 'Myth', explores some mythological topics that are important in storytelling but widespread in other media too. The second section, 'Storytelling', more narrowly addresses contemporary oral storytelling; it includes, among other things, some of the reviews I've been inspired to write by Ben Haggarty's pamphlet *Seek out the Voice of the Critic*, which calls for the critical scrutiny of modern storytelling. In the final section, 'Ecobardic', the focus widens again to encompass other art forms as well as the particular contributions that storytelling might make to the challenges we face in coexisting with the rest of the ecosystem. Essays in this section expand upon aspects of my monograph *Storytelling and Ecology* and upon the Ecobardic Manifesto that I co-authored with other members of Fire Springs, the company that's been so much a part of my journey as a storyteller.

Where possible, in revising the essays, I've tried to eliminate the repetition of ideas, but each piece is a discrete entity and so some repetition has had to remain in order to preserve the integrity of argument. I've inserted cross-references to link ideas mentioned in one place to discussion of them somewhere else. These cross-references and restatements may alert the reader to the book's central preoccupations.

I'll say no more about those preoccupations here except to say something about that word 're-enchantment'. The modernisation of the way we think has brought many benefits but at the same time has relegated metaphysical understandings of our lives and the world into the realm of irrational superstition, leaving us in a condition that Max Weber called 'Entzauberung' (disenchantment), in which our sense of the significance and agency of ourselves and what's around us is diminished. A big part of my motivation, my desire, as a storyteller and writer is a belief that stories can re-enchant our lives, and the places we live in and the creatures with which we share the earth, with a sense of heightened significance: that each one of us, each one of them, is special and worthy of love. If that means I must be labelled a 'romantic', then I accept the label.

**Anthony Nanson**

# Myth

# Mythscapes of Arcadia

> In Greece, the myths are still very much alive. And in amongst them sits your own ... patiently waiting for you to live it. Live your myth in Greece.

So says the caption above a godlike young couple bathing at the edge of a wine dark bay behind which gently curving hills fade into the mist. In its cheesy way this Greek National Tourism Organisation advertisement taps into the longing for paradisal joy, amidst unspoilt natural beauty, which propels people on holidays far from their homes, or even to de-camp more permanently to a place where a life a bit closer to paradise seems possible. That was, I admit, one of our motives for spending a year in Greece. There were others. My spouse Kirsty Hartsiotis is half Greek by ancestry, though all English by upbringing, and wanted to investigate that lost half of her heritage. Since the cost of living was lower than in Britain, we could devote more time than usual to purely creative work. And as storytellers we were keen to explore the landscape that gave birth to Europe's best-preserved ancient mythology.

That last motive dictated our choice of which region of Greece we'd make our home: the Peloponnese, which has the densest concentration of Mycenaean ruins and other mythic locations. Moreover, Kirsty was planning a museological research project comparing the Roman Baths Museum in Bath and the archaeological site and museum of Epidaurus, in the Argolid. Both these sites had been sacred sanctuaries centred on a spring whose healing properties are explained in local myths: the stories of Bladud and Asclepius, respectively, which Kirsty and our Fire Springs[1] colleague Kevan Manwaring had included in a show called *Healing Waters* they devised for a museum exhibition about Bath's spa. We ended up living an hour's drive south from Epidaurus, in a village on the coast of a mountainous district that has the same name today as it did millennia ago: Arcadia.

In exploring Greece's mythological landscape, and its multilayered historical landscape too, we were inspired by Hugh Lupton's and David Abram's perception that everywhere a web of stories is draped over the physical landscape.[2] Though the Greek myths have been familiar to me since childhood,[3] I hadn't appreciated how thoroughly the events in these stories are located in actual (though sometimes disputed) geography. A great aid to such explorations is Pedro Olalla's *Mythological Atlas of Greece*, which exhaustively plots the bones of each of the stories on a set of road maps covering the whole of Greece.

You can experience the mythscape in various ways. Firstly, the obvious one of visiting the locations where events in the stories took place. Sometimes these can be pinpointed: the plane tree at Gortys, in Crete, where Zeus made love with Europa (the tree's still there!); the stone at Troezen, in the Argolid, beneath which Theseus found the sword left him by his father; the stagnant pool at Lerna where Dionysus descended to the underworld and maybe where Core too was spirited down by Hades. Other times the stories confront you with larger geographical features: the Langada Pass by which Telemachus crossed the Taygetos mountains to reach Sparta; Mount Parnassus where Apollo frolicked with the Muses; Lake Stymphalis – the remnant of it not yet drained for agriculture – from whose marshy shores Heracles drove away a flock of man-eating bronze-winged birds.

Secondly, you can imbibe the landscape in a more general way – the play of light on the textures of rock and sea, the colours and aromas of the native flora through the changing seasons, the summer-long drone of crickets, the birdsong in winter – to inform your sensual imagining of the stories. It's true, though, that the landscape has changed a bit since the Mycenaean age, more than three millennia ago, in which the myths are set. I have in mind not only the recent impacts of fast roads, urban sprawl, and industrialised agriculture but also the deforestation that, even in classical times, had made Greece a harsher, drier land than it once was and caused Plato to complain about the erosion of topsoil.

Thirdly, you can visit archaeological sites. At Tiryns, Mycenae, Pylos, Knossos, you can walk among the prehistoric remains of the very palaces where Perseus, Agamemnon, Nestor, and Minos dwelt. Even sites that do not feature in the myths can help you to imagine the human element in the ancient landscape. Many ancient settlements are remote from present-day centres of habitation. We enjoyed seeking out obscure archaeological sites in our local area. Whereas the major sites are extensively excavated and often crowded with busloads of visitors, these lesser sites – goat-haunted fragments of masonry poking out of the oak and myrtle bushes – open your imagination not only to antiquity but also to the experiences of those romantic travellers immortalised in eighteenth-century prints.

The ancient temple sanctuaries are usually located in powerfully numinous places in the landscape. This numinous quality evokes for me a sense of the gods as potent elemental spirits, in contrast to the typically anthropomorphic depiction of the gods in the myths, which tend often to be told from a humanist standpoint that ill-favours the gods. I felt this most strongly in the sanctuaries of Apollo, the Greek god to whom I feel most affinity: at Delos, Delphi, Vasses, and Tyros (a minor site on the Arcadian coast) I felt uplifted by the brilliance of the sunlight, the clarity and animation of the air, the scale of space and panorama.

During the year before we moved to Greece I'd conducted a research project for the Society for Storytelling about storytelling and ecological awareness; I wrote the first draft of *Storytelling and Ecology* while we were there. This made me keen to spend time in nature and very sensitive to the condition of the environment I saw around me. The paradisal image of Greece promoted by the holiday industry does not quite match the reality. The classier resorts try to keep their beaches clean and their development tasteful, but any undeveloped beach that's accessible by car is likely to be thickly littered with plastic bags and bottles, used condoms, even abandoned fridges. On one such beach the sight of delicately beautiful sea daffodils growing among the rubbish made me burst into tears. When you stop at a lay-by to enjoy a lovely mountain view, you're likely to find the ground strewn with litter and see a huge fan of garbage tipped down the slope below. The archaeological site of Eleusis – venue of sacred mystery rites, where Core was reunited with her mother Demeter upon returning from the underworld – is a tiny oasis of green surrounded by the stink and pipework of petrochemical facilities. But if you head out on foot where cars can't go you'll discover beautiful pristine landscapes where the archetypal vision of Arcadia – flower-spangled meadows, wooded hills, steeple-tall cypress trees, and sun-browned herdsmen watching their goats – remains a reality.

I was fortunate to have an introduction to WWF-Greece and there meet Greeks who do care about the environment; in particular the lovely Eleni Svoronou, who uses storytelling in her work for WWF and has written, among much else, an ecological fairy tale for children.[4] Keen to promote storytelling, she arranged for me to run an intensive weekend workshop at the WWF office in Athens. The participants, who included ecologists, educators, and communicators influential in their own fields, were extremely enthusiastic. I felt sure I'd sown seeds in soil that would bear fruit.

Given our limited knowledge of Greek, we didn't really encounter the living oral tradition, though any of the octogenarian goatherds we exchanged pleasantries with on our hikes could well have had a head stuffed with folktales. But one of my students in Athens, a tour guide from Chios, had inherited traditional tales from his storytelling great-aunt – and told me about a scholarly conference about Homer, held on Chios (where the bard was supposedly born), at which an aged, almost senile local woman had turned up uninvited, claiming to be in possession of an oral tradition of Homeric tales, and regaled the startled scholars with a folk version of the life of Homer.

The garbage problem shocked all our visitors from Britain. Not least Kevan, who with his friend Cathy accompanied us on an intense ten-day tour of mythic mountain adventure. Kevan's a great person to travel with because he has a remarkable sense of the joy of the moment and, where another traveller might just look at the view, he likes to engage as interactively as he can with whatever place he's visiting. Take him to a healing spring and he'll strip off to take the waters. Take him to an ancient theatre and he'll resonantly recite a poem to win a round of applause from the other tourists. Take him to an ancient temple and he'll boldly invoke whichever god was worshipped there. Take him to Olympia and he'll sprint round the stadium. Take him to the Styx ravine and he'll try to reach the cave said to be the source of the Styx, even at risk of a one-way plunge down the cliffs to Hades.

We packed many sights into that trip; but the highlights were two long walks: the one to the Styx; and one to the Corycian Cave (on Parnassus), sacred to both Pan and Apollo, also a venue for orgiastic Dionysian rites – and even today, to judge by the evidence we saw, a place used in pagan ritual. In both cases the mythic resonances of the landscape impinged powerfully upon the exercise of going for a mountain hike. Our experience at the Styx ravine was a more intense example of the general awareness of easy access to death that you get when travelling around the Peloponnese, partly because of the risk-taking audacity of many drivers and partly because the landscape is so precipitous and unforgiving: one false move, whether you're driving or walking, and you could dive hundreds of feet to your doom. This compels a Zen-like intensity of focus on what is happening in the moment. Perhaps too it suggests a link between landscape and psychology in the twentieth-century Greek writer Nikos Kazantzakis's notion of 'the Cretan Glance' – that courage to look death in the face and live in creative defiance of one's personal annihilation, which he regards as a perennial characteristic of the Greek mind since ancient times.[5] Et tu in Arcadia ego.

When, in England a year later, Fire Springs began to plan a new storytelling epic based on Greek mythology, titled *Return to Arcadia*, our ambitions converged on the two big themes mentioned above: ecology – already an important theme in our previous ecobardic epics, *Arthur's Dream* and *Robin of the Wildwood* – and death, especially as confronted by the ancient Greek mystery religions that endeavoured to prepare the soul for the realm beyond death. The stories of Orpheus and Core/Persephone are key myths – associated with, respectively, the Orphic and Eleusinian Mysteries – that connect these two themes. We decided to weave those two stories into a single mythopoeic arc, along with three other tales – of Aristaeus, Erysichthon, and Arkas – in which nymphs mediate between nature and humankind. In preparing the stories we drew upon our memories of the Greek landscape, including locations such as Eleusis, Lerna, and Cape Taineron that feature in these stories, and also tried to honour the gods as powerful spirits of nature in the way we'd perceived them outdoors in Greece.

There was a danger that all this could get too heavy and mystical, so we earthed the mythological strands with a parallel storyline of highlights from the journey Kirsty and I made with Kevan and Cathy, told in a more relaxed anecdotal style. The shifts between narrative moods – from the divine level of Persephone's story, to the more human stories of Orpheus, Aristaeus, and co., to our own humble travellers' tales – were facilitated by David Metcalfe's guitar-work. This experimental combination of material works, we think, to guide the audience's imagination into both the mythology and the Greek landscape. For me, it also makes a connection between the personal quest for some arcadian quality in one's own life and the utopian dream that peaceful coexistence between humankind and nature might somehow come to be.

That dream takes us beyond our own time and our own death into a metaphysical realm where environmental politics merges with religious hope and rational discourse becomes tricky. That's where the myths serve us, rather like the icons that retain an important place in Greek Orthodox spirituality, providing a doorway for the imagination to engage with mysteries that cannot fully be known this side of paradise (see pages 165–9).

---

[1] Fire Springs is a company of storytellers, formed in 2000, comprising: Kevan Manwaring, David Metcalfe, Kirsty Hartsiotis, Richard Selby, and Anthony Nanson.

[2] Lupton, *The Dreaming of Place*; Abram, *The Spell of the Sensuous*.

[3] I was introduced to them in a most compelling way by Dudley Green, my classics teacher at Clitheroe Royal Grammar School.

[4] Svoronou, *Ο Τζιτζίκο-Περικλής μεγάλος συνθέτης της Ελλάδας!*

[5] Friar, 'Introduction'.

# Mythic Patterns in Popular Entertainment

It's easy to feel cynical about the bestsellers and blockbusters, those products of the culture industry that achieve huge mass-market commercial success. Crass many of them are, but there are some that are truly great works of art. They are seminal in their respective genres, yet never bettered by their imitators, and so enormously popular that they achieve cult status within our culture as a whole. They capture the public's imagination in a special way, by presenting characters and patterns of events which have a profound resonance with our deepest longings. In modern society the traditional symbols of religion have lost much of their power to stir people's hearts, and yet people retain the capacity to be touched by the mythic symbols found in great narrative art. In this essay I shall outline and compare such archetypal patterns in three colossi of popular entertainment.

The Waterstone's poll of 1995 and the BBC poll of 2000 both voted Tolkien's *The Lord of the Rings* the nation's favourite book of the twentieth century. Bookshops have at times had a whole section devoted to Tolkien's imaginary world of Middle-earth. Critics may decry the novel's lack of psychological realism and its archaic use of language, but they miss the point. The whole story is steeped in the richness of geography, history, language, and lore that Tolkien had spent half a century creating, and in his professional knowledge of European mythology. That's why no other fantasy novel can compete with its mythopoeic depth. For Tolkien's wish was to reconstruct, by back-extrapolation from the fragments that have survived, a pre-Christian mythology for England, to replace the original mythology lost in the course of the Anglo-Saxons' migration across the sea to Britain and subsequent rapid conversion to Christianity. Middle-earth represents Europe in the distant past, before the ice sheets sculpted the present shape of the continent, before anything was known of Jehovah. In creation and providence and the hearts of people, God is present, but God is not articulated in religious terms.

The *Star Wars* trilogy projects the mythic into what seems a starfaring future – and yet each film begins, 'A long time ago in a galaxy far, far away ...' A hint, perhaps, that the space-age dream of humanity's endless expansion into space may never come to pass. *Star Wars*, the epitome of space opera, inhabits an outer-space mythos of a never-never future that might as well be a heroic age of the past. Its heroes, like Middle-earth's, have no knowledge of God, and yet the Force is with them – 'feel the Force around you ... between you ... me ... the tree ... the rock ... everywhere'[1] – an intangible power reminiscent of South Seas mana and in some ways of the Holy Spirit.

The adventures of James Bond take place in a glamorised version of our own contemporary world. The milieu is totally secular. The secret agent fights alone, without God, and in this the audience identify with him, for in the late twentieth century it is increasingly people's experience that in the battles of life they are on their own. With the collapse of the church's influence, British society lost its traditional framework of values for evaluating right and wrong, yet evil-doing has not ceased to torment the world; people still want myths in which they can see evil objectified – as SMERSH, SPECTRE, Mordor, the Empire – and discover that it cannot be vanquished on its own terms. By taking a via negativa akin to Christ's surrender on the cross, the heroes of Middle-earth defeat Sauron by destroying the One Ring that they might have tried, disastrously, to wield against him; and Luke Skywalker resists the temptation to turn to the dark side of the Force, and by exposing his own vulnerability allows even his corrupted father, Darth Vader, to be redeemed.

It may stretch credulity to make such lofty claims for the Bond movies, which have been salted with irony since Sean Connery's first charming smirk at Miss Moneypenny, and homogenised by the dictates of commercial formula; but Ian Fleming's novels, for all their transgressions of political correctness, contain surprising moral depths.

In the first, *Casino Royale*, Bond reflects that 'there's a Good Book about goodness and how to be good ... but there's no Evil Book about evil and how to be bad ... no book from which we can learn the nature of evil in all its forms'.[2] Ann Boyd, in *The Devil with James Bond*, claims that the complete sequence of Bond novels constitutes Fleming's attempt to write such a book. In his foreword to a book entitled *The Seven Deadly Sins*, Fleming proposed that in the modern world the evil of the seven deadly sins traditionally upheld by the church – envy, pride, covetousness, gluttony, sloth, lust, anger – is greatly exceeded by that of 'seven deadlier sins': avarice, cruelty, snobbery, hypocrisy, self-righteousness, moral cowardice, and malice.[3] These deadlier sins characterise the villains of Fleming's novels. But the most demonic of Bond's foes – Dr No, Mr Big, and especially Blofeld – embody an eighth deadlier sin, accidie, or extreme apathy, which Fleming regarded as the worst failing of modern society. In the face of such evil, Bond's susceptibility to some of the traditional sins comes across almost as virtuous. His patriotic pride, violent anger, and weakness for women make him human and empower his fight against the cynical schemes of his enemies.[4]

A similarly roguish hero appears in *Star Wars* in the form of Han Solo, but throughout the movie trilogy George Lucas deploys the device of twin heroes to provide a plot–counterplot structure: Solo the worldly trickster stands in contrast to Luke Skywalker, the saintly youth. *The Lord of the Rings* complicates its story structure by use of three primary heroes: Frodo the saintly hobbit, Aragorn the warrior who would be king, and Gandalf the wizard, who from other characters' point of view functions also as the archetypal wise old man, a role fulfilled by Obi-Wan Kenobi in *Star Wars* and by M in the Bond stories.

In devising *Star Wars*, Lucas was strongly influenced by the Jungian mythologist Joseph Campbell. His heroes follow the mythic hero cycle of separation, transformation, and return described in Campbell's *The Hero with a Thousand Faces*. You can tease out some version of this pattern for all the major characters in the trilogy[5] – as indeed you can in *The Lord of the Rings*[6] – but the correspondence of the pattern to an adolescent's initiation rite makes it most strongly apposite for Skywalker, whom we see powerfully transformed from the gauche youth in the first film to the grave, self-assured knight in *Return of the Jedi*. The audience of stories that fit Campbell's 'monomyth', in identifying with the hero, vicariously share in his experiences and at some level of their psyche they may, perhaps, be transformed as he is transformed in the fulfilment of his quest.

I used the masculine pronoun in that last sentence because the hero in this scheme seems ubiquitously male. Not always, though. The story of Psyche fits it very well, and Maureen Murdock has adapted the monomyth into a 'heroine's journey' that better matches the challenges of women's lives.[7] But in the typical heroic story female characters (young ones anyway) are likely to symbolise the male anima; they feature as the archetypal princess who inspires the hero's struggle and becomes his final reward. The elvish lady Arwen plays this role for Aragorn, though the theme of their love is understated in *The Lord of the Rings*; only in an appendix is the full story told. Princess Leia is a feistier heroine in *Star Wars* – she knows how to use a blaster – but she *is* a princess and her main function in the plot is to motivate Skywalker's and Solo's commitment to the rebel cause. The same goes for the Bond girls; indeed Fleming repeatedly compares Bond to St George, the quintessential archetype of knight killing dragon to rescue princess.[8]

The hero's journey begins with a departure from the familiar everyday world to an exotic world of adventure. Skywalker, compelled to leave his uncle's desert farm, is hurled into the fray of an interstellar war. Frodo has to depart from his beloved Shire on a journey through the wilderlands. For Bond every mission takes him away from London to some exotic place of danger. In the bigger picture of his career as a

whole, as a secret agent with blood on his hands, he is perpetually separated from normal society and the innocence of his childhood, poign-
antly remembered at the beginning of *On Her Majesty's Secret Service*.

The War of the Ring raises Aragorn to sufficient heights of heroism
to be worthy of 'returning' to Gondor's capital to claim the throne of his
ancestors. Gandalf, in confrontation with the most terrible of the servants of darkness, is revealed to be an angelic being, whose true home is
in the Undying Lands across the western sea. Frodo, having achieved the
Ring's destruction, returns to the Shire bearing an aura of holiness. In
the end he is too changed, too wounded, to remain in Middle-earth and
accompanies Gandalf to the Undying Lands. By the end of the *Star Wars*
trilogy, Skywalker is a fully fledged and proven Jedi knight and at last
can relax in fellowship with his companions, including the spirits of the
deceased Kenobi and Vader. Meanwhile Solo has grown to care about
things beyond his own self-interest – and won the princess's love.

But James Bond can never come home. The novels ceased only when
Fleming died. The films continue production even though the stock of
Fleming titles – and concepts – is exhausted. Near the end of *On Her
Majesty's Secret Service*, Bond finally marries his princess, dreaming of a
normal happy life – till a SPECTRE agent murders the girl. There is no
escape for him. The struggle must continue. It seems fitting that it is the
example in a contemporary setting which fails to complete the 'return' in
Campbell's hero cycle. The present is ongoing and inescapable except by
death. The secret agent, always lonely, always hiding behind a mask,
always having to think on his feet, is the archetypal hero for our time.

---

[1] Yoda in *The Empire Strikes Back* (1979).
[2] Fleming, *Casino Royale*, pp. 144–5.
[3] Fleming, 'Foreword'.
[4] Boyd, *The Devil with James Bond!*
[5] Henderson, *Star Wars*.
[6] Petty, *One Ring to Bind Them All*.
[7] Murdock, *The Heroine's Journey*.
[8] Boyd, *The Devil with James Bond!*

# The Metaphysics of Imaginary Worlds

Whereas science fiction is characteristically set in a materialist universe – one in which the only reality is physical matter and energy – where all imaginative or marvellous elements are made to seem scientifically plausible,[1] fantasy justifies the marvellous by means of alternative, metaphysical assumptions about the nature of the universe. For a fantasy story to be coherent and convincing, the author has to determine what specific metaphysics operate in the world in which the story is set, including the cosmology that structures that world. We may think of this as the upper level of the imaginative work of world-building; the middle level being the devising of the historical, geographical, social, and cultural setting, and the lower level the detailed sensory imagining of each scene. There are a number of basic patterns of such metaphysical imagineering, whose antecedents can be traced back to folklore, mythology, and religious cosmography.

Tolkien distinguishes between the 'primary world' – the real world that we inhabit, which for Tolkien, as a Christian, itself has a metaphysical dimension – and a 'secondary world' in which a story takes place.[2] Strictly speaking, *any* fictional world is a secondary world, since it exists only in the imagination of the storymaker[3] and the audience, but the term 'secondary world' is generally used to refer to an imaginary world that is manifestly different from the primary world: a world with its own geography and history and in which beings and powers may exist that defy the laws of nature that govern the primary world. In some stories, like C. S. Lewis's *The Lion, the Witch and the Wardrobe*, characters cross through some kind of 'portal' between the primary world – to be precise, a fictional simulation of the primary world – and a secondary world. Conversely, there may be, as in Susan Cooper's *The Dark Is Rising*, and many horror stories, an 'intrusion' of beings or supernatural phenomena from another world *into* the primary world. Other, 'immersive' fantasies, such as Ursula Le Guin's *A Wizard of Earthsea*, and many fairy tales, are set entirely within a secondary world and may make no mention of our own world.[4] Worlds like Lewis's Narnia and Fritz Leiber's Nehwon[5] coexist with the primary world and are distanced from it through something akin to a spatial dimension. Others, such as Tolkien's Middle-earth and Robert E. Howard's Hyboria,[6] are distanced from our world into the distant past. Yet others are distanced as alternative versions of the primary world – whether in an alternative present day, as in Philip Pullman's *Northern Lights*, or an alternative historical past, as in Jacqueline Carey's *Kushiel's Dart*.

Most people in most cultures throughout the world through most of history have inhabited a thought-world in which the existence of supernatural entities, that post-Enlightenment thought would regard as fantasy, has been normative. Some kind of otherworld or spirit world has typically been seen as the source of them.

In British and Irish tradition – in both ancient myth and more recent folklore – the otherworld is variously located under the sea, underground, in the depths of forests, and on islands across the western sea. Access between the familiar world and this otherworld may involve physical travel – venturing into a forest, sailing across the sea – but there's also a notion that a metaphysical veil lies between the two worlds and that at certain liminal times, such as Halloween or Beltane, this veil becomes especially thin, permitting lively traffic between them. Moreover, the veil may be especially thin in certain localities that have a numinous or liminal quality – certain coves, caves, pools, mountain tops, barrows, cromlechs, trees – and consequently can serve as portals. We can see the origins of intrusion and portal fantasies in traditional stories like 'Thomas the Rhymer' and 'Oisin and Niamh' that tell of people (typically, young men who are too good-looking for their own good) who are carried away (typically by an otherworldly woman of overwhelming beauty) into an otherworld in which space and time are distorted. The landscapes of the otherworld, as they are experienced from the inside, open out to be more extensive in scale than could fit into the geographical area as perceived from the outside, a concept beautifully rendered in Robert Holdstock's novel *Mythago Wood*. Time there may move at a different speed than it does in the primary world: so when Oisin goes home to Ireland after his sojourn in Tir na nOg with the fairy princess Niamh, he discovers that three hundred years have passed and he himself has become a figure of legend.

Greek mythology perceived the otherworldly in terms of a triple-tiered cosmos. Deep underground is the underworld of the dead, accessible to the bold via certain of the ravines and caves with which Greece's mountainous karst landscape is riddled. On the summits of the highest mountains – Olympus, Parnassus, Helicon – is the overworld of the gods and their attendants, an idea given conviction by the sight of these summits clear above a layer of cloud and sometimes even magnified by the optical effect of dust particles in the air.[7] In the wild places of the middle world between, the world that humans inhabit, dwell fantastic beings like nymphs, satyrs, centaurs, and river gods: 'exotika' that have retained a place in Greek folklore analogous to the fairies in the British Isles. Complicating our ability to visualise this scheme, the Greek paradise of Elysium, though theoretically part of the underworld, is located like Tir na nOg across the western ocean, among the Fortunate Isles (see pages 26–7).

Norse cosmography pictured nine interconnected worlds arranged in three tiers around the axis of a gigantic ash tree, Yggdrasil.[8] The upper tier comprises: Asgard, where the Aesir (warrior gods) dwell; Vanaheim, realm of the Vanir (fertility gods); and Alfheim, realm of the light elves. On the middle level are: Midgard (Middle-earth), where we humans dwell; Jotunheim, land of the giants; Nidavellir, land of the dwarves, and Svartalfheim, land of the dark elves. At the bottom are Hell and Niflheim, two realms of the dead whose metaphysical distinction is unclear; the best I can make out is that if you're in Hell you're dead, and if you're in Niflheim you're really dead. Midgard is connected to Asgard by the rainbow bridge Bifrost. This cosmography probably helped to inspire the system of interconnected worlds in Lewis's Chronicles of Narnia. You can also see its influence in Tolkien's division of his world into Middle-earth (home of humans, dwarves, ents, and dark elves) and the Undying Lands (home of the light elves and godlike or angelic beings called the Valar and Maiar).

In African metaphysics, typically, the spirit world is spatially coextensive with the material world, so that the elemental and ancestral spirits that inhabit it are in some way present among the living community and may sometimes be manifest to them. As the number of living people who remember any particular deceased person diminishes to vanishing point, that person's spirit fades away from the 'sasa' (the now) into the mythic 'zamani' (the long ago).[9] Such a weltanschauung informs Ben Okri's novel *The Famished Road*, whose child protagonist is able to perceive spirit beings who are invisible to most of the community. In 'magical realism' of this kind the notion of a distinct secondary world breaks down. The marvellous elements of the story are presented as more or less part of the primary world, as perceived according to the traditional beliefs of a non-Western community, be that in Africa, India, Latin America, or, say, a Native or African American community in North America. Magical realism is thereby seen as challenging the intellectual hegemony of Western materialism, though to what extent a particular author or storyteller actually believes in the metaphysical reality of what they describe may well be impossible to determine from their stories.[10] At a bookshop reading, I once saw Okri questioned directly about his spiritual beliefs: his response was evasive, and I sensed that he regarded the uncertainties of the metaphysical as something that could only be expressed through imaginative literature.

Between magical realism, in which the 'marvellous' is presented as truly supernatural, and 'uncanny' realism, in which it's made clear in the end that any hints that something is supernatural are in fact false – for example, Ann Radcliffe's Gothic novel *The Mysteries of Udolpho* and the TV exploits of Scooby Doo – the critic Tzvetan Todorov has defined a form he calls the 'fantastic', in which the reader is left hesitating between supernatural and mundane interpretations of what's happened.[11] An example is Henry James's *The Turn of the Screw*: were there really ghosts, or were there not? This use of the term 'fantastic' seems to me unfortunate, in that it ignores the existence of the prolific genre of 'fantasy' in which the existence of supernatural phenomena is quite explicit. Farah Mendelsohn, a critic who is engaged with this genre, has coined the category of 'liminal' fantasy to encompass the kinds of strategies referred to above as 'magical realism' and the 'fantastic'.[12]

Which brings us to something rather neglected in discussions of magical realism, perhaps because the premise of materialism is taken for granted in critical discourse and because 'genre' fantasy and indigenous European folklore tend to be ignored: that some Western liminal fantasy set in the primary world is metaphysically equivalent to non-Western magical realism and in some cases may even be written by authors who believe in the metaphysics they're presenting, whether literally or as metaphor of some dimly understood higher reality. Alan Garner's *The Weirdstone of Brisingamen* depicts contemporary Cheshire as frequented by marvellous beings derived from native folklore – whose actual existence local people must once have believed in, even if the author himself does not. Charles Williams's supernatural thriller *War in Heaven* expresses, albeit in symbolic imagery, the Christian metaphysics this author did believe to be real. Liminal fantasy, then, can lure our imagination towards the *possibility* of metaphysical reality which myth and folklore have mediated throughout the millennia of human consciousness.

Whereas pagan mythological traditions tend to look back to a paradisal golden age and/or warlike heroic age located in a distant past in which gods were active agents, the Judaeo-Christian–Islamic metaphysics of medieval and later imaginative work not only recalls a golden age and a cosmic struggle in the distant past, and a spiritual realm of angels and devils that – like fairies, exotika, spirits – coexists with the material world, but also emphasises the prospect of a restored paradise sometime in the future.

Tolkien's fictional cosmology, as narrated in *The Silmarillion*, attempts to harmonise ingredients from pagan European mythology and Judaeo-Christian theology. The relationship between the metaphysics of his secondary world, which he knew he had invented, and the primary-world Christian metaphysics in which he actually believed is complex.

'Subcreation' is his term for a writer's work of constructing a secondary world, by analogy with the 'creation' performed by God. Tolkien believed the secondary world should be internally consistent and culturally coherent; for this reason he disliked the eclectic combination of tropes from diverse sources in Lewis's Narnia. Not only was Tolkien's secondary world finely and intricately crafted as a work of subcreation – geographically, historically, and linguistically 'encyclopaedic', as Tom Shippey describes it[13] – but 'subcreation' (in a wide sense encompassing other crafts besides writing) is itself a central theme of the stories set in that world: consider the importance of the silmarils (finely wrought jewels) in *The Silmarillion* and the rings of power in *The Lord of the Rings.*

Tolkien's fantasy, especially *The Lord of the Rings*, is encyclopaedic also in the way it incorporates diverse notions about the otherworld to be found in European mythology: from the hobbits' perspective everything outside the Shire is effectively the otherworld; the Undying Lands represent the paradise imagined to lie beyond the western sea; Lothlorien, Rivendell, the Old Forest, and Fangorn are sylvan fairylands, inhabited by enchanted beings, in which time and space seem to distort; and bearing (and especially wearing) the Ring gives Frodo glimpses of a hidden world that coexists with the material world:

'I thought that I saw a white figure that shone and did not grow dim like the others. Was that Glorfindel then?'

'Yes, you saw him for a moment as he is upon the other side; one of the mighty of the Firstborn.'[14]

Moreover, in Tolkien's theory of 'mythopoeia', the metaphors deployed in fantasy such as his provide inklings of insight into the greater metaphysical reality that he believed we inhabit (see page 147).[15] A psychoanalytic analogue to this idea is to see the landscape and beings of the secondary world as expressing in symbolic form the contents of the unconscious.[16]

In much fantasy the symbolic significance of elements of the secondary world, whether metaphysically or psychoanalytically conceived, operates without disturbing the realism of a generally earthlike world in which the author may take for granted our knowledge of many things – trees, horses, kings, inns – familiar from the primary world. In didactic allegories, like John Bunyan's *Pilgrim's Progress* and Lewis's pastiche *The Pilgrim's Regress*, and in the teaching fables of many cultures, the very blatant symbolism tends to overpower the secondary world's verisimilitude. In 'surreal' fantasies, on the other hand, such as Lewis Carroll's *Alice in Wonderland* or Angela Carter's *The Infernal Desire Machines of Doctor Hoffmann*, the resemblance to the primary world begins to be left behind as imagery akin to the dreamscape of the unconscious takes over. The task of persuading us to suspend our disbelief then becomes more challenging; but even in this approach a writer as skilled as Carter can present a secondary world that, if bizarre and fluidly mutating, yet comes alive before our mind's eye, just as do the worlds sculpted in our imagination by Tolkien's myth-making, by Le Guin's pellucid realism, and by the gifted storyteller who speaks to us face to face.

[1] Roberts, *Science Fiction*.

[2] Tolkien, 'On Fairy Stories'.

[3] I use 'storymaker' to refer collectively to storytellers, story-writers, playwrights, and film-makers.

[4] On the terms 'portal', 'intrusion', and 'immersive', see Mendlesohn, *Rhetorics of Fantasy*.

[5] Nehwon = the setting of Leiber's stories about Fafhrd and the Gray Mouser.

[6] Hyboria = the setting of Howard's stories about Conan.

[7] Seltman, *The Twelve Olympians*.

[8] See Crossley-Holland, *The Norse Myths*.

[9] Mbiti, *African Religions and Mythology*.

[10] Bowers, *Magic(al) Realism*.

[11] Todorov, *The Fantastic*.

[12] Mendelsohn, *Rhetorics of Fantasy*.

[13] Shippey, *J. R. R. Tolkien*.

[14] Tolkien, *The Fellowship of the Ring*, p. 292. In Peter Jackson's film adaptation of *The Fellowship of the Ring* (2001), this vision of the Elven lord Glorfindel is replaced by a comparable vision Frodo sees of Arwen, white-robed and radiant in her otherworldly glory, shortly after his wounding by the Nazgul. The next camera shot reveals a more homely-looking Arwen as she is in the material world, dressed in dark travel clothes.

[15] Tolkien, 'On Fairy Stories' and 'Mythopoeia'.

[16] Moorcock, *Wizardry and Wild Romance*.

# Lost Islands: myth and reality

Atlantis, Lemuria, Mu, Thule, Hy-Brasil, the Fortunate Isles, Tir na nOg, Lyonesse, Ys ... Avalon. The very names of these mythic islands that never were mesmerise us. They're an irresistible magnet to all manner of wildly speculative thinking that tries to demonstrate these lands' concrete existence sometime in the mists of the past. Some of this is unashamedly cranky, presented with complete disregard for scientific standards of validation. On the other hand, books by the likes of Graham Hancock, Charles Berlitz, and Erich von Däniken have tapped a lucrative seam of 'mysteries' journalism that dresses up imaginative speculation in a pseudoscientific guise that can seem persuasive to the gullible. Why does this sort of thing have such an appeal? It seems to me a consequence of the prevailing assumption today that only that whose material reality can be scientifically demonstrated has any claim to truth or value. The pseudoscience attempts to download myths such as those of Atlantis and Avalon from the realm of the imagination into the material world that the ruling voices of our culture tell us is the only reality that exists.

Kevan Manwaring's *Lost Islands* is not that kind of book. The author is at pains to distance his work from the flawed reasoning of pseudoscience. He embraces Keats's 'negative capability': that is, he accepts, and finds inspiration in, the impossibility of sure knowledge about some aspects of the world; something that goes against the grain of our materialistic society's impulse to know certainly in order to control absolutely. He discriminates between mythology – the realm of the imagination – and geology and archaeology, the realm of the actual. This is not the same as a distinction between falsehood and truth. The contents of the imagination may well be 'true', whether materially or psychologically or in some metaphysical way; only we can't know their truth with the same kind of certainty with which we can try to pin down scientific data. They may also be just as valuable.

I do not mean to define too rigid a dualism. The frontiers between the actual and the imagined are themselves uncertain, like the boundary between sea and land in the intertidal zone around an island. The implication of Kevan's book is that to face up to the world's deepening ecological crisis we must transcend this dualism. In my view, there's a divergence even within the green counterculture between an otherworldly naivety – the attitude that dodges political responsibility by declaring that, at some spiritual level, each one of us chooses everything that happens to us – and the earnest mobilisation of science and politics to try to save the planet from the destructive impacts of the ever-growing human population. The weakness in the latter stance, laudable and necessary though it is, is that it often fails to take seriously the existential challenges arising from the fact of human mortality. Effective response to the crisis requires us, as individuals and collectively, to constrain our lifestyles and our procreation for the sake of people, places, creatures we may never see, for the sake of children who won't be born till after we're dead, for the sake of processes of ecological recovery that may not bear fruit within our lifetime. The ingredient often missing from the discourse of environmentalism is 'faith' – some kind of myth or metaphysics that can sustain our commitment to the struggle and can keep our lives joyful in the face of challenges so dispiriting and awesomely long-term (see pages 165–9).

Kevan's attempt to tackle this dialectic between myth and science is explicit in the threefold structure of his book. In the first part, 'The Allure of the Imaginary', he approaches the mythology of lost islands by way of the ancient Irish notion of 'immrama', wonder voyages that are as much spiritual as physical journeys and have been interpreted as a kind of shamanic reconnaissance of the metaphysical pathways between our mortal existence and whatever lies beyond the veil of death.[1] The island paradises encountered by the voyagers – with their ecological perfection, their peacefulness, their beautiful and unageing inhabitants – represent an idealised world that we seek seemingly in vain in our mortal lives and traditionally have hoped to find beyond the grave (see pages 25–9).

In the second part, 'The Cold Light of Day', Kevan examines the geological and ecological history of actual islands, emphasising in particular those which really have disappeared, for example during the rise in sea level at the end of the last ice age (though some of his examples are really flooded coastal regions rather than flooded islands); and those, such as Easter Island, which though still above the waves have suffered ecological meltdown; and those, like many Pacific atolls, which are expected to be lost to sea-level rise caused by global warming in our own time. In both ecology and myth the island is such a potent symbol because it is in microcosm a whole world, its resources visibly finite within the bounds of its coastline. As Kevan points out, the photographs of the earth's globe taken by the Apollo astronauts clarify for us that the earth is itself an island, of finite resources, isolated in a barren sea of space.

In the final part, 'When Worlds Collide', the actual and the imagined are brought together and Kevan makes an object lesson of the European impact on America, that vast and bounteous continent discovered to actually occupy the geographical space, across the western sea, where Celtic and Greek myth imagined the islands of paradise to lie. He makes us confront the distressing futility of seeking paradise on earth: it seems that everywhere human beings go, and however impressed we are by the beauty of what we find, and however good our intentions, we end up causing ecological destruction – and are now doing so on a scale that threatens the future of our civilisation.

This grim diagnosis begs two questions relating to the two sides of the dialectic. Firstly, having had our consciousness raised – about global warming, habitat destruction, species extinctions, the human suffering that results when resources are exhausted – what are we, individually and collectively, going to do about these things? Because we have to do something. Because the ecological crisis is actually happening. Because we'd be less than fully human if we said we didn't care. That is the hands-muddying task of politics and science to which I've already alluded. Secondly, how can the mythology help us to keep going, to find consolation in the face of despair (see pages 154–6), without evading the duty thrust upon us by the first question?

Kevan's answer to that second question, I believe, is implied in the frame story within which he's parcelled the whole book: the Irish legend of 'Oisin and Niamh'. For Oisin comes back from the paradise of Tir na nOg and has dialogue with St Patrick. There's a synthesis between pagan celebration of the earthly here and now and Christian concern for our spiritual destiny, between an earthly paradise that may be sought beyond the sea and an eternal paradise hoped for beyond death. It won't do to simply argue the case for one side of the dialectic. You need to do the political work *and* have spiritual faith. You have to accept both sides, embrace the paradox, in faith that out of doing that will spring hope and wholeness and possibilities you might never even have imagined.

---

[1] Matthews, 'The Circuits of the Soul in Celtic Tradition' and 'The Quest as Shaman Journey in Celtic Tradition'.

# Wonder Voyages

A crew of sailors voyages through unknown waters, encountering marvels unseen in the everyday world, calling at strange islands, some terrifying, some that fulfil the deepest desires of one's heart, and eventually returns home to tell the tale. Such stories occur in a number of maritime cultures. Though filled with unearthly wonders, they also intersect with true-life stories of exploration. How are we to discriminate what's true from what's imagined? What kind of truth is at stake? What kinds of meaning can we find in these wildly imaginative wonder voyages?

Stories of this kind are found particularly in cultures possessing superior maritime technology, a bold exploratory impulse, and a sophisticated mythological tradition. They occur in the pre-modern stage of cultural development, before the blank areas on the map have been filled in with scientific knowledge: most notably in ancient Greece, early medieval Ireland, and pre-contact Polynesia. When the Norse came to range across the North Atlantic in the tenth century, the imaginative wonder voyage began to surrender to more prosaic accounts of actual voyages, and yet, as we shall see, the memory of the wonder voyage has continued to inform people's journeying and dreams.

For ancient and medieval Ireland, located on the extreme western seaboard of the known world, it was natural to look westwards across the ocean into the vast space of the unknown. The setting of the sun over the sea horizon was symbolic of the passing of one's soul from life into death. Fishing boats would venture as far as they dared in search of fish, and sometimes storms took them and their crews never returned. So it was an obvious step of the imagination to conceive of lands across the western sea as an otherworldly realm, abode of the souls of the dead. Multiplying populations on the Eurasian continent exerted a relentless westward pressure, and so people in Ireland may also have gazed into the west with a longing for new lands to settle. Though it was not feasible to migrate en masse at that time, small numbers of intrepid Irish monks did, in their ox-hide currachs, seek contemplative solitude on islands beyond the waves, reaching as far into the Atlantic as Iceland and possibly Greenland – the 'Great Ireland' known to the Vikings.[1] These circumstances, together with a literary knowledge of older Greek myths of islands in the west, produced the genre of 'immrama' – wonder voyages into the west, which were at the same time symbolic of the journey of the soul.

Among the immrama, 'The Voyage of Bran' takes place in an explicitly pre-Christian setting. Bran's journey is mediated by an otherworldly woman who beckons him come to Tir na mBan (the Land of Women), and by the guidance of Manannan mac Lir, the sea god. It echoes other stories – called 'echtrai' – from pagan Ireland which dwell more on the hero's experience in the otherworld than on the journey to get there. In some echtrai the otherworld is a land across the western sea: the Tir na nOg (the Land of Youth) to which Oisin is taken by the beauteous Niamh, or the Tir na mBeo (the Land of the Living) visited separately by Ciabhan of the Curling Hair, Connla of the Red Hair, and Tadg son of Cian. In others it's located underwater (evoking the trope of a land lost beneath the sea), underground (as in the enduring folklore of the sidhe dwelling within barrow mounds, or 'fairy forts'), or simply beyond a veil of mist (see page 16).

Other immrama are set in a Christian milieu. The extant stories are: 'The Voyage of the Ui Chorra', 'The Voyage of Snedgus and Mac Riagla', 'The Voyage of Mael Duin' – the longest one, in which the eponymous hero seeking his father's slayer tours twenty-nine weird and wonderful islands – and, best known, 'The Voyage of St Brendan', which brings together explicit theological content, plus a cycle of journeys mapped on to the calendar of feast days, with authentic nautical and geographical knowledge of the reality of sailing in the North Atlantic. From information in 'The Voyage of St Brendan' it's possible to confidently identify certain places mentioned in the text with real places: the Island of Sheep and the Paradise of Birds are, respectively, the islands of Streymoy and Vagar in the Faeroes; the Island of Smiths appears to be Iceland.[2] Those of a romantic persuasion like to think that Brendan's ultimate destination, the Land of Promise, must be America; Tim Severin's transatlantic voyage in 1978 in a replica currach demonstrated that Brendan or other sixth-century Irishmen could conceivably have got there; but neither the text of the story nor any other evidence proves that they did, and the Land of Promise has been speculatively identified with other locations, such as the Azores.[3]

The composition of 'The Voyage of St Brendan' dates to c. 910, less than a century before the documented discovery of America by the Norseman Leif Ericson in c. 1000. The existence of a transatlantic land was an idea whose time had come. Two sagas describe the Norse voyages from Iceland to Greenland to America: 'The Saga of Eric the Red' and 'The Saga of the Greenlanders'. They may have a faint whiff of the wonder voyage – there's a consultation with the seeress Thorbjorg, and feisty Freydis scares off some Native Americans by slapping a sword on her bared breasts – but they're essentially plausible accounts of the experiences of seamen who had the means to undertake accurate transatlantic navigation. However, these texts languished unknown in Iceland for centuries, and Christopher Columbus had to start out from scratch, using 'The Voyage of St Brendan' as his inspiration, and first investigating the northern route via Ireland and Iceland before he embarked on his bold voyage straight across the mid-Atlantic to reach the Caribbean.

The Celtic theme of the otherworld across the sea recurs in Arthurian myth: in the isle of Avalon, associated with enchantresses such as the Lady of the Lake and Morgan le Fay, where the wounded King Arthur is taken after his last battle; in the Fortress of Annwn (the Welsh underworld) to which Arthur voyages in quest of the magical Cauldron of Annwn; in Corbenic, the Grail castle to which the quest knights sail on an enchanted ship (see page 34). Real islands to the west of Britain, such as Bardsey and the Isles of Scilly, do have the tangible association with the underworld of having been used in ancient times as burial grounds.[4]

These Irish and British notions of otherworldly islands in the west were probably influenced by the older Greek legend of the Fortunate Isles: islands located beyond the Pillars of Hercules (the Straits of Gibraltar) and inhabited by nymphs (the Hesperides, tending a garden of apples trees), the sleeping titan Cronos, and the souls of the virtuous – or at least the noble – sporting in the Elysian Fields. The Greek wonder voyages of Odysseus and Jason begin eastwards, to Troy and Colchis, respectively, and within the bounds of the Aegean and Black Seas; but their return journeys – and for Odysseus this is the main event – are more circuitous and some of the islands they visit lie far to the west of Greece. The locations of these islands are debatable, but Odysseus's visit to the underworld takes him beyond the Pillars of Hercules into the Atlantic, and some would place Ogygia, island of the nymph Calypso with whom Odysseus dallies awhile, among the Fortunate Isles.[5]

Though wonder voyages include diverse trials and tribulations, their quintessential destination is an earthly paradise. Whether it's the Land of Youth or the Land of Women, the Land of Promise or the Land of the Living, Avalon or Corbenic, the isles of Circe, Calypso, Nausicaa, or the Hesperides, or even Lemnos or Samothrace as depicted in the *Argonautica* (the voyage of Jason and the Argonauts),[6] these islands are places where the weather is clement, the trees are always in fruit, the flowers in bloom, everything is lovely and healthy, and there's no disease, death, or war, only a delightful coexistence of rustic civilisation and wild nature, in which people live in harmony with each other and the beasts, as in Eden, eating only vegetables, and enjoying each other sexually in freedom and purity.[7] There's much emphasis on the islands' female inhabitants, whether this derives from the fantasies of sex-starved mariners or the memory of a goddess-centred culture,[8] though in the Christian immrama we see a shift from sinless sensuality to sinless celibacy.[9] The earthly paradise is a dream of what people long for in this life, imagine to have existed in a past golden age, and hope for in the world to come.

Symbolically, this dreamy otherworld is located an unattainable distance beyond the western horizon. In more recent sea lore, memories of the Celtic and Greek paradise islands became blended in the legend of Hy-Brasil, which it was said could be glimpsed faintly through the mist once every seven years.[10] In ancient and medieval times people did not readily distinguish between symbolic and physical geography. They also had a rival conception of where people go when they die: underground, into the caverns of Hades or the barrow mounds of the sidhe. Both Greek and Irish cosmography depicted a seemingly contradictory picture of the otherworld or underworld being located both underground and across the western sea. John Carey makes sense of this in terms of antiquity's muddled understanding of the world, in which geographic and metaphysical ideas were interwoven: both Greeks and Irish had some notion of the earth being a sphere and hence that it would have an underside, which might conceivably be reached either by sailing around the curved surface of the ocean or by delving down through underground caverns, and might be inhabited by Antipodean beings.[11]

What neither the Greeks nor the Irish could know was that the Antipodes of the planet – the South Pacific – were indeed inhabited by people whose environment and way of life had quite a bit in common with the paradise islands that European mythology had imagined. At the beginning of the European age of discovery, in 1492 when Columbus crossed the ocean blue, it was still possible to imagine that God's paradise, the prelapsarian Eden, still existed in some remote part of the earth. Contempories of Columbus made serious efforts to find the island of Hy-Brasil. Columbus himself, though commissioned to seek a seaway to India, was obsessed with the idea of paradise; when he discovered tropical America, and its native people living naked and free in the rainforest, he believed he was close to Brendan's earthly paradise, which he computed lay south and west of the mouth of the Orinoco.[12] This kind of expectation continued as late as the eighteenth century, when the discovery of the Polynesian inhabitants of the South Pacific islands, especially Louis Antoine de Bougainville's description of Tahiti, led some in Europe, influenced by Rousseau's idea of the 'noble savage', to conclude that a prelapsarian people really had been found dwelling in paradise. The balmy climate, the lovely scenery, the abundance of food, the white-teethed and golden-skinned beauty and health of the people, and the willing sensuality of the women were a striking fulfilment of wonder-voyage dreams – until blighted by the impact of European exploitation.

Polynesian oral tradition contains many stories, like the Norse sagas, chronicling their ancestors' exploration and colonisation of the islands, and maritime raids and feuds between them. Their cosmography of the otherworld is complex too. There's a pervasive myth of 'Hawaiki', the island in the west from which their ancestors originally sailed, which actually corresponds to a whole sequence of islands from which the Polynesians progressively embarked as they colonised further and further through the Pacific. And there's a notion of an earthly paradise inhabited by gods and/or the spirits of the dead: for example, the paradise of Rohutu Noanoa above a mountain on Raiatea (one of the islands equated with Hawaiki), and various manifestations of the floating island of Kanehunamoku, which, like Hy-Brasil, can sometimes be glimpsed faintly on the horizon at sunset or sunrise: a destination that many seekers have sought, where there's a pool that can heal all illness and sustain one's youth. In some stories this island rises or sinks beneath the sea.[13] The story of 'Tiaitau's Veil' tells of a magical voyage to the Kingdom of the God of Night, which is plainly a metaphor of death.[14]

In this Polynesian mythos we are closer to a shamanic understanding of the symbolism of wonder voyages. Caitlin Matthews argues that the Celtic immrama and echtrai may be understood as memories of a shamanic conception of spirit and otherworld that once prevailed in the British Isles too. Instead of seeking, as the modern vogue is, to demythologise stories in terms of real places, real people, and physical journeys that may actually have taken place, she invites us to experience these stories as a kind of reconnaissance into the spiritual realm that our souls will some day have to navigate when we die.[15] I take this to be a symbolic reconnaissance, through the waters of our own imagination, in which the ocean symbolises death or the unconscious, the islands symbolise states of being we might hope to attain, and the voyaging boat symbolises the individual soul. One can interpret all this in psychoanalytic terms of getting to grips with mortality: Peter Connor sees the wonder voyage as expressing the key psychological task to be accomplished between the tasks of marriage and death – the mythology of the midlife crisis.[16] But one can also view this imaginative symbolism as an interface with a spiritual reality, which we can already experience in the spiritual dimension of our lives, as through a glass darkly, and which we'll experience more profoundly when we die.

This line of thought implies it might be worthwhile to engage with some of the wonder-voyage stories in a deeper, more meditative way than merely enjoying them as diverting entertainment. The same is surely true of other mythic stories, but, as we've seen, the voyage narrative works especially well as a metaphor of the spiritual journey. Not all wonder-voyage tales, however, lend themselves to such use: the voyages of Sinbad in *The Thousand and One Nights* place the emphasis on adventure and the winning of riches; their subtext endorses mercantile values rather than spiritual ones.[17] In the twentieth century C. S. Lewis understood the spiritual potential of the wonder voyage when he wrote *The Voyage of the Dawn Treader*, which is as laden with theological significance as the Christian immrama. His friend Tolkien wrote a poem, 'Imram', which links Brendan's quest for the Land of Promise with Tolkien's fascination, in his own myth-making, with the idea of a seaway into the west by which one might sail to the Undying Lands, inhabited, like Tir na nOg and the Fortunate Isles, by immortal beings and symbolic of the realm beyond death. In spacefaring science fiction, meanwhile, the wonder voyage has found a new lease of life. *Star Trek* displays the influence of both the *Odyssey* and the eighteenth-century voyages of Captain James Cook, as Captain James T. Kirk's starship wanders between planets suspended like islands in the ocean of space.

Tolkien shared with the author of 'The Voyage of St Brendan' the challenge of how to square the reality of the material world in which we live with the unseen spiritual reality in which both these authors believed and the imaginative world in which the stories take place. When he reaches the Land of Promise, Brendan is told, 'Fill your ship brim-full with precious stones and return to the land of your birth. The day of your final journey is at hand; you shall soon be laid to rest with your fathers. After many more years have rolled by, this island will be revealed to your successors at the time when Christians will be undergoing persecution.'[18] Sounds like a prophecy of the European discovery and settlement of America. Back in Ireland, Brendan does indeed soon give up his spirit to the Lord. Where does his 'final journey' take him? Not across the Atlantic to America, or to the story-world's Land of Promise; but out of this world to a place ultimately beyond our imagining.

A recurring theme in the wonder voyages is the impulse to return home: Brendan is commanded to; Bran is persuaded by one of his men to do so; Oisin can't resist his homesick longing; Odysseus spends ten years negotiating the perils and pleasures of monsters and women to get home to Ithaca; among the knights who win the Grail, it's important that one of them, Bors, does go home to tell the tale. This theme bespeaks a tension of desire between staying in paradise and returning to the mundane world. There's implicitly something of value in both. A reminder perhaps that it's not just our spiritual redemption that matters. The state of the material world matters as well.

Tahiti, more than any other island in the world the focus of European dreams of paradise, has been ruined by the projection of those dreams, so that today almost its entire circumference is ringfenced by concrete and tarmac development and its inland forest is being destroyed by the hypertrophic growth of an introduced garden plant. Iona, by contrast, thanks to its cooler climate and to the Iona Community that has restored the abbey and thereby renewed the island's holiness, is beautifully managed as a place that can provide a genuine balm to the soul. My own speculation is that the way we treat the material world matters at some profound metaphysical level, and that what we imagine matters as well, and that what we can imagine – even the deepest desires of our heart – we can perhaps make true, with God's blessing, if not fully in this world then in the next.

[1] Ashe, *Land to the West*.

[2] Ibid.; Wooding, 'Monastic Voyaging and the *Navigatio*'.

[3] O'Meara, 'In the Wake of the Saint'; Van de Weyer, *Celtic Fire*.

[4] Manwaring, *Lost Islands*.

[5] Ashe, *Land to the West*; Baring-Gould, *Curious Myths of the Middle Ages*.

[6] Especially as amplified in retellings by William Morris (*The Life and Death of Jason*) and Robert Graves (*The Golden Fleece*).

[7] Walker, *The Golden Feast*.

[8] Ashe, *The Mythology of the British Isles*.

[9] Mac Cana, 'The Sinless Otherworld of *Immram Brain*'.

[10] Johnson, *Phantom Islands of the Atlantic*.

[11] Carey, 'Ireland and the Antipodes'.

[12] Bartosik-Vélez, 'The Three Rhetorical Strategies of Christopher Columbus'; Flint, *The Imaginative Landscape of Christopher Columbus*.

[13] Beckwith, *Hawaiian Mythology*.

[14] Tessadri, *Legends from the South Seas*, pp. 73–83.

[15] Matthews, 'The Circuits of the Soul in Celtic Tradition' and 'The Quest as Shaman Journey in Celtic Tradition'.

[16] O'Connor, *Beyond the Mist*.

[17] Flint, *The Imaginative Landscape of Christopher Columbus*.

[18] Webb, 'The Voyage of St Brendan', p. 245.

# The Myth of King Arthur: a creative tradition

Did King Arthur really exist? It's an obvious question to ask and ultimately an impossible one to answer. The desire to find an answer is characteristic of our time. For all the postmodernists' subtle anxieties about 'truth' and 'reality', most of us, in Britain at least, have been conditioned to believe in material reality and the power of science and reason to tell us what is true. Earlier ages were less exercised about questions such as whether King Arthur existed. They just told the story – and changed it as they wished to fit the needs of the day.

In A.D. 407 the last Roman legions stationed in Britain departed. In 410 the city of Rome fell to the Goths. The people of Britain – Christian and long accustomed to Roman administration – found themselves on their own. They were under attack from the Irish in the west, the Picts in the north, and – worst of all – the Anglo-Saxons invading across the North Sea. The latter had already established a beachhead on the 'Saxon Shore' before the Romans left – and maybe even before the Romans came. During the next three centuries the Saxons inexorably colonised the whole of lowland Britain, driving the Romano-British (soon to be known as the 'Welsh') into their final refuges in Wales, Cornwall, and over the sea to Armorica (which thereby became 'Brittany').

For a short period in the late fifth and early sixth century the British managed to arrest the Saxon advance; after that they were always on the retreat. The inference is that during that time some charismatic leader must have arisen to weld the fragmented British kingdoms into a united front to resist the invaders; and that he was probably a cavalry commander, to have been able to range between regions as distant as Cornwall and Scotland.

According to Gildas, a historian writing at that time, that leader was the Roman nobleman Ambrosius Aurelianus. According to Nennius, writing three centuries later, the British 'dux bellorum' ('war duke') was Arthur. Neither source is entirely trusted. The only other documentation of Arthur's existence is a skimpy list of battles, probably drafted in the tenth century, which names Arthur as having defeated the Saxons at the battle of Badon Hill in 516 and fallen, with Mordred, at the battle of Camlann in 537. In short, the period in which Arthur is supposed to have lived is the least documented of any since the Roman conquest.

This void of knowledge has been a cauldron of inspiration for storytellers and writers ever since.

That stories about Arthur have had a long-lived place in folklore is apparent from the numerous landscape features (Seats, Beds, Caves, Stones) named after him; only the Devil is more celebrated in the British landscape. The legend grew like a snowball: the more famous Arthur's name became, the more stories became attached to him. Folk memory commonly conflates personages or events from different times in the past. The memory of an Arthur – let us say the sixth-century dux bellorum – became conflated in the folk imagination with the memory of earlier figures: Ambrosius, for one; and Magnus Maximus, self-appointed emperor of the West who captured Rome with British troops in 388; and Lucius Artorius Castus, a Roman cavalry commander on Hadrian's Wall in the second century who subsequently quelled an uprising in Armorica; and Arwîrac (known to history as 'Caractacus'), leader of the 'feini' warband, who resisted the Roman invasion of Britain in the first century and supposedly bore the title 'Arctur' ('the Bear');[1] and perhaps even a mythic titan, Albion, who gave his name to the land.[2] Another likely contributor to the legend, suggests Geoffrey Ashe, may have actually *been* Arthur: 'Riothamus' ('Supreme King') was the title of an anonymous British war leader who campaigned in Gaul in the late fifth century and was last heard of near the town of Avallon in Burgundy.[3]

The appeal of the legend for the Welsh was that it recalled a time when their ancestors had stood firm against the invaders and kept alive something of the splendour of Roman civilisation – and that it held out the hope that Arthur might yet live, sleeping in one of the many 'hollow hills' that claim that distinction, and someday return to lead them to regain the land they'd lost. This legend of the sleeping king taps into the more ancient myth of a sleeping giant embedded in the land and recurs in other countries: Finn mac Cumhail in Scotland; Frederick Barbarossa in Germany; Constantine Palaeologus in Greece. The folkloric Arthur passed into some early Welsh poetry, some lives of saints, and one lengthy prose narrative, 'How Culhwch Won Olwen'.[4] Here Arthur comes across not so much as dux bellorum or high king as leader of a wild band of warriors – reminiscent of Finn mac Cumhail's Fianna – who deal out harsh justice in a world of supernatural marvels.[5]

The legend of Arthur travelled to Brittany with the Britons evacuating from Cornwall before the Saxon advance. From there it came back into England with the Norman conquerors. A knowledge of folktales from both Wales and Brittany, as well as of Nennius, informs Geoffrey of Monmouth's *The History of the Kings of Britain*, the seminal work of fiction masquerading as history, completed in Oxford in 1136, that established the template of Arthur's career for all later literary treatments.

Merlin enters the narrative to arrange by sorcery Arthur's conception. Arthur not only unites Britain to fight off the Saxons, but invades Gaul to fight the Romans. After Mordred's treachery and the final battle at Camlann, the mortally wounded king is carried away to the Isle of Avalon 'so that his wounds might be attended to'.[6]

Geoffrey's book opened the floodgates to the vogue for Arthurian romance that was an important ingredient of the twelfth-century renaissance. From Brittany, Arthurian tales entered French literature in the romances of Chrétien de Troyes, Marie de France, and the writers who came after them. In the shared francophone literary culture of France and England, Arthur and his men were uprooted from their Romano-British origin and reinvented as knights of chivalry with all the shiny armour and courtly manners and jousting tournaments of the high Middle Ages. In a manner analogous to a folk tradition – and without any anxieties about plagiarism – successive writers endlessly reworked the stories, translating them from one language to another, adapting them from prose to poetry or vice versa, and adding new scenes and emphases as they fancied.

Arthur's fame was further boosted by the discovery of his grave at Glastonbury Abbey in 1191. This 'discovery' was almost certainly fake: it served the political interest of demoralising the truculent Welsh's hope that Arthur would return, and the economic interest of attracting pilgrims to the monastery, which had suffered a damaging fire. As the popularity of Arthur's legend grew, and became the vogue throughout Western Europe, it exerted a gravitational effect that pulled other, once quite separate stories – such as the Cornish tragedy of Tristan and Iseult – into the Arthurian framework. The same process can be seen elsewhere, as in the accretion of stories around Robin Hood; or around Prince Vladimir of Kiev, whose court of venturesome knights much resembles Arthur's; and indeed in the coopting of many classic science fiction plots by *Star Trek.*

It was Chrétien de Troyes who began, but died before completing, the first known version of the quest for the Grail: 'Perceval'. The incomplete state of this romance prompted a spate of lengthy 'continuations'; a Welsh version of the story appeared too, incorporating many indigenous Welsh elements, including, most dramatically, a severed head borne on the Grail.[7] The legend of Arthur expanded as a matrix of possible storylines through the countless permutations of characters and incidents. The different narratives fed off each other but did not attempt to maintain any consistency of detail as, say, contributions to the *Star Trek* mythos are required to do today. The most grandiose compilation was the Vulgate Cycle, of uncertain authorship, a five-part Latin epic in which Lancelot and the Grail provide the principal story arcs. The definitive treatment in English, distilled from the Vulgate Cycle and all that had gone before, came in the fifteenth century: Thomas Malory's *Le Morte D'Arthur*. Printed by William Caxton in 1485, this is the version by which Arthur's story has been principally known ever since, the basis of countless adaptations for younger readers.

Once Arthur is established by Merlin as high king and has inaugurated a regime of peace and prosperity, he withdraws from active duty and delegates to his knights the task of responding to any threats to the kingdom's tranquillity. The knights' adventures often take them into otherworldly situations located beyond the frontiers of the kingdom or in enchanted enclaves within it. Chief instigator of supernatural challenges to test the Round Table's mettle is the King's half-sister, the sorceress Morgan. She represents one of the insidious threads of tension within the kingdom which propel the story arc of the epic as a whole. So does Arthur's other half-sister, Morgause, also a sorceress and in some accounts conflated with Morgan, both of them ultimately deriving from the same Celtic goddess. Early in his career Morgause manages to conceive a son by her unwitting brother, and, Herod-like, Arthur tries to have the infant killed. These sisters' strained relationship with Arthur traces back to the deception of their mother, Ygerne, that facilitated his own conception, and reflects the fact they have sons of their own – including poor incest-spawned Mordred – who stand in line to the throne. And then there's Guinevere, Arthur's barren queen, who's been in love, since the moment their eyes first met, with his right-hand man, his greatest knight, unbeatable in battle: Lancelot. Thus the whole edifice of this utopian kingdom is built upon a foundation of human frailty. The mythopoeic logic dictates the onset of lassitude and decadence. Peace brings its own peril, it seems, for men whose sense of worth hinges upon their hyper-masculine prowess in battle.

Into this void of purpose, this angst of festering sin, comes a vision of the Holy Grail. Triggered by Morgause's impetuous eldest son, Gawain, the knights scatter to the four winds on the ultimate quest. Only Arthur has the wisdom to realise that this obsessive quest for an otherworldly ideal must destroy his kingdom of peace on earth. The Grail quest takes its protagonists into a more obviously otherworldly realm than any of their previous adventures. They travel strange dreamlike landscapes in which their lust and war skill leave them struggling to cope with trials that are ultimately spiritual, in which they don't know where to go or what to do, in which many of them die. They encounter a wasteland that has lost its fertility in what seems a prophetic vision of the ecological disasters of our own time. A handful of knights, the purest in heart, cross the sea to an enchanted castle whose inhabitants seem to dwell outside time. Here the purest of all are granted a glimpse of the enigmatic Grail.

Lancelot's secret love for the Queen dooms him to failure in the quest. When he returns, the two succumb at last to the desire they've fought to contain for so long. Mordred exploits this situation to unleash the tragic events that destroy the kingdom and lead inexorably to the last battle, where Arthur slays his own son and takes a mortal wound in return. Malory's conclusion holds out one ambivalent tendril of hope:

> Yet some men say in many parts of England that King Arthur is not dead, but had by the will of Our Lord Jesu into another place; and men say that he shall come again ... I will not say that it be so, but rather I will say, here in this world he changed his life. But many men say that there is written upon his tomb this verse: HIC IACET ARTHURUS, REX QUONDAM REXQUE FUTURUS.[8]

After the close of the Middle Ages, there was a lapse of interest in King Arthur. Milton chose to write *Paradise Lost* instead of his planned *Arthuriad* and there were no major new treatments of the legend until, in the glory days of the British Empire, the nineteenth-century Arthurian revival spearheaded by Tennyson's *Idylls of the King* and the paintings of the Pre-Raphaelites. Since then the production of new poems, novels, studies, and films has grown exponentially and it shows no sign of ceasing. The stories are once again being told orally too, as in Fire Springs' epic *Arthur's Dream* and Eric Maddern's *Telling Merlin* (see pages 50–2).

Since the 1960s, breakthroughs in archaeology have prompted a new emphasis in much of this output. At many sites associated with Arthurian legend – Tintagel, Castle Dore, Glastonbury Tor, Cadbury Castle, Dinas Emrys – archaeologists have discovered evidence of activity during the period when Arthur is supposed to have lived. Excavations at Cadbury Castle, one of the hollow hills where folk believed Arthur slept, demonstrated that this prehistoric hill fort was heavily refortified at about the right time to have made a fitting headquarters for Arthur as dux bellorum.[9] These discoveries inspired a vogue for fiction that tries to reconstruct the story of the 'real' historical Arthur: Rosemary's Sutcliffe's *Sword at Sunset* and Mary Stewart's *The Crystal Cave* were the trailblazers; many others have followed (see pages 40–7). Hollywood caught up with this trend in 2004 with *King Arthur.*

Each generation of writers has imposed its own agendas and needs on to the legend – and its own unexamined assumptions. The medieval treatments were written in a milieu that was unquestionably Christian and patriarchal and accorded much virtue to martial strength; women tended to be stereotyped as either passive victims or seductive enchantresses. Our current fascination with the 'real' Arthur seems to me to express the prevailing assumption that the material world accessible to science and senses is the only reality that exists (see page 84). We feel we ought to prefer the gritty reality to the romanticised myth. I don't mean to put down the value or fascination of historical investigation; it's the job of historians to find out whatever we *can* know about the past and to clarify what we *cannot*. But when stories' historicity can't be proven we don't need for that reason to discard them; we can accept them *as stories* and respond to them creatively as bards and writers have always done.

Am I saying we ought to feel free to change the traditional stories howsoever we please? The paradigm of artistic freedom might seem to demand that. But if we want to retell them in a way that harnesses the strengths and wisdom that have been forged by successive previous retellings, then there's a need to respect the tradition at the same time as we subvert it. Let's consider some Arthurian films.

*Excalibur* (1981) essentially follows Malory, but simplifies his epic greatly to condense it into two hours: for example, the film conflates Morgause with Morgan, and the wounded Fisher King of the Grail castle with Arthur, and reduces Malory's three Grail winners to Chrétien's one. *The Mists of Avalon* (2001) follows Marion Bradley's novel of the same name, which takes the sixth-century Romano-British setting of Sutcliffe and Stewart, reinjects it with magic and an otherworld Avalon located beyond a supernatural veil of mist, and stunningly inverts the sensibilities of the Matter of Britain by telling the story from the perspective of the female characters and the remnants of an indigenous pagan faith. The heroine is Morgaine (Morgan), a priestess of the old religion, who does indeed possess magical power and allure, but is extremely sympathetic and a tragic victim of events that conspire against her happiness.

*First Knight* (1994) and *King Arthur* (2004), on the other hand, adhere to Hollywood's conventions for a romantic adventure movie. The requisite happy endings seem oblivious of the essentially tragic nature of Arthur's story. *First Knight* resolves the love triangle between Arthur, Guinevere, and Lancelot by having the aged Arthur die nobly out of the way of the lovers' happiness together. So much, alas, for the once and future king, sleeping in Avalon or the hollow hill, waiting to return! *King Arthur*, in its wildly inaccurate pursuit of the 'true story', jettisons nearly everything from the tradition bar the characters' names and then fails to dream up any meaningful plot to fill the dramatic void.[10] The first two films, in very different ways, respectfully and knowledgeably rework the tradition. The second two don't; this is the reason they are much weaker films.

C. S. Lewis writes about 'myth' as the structure of motifs that underlies – and could exist independently of – the literary or performed presentation of a story.[11] This notion of mythic structure concerns not just the dramatic structure of plot climaxes and conflict, but also the patterns of characters, locations, incidents, and symbols which have developed through successive retelling of the story. An analogy may be drawn with language. It is possible to lump together words in ways that disregard the principles of syntax and style that have been forged as a language has developed; but the most eloquent speech and writing evince a mastery of these principles, upon the foundation of which the speaker or writer may make innovations that advance the language further. When it comes to the manipulation of myth that has developed over time, the writer, storyteller, or film-maker would likewise do well to base their work on knowledge of and respect for the tradition they're exploiting.

One way of getting to grips with a story's mythic structure is in terms of what Vladimir Propp calls 'functions' – unit events involving fundamental characters such as the hero, the villain, the helper: 'An interdiction is addressed to the hero'; 'The interdiction is violated'; 'The villain receives information about the hero'; and so on.[12] Another approach is to explore the relationships between the characters in terms of the archetypes of the unconscious that were identified by Jung. In the climactic sequence of *Excalibur* there's a remarkably clear illustration of the symbolic 'integration' in one psyche (represented by Arthur) of Jung's four basic archetypes: the *ego*, embodied in the quest knights, especially Perceval, the Grail winner; the *anima*, embodied in Guinevere, with whom Arthur is reconciled when he visits her in the convent she's withdrawn to and forgives her adultery with Lancelot; the *self*, wise old Merlin who returns as 'a dream' to give Arthur strength on the eve of his last battle; and the *shadow*, embodied in Mordred, with whom Arthur is united in the embrace of mortal combat.

These forms of analysis are interesting and useful, but note that they're also reductive. The sum of the parts is less than the whole. There are likely to be aspects of a story's mythopoetics that can only really be grasped by experiencing the whole story in your imagination, through listening to it, reading it, meditating on it.[13] Psychoanalytic interpretation is, like the search for the 'real history' behind a mythic story, a means by which modern secular culture tries to contain myth within a materialist understanding of the world. But in their traditional form the Arthurian stories repeatedly and profoundly invoke otherworldly concerns. It seems to me that at some level we disrespect what the stories are actually about – and the intentions of many of their authors – if we must always demythologise them in terms of history or psychology. A story's metaphors may allude to spiritual matters as well as material ones.

The Grail's evolution from a pagan cauldron of rebirth in early Welsh tales to the chalice used by Jesus Christ at the Last Supper reflects the potent blending of pagan and Christian ingredients in both the story of the Grail and the Arthurian mythos as a whole. The Grail's precise spiritual significance is elusive. Jessie Weston proposed in 1919 that the Grail quest preserved the memory of an ancient fertility rite that, in Gnostic Christian form, had survived into the Middle Ages.[14] Caitlín Matthews believes that the journeys to the Grail castle and the Isle of Avalon represent, like the Irish wonder voyages, shamanic journeys through the spirit world (see page 28).[15]

Such interpretations, though attractive, may risk a degree of wishful thinking about the past. If one wishes to promote feminist or environmentalist values today, or a particular form of spirituality, it can be tempting to believe that a matriarchal or ecological utopia, or a ritual tradition of a particular kind, once really existed. One may advance such hypotheses with greater claims of certainty than are warranted by the data – mythological stories – on which they're based. Belief in the literal truth of biblical narratives is an example of the same thing. I would suggest that even people who believe in a spiritual dimension to reality, when they make such claims about the past, unwittingly pander to the contemporary demand that we seek out the material truth that will explain away the myth.

It's not in the nature of mythological stories to yield such certain knowledge. What they can do is inspire our imagination in ways that serve both our political and our spiritual needs; they can do that *as stories* without any conclusive elucidation of their origins. Ashe explains how the myth of the 'golden age' in cultures worldwide, and of Arthur's kingdom in particular – an idealistic and benevolent society in equilibrium with its environment, transcending for a time the baser impulses of human nature and raising the hope that something like it may someday 'return' – appeals to our deepest longings, for well-being in this world and for paradise in the hereafter.[16] The parallel to the story arc of the Bible is obvious. Moreover, the mythopoeic linkage between the spiritual health of King Arthur's regime and the ecological condition of the wasteland speaks to the ecological crisis of our own time – and the question, rarely discussed, of what relationship may exist between this crisis in the material world and our spiritual destiny (see pages 165–9).

In some versions of the Grail quest, upon arriving at the otherworld castle the quest knight is expected to ask a question, one whose asking will heal the Fisher King and thereby heal the wasteland. The question is, 'What ails thee?' It is the asking of the question that matters more than any answer.

---

[1] Whitehead, 'Arwîrac of Glastonbury'.
[2] Ashe, *Camelot and the Vision of Albion*.
[3] Ashe, 'Riothamus'.

[4] Gantz, *The Mabinogion.*

[5] Padel, *Arthur in Medieval Welsh Literature.*

[6] Monmouth, *The History of the Kings of Britain*, p. 261.

[7] 'Peredur Song of Evrawg', in Gantz, *The Mabinogion.*

[8] 'Here lies Arthur, once king and future king.' Malory, *Le Morte D'Arthur*, Vol. 2, p. 519.

[9] Alcock and Ashe, 'Cadbury'.

[10] Nanson, 'Not Quite Camelot'.

[11] Lewis, *An Experiment in Criticism.*

[12] Propp, *Morphology of the Folktale.*

[13] I'm indebted to Simon Heywood for introducing me to this idea.

[14] Weston, *From Ritual to Romance.*

[15] Matthews, *Arthur and the Sovereignty of Britain.*

[16] Ashe, *Camelot and the Vision of Albion* and *King Arthur.*

# The Promise and Pitfalls of Christian Agenda in Stephen Lawhead's Pendragon Cycle

As a Christian writer whose fantasy novels have sold well in the secular marketplace, Stephen Lawhead follows in the footsteps of Tolkien and C. S. Lewis. After some mediocre early work, he hit the big time in the late 1980s with the Pendragon Cycle, a three-volume retelling of the legend of King Arthur, later expanded by two further novels.

The first book, *Taliesin*, tells the parallel stories of Charis, a princess of Atlantis who escapes her war-torn homeland when it sinks beneath the ocean, and Taliesin, a gifted Welsh bard living at the time the Roman legions withdrew from Britain. The two strands merge in a love story, whose offspring is the subject of the second volume, *Merlin*. Having earned a reputation as prophetic bard and berserk warrior, Merlin is propelled into an exile of insanity. He eventually returns to orchestrate Britain's defence, under a Christian king, Aurelius, against the invading barbarians. After that king's untimely death, Merlin is left with his baby heir, who turns out to be the nation's real hope. The third book, *Arthur*, traces this child's rise to power and the brief establishment of the longed-for Kingdom of Summer before it is undermined by the machinations of the sorceress Morgian and her son, Medraut.

Among modern fictional treatments of the Matter of Britain, Lawhead's is distinctive in its overtly Christian outlook. The Pendragon Cycle made Lawhead the flagship author of Lion Publishing's mission to sell Christian books into a secular market largely hostile to Christianity. The novels' excellent Celtic-romantic cover designs certainly contributed to their success; but what is the strength of Lawhead's writing, how has he managed to rework the Arthurian legends in a way that both communicates his faith and engages a broad readership, and what are we to make of the *kind* of Christianity he's mediating?

*

Lawhead writes with fluency and clarity. You always know what's happening; your mind's eye beholds each scene as on a floodlit stage. The imagery is neatly defined, colourful, simplified, almost like an animated film. The narrative tone is suitably epic. The characters, most of whom are nobles, speak with understated formality. There are just a few incongruous slips into modern American idiom. Lawhead varies the tone by varying the narrator. *Taliesin* is told in an omniscient storyteller's voice. Merlin tells his own story in the second book, inviting perilous comparison with Mary Stewart's superb Merlin character who narrates the whole of her Merlin Trilogy.[1] In the central part of *Merlin*, Lawhead also nicely varies the narrative tone by having Merlin, in his madness, deliver a series of charged outbursts, prophecies, and increasingly lucid memories of the dreadful events that precipitated his madness.

The charisma and enigma of Merlin, as others perceive him, are more apparent in *Arthur*, whose three parts are narrated by three different characters: Pelleas, Bedwyr, and Aneirin. Of these only Bedwyr, one of Arthur's captains, has sufficient character to add zest to his narrative. Breezy and spirited, his voice conjures images of galloping horses and of cloaks and unbound hair flying in the wind. Pelleas seems devoid of personality – through Bedwyr's eyes almost robotic – and both Pelleas and Aneirin function as little more than foils for Merlin.

Touches of humour occasionally lighten the epic tone: for example, the comic naivety of two monks, one of whom is not very bright, when upon first encountering the lovely Charis they take her for a vision of the Virgin Mary. There may be some gentle mockery of Roman Catholicism here, but the more intelligent monk, Dafyd – none other than St David of Wales – is an instrumental figure in the Christian conversion of Taliesin and the Atlantean refugees, and in supporting Merlin's plans for the Kingdom of Summer.

There's also a comic glimpse at the domestic behaviour of some Saxons after Arthur has made peace with them:

The Saecsen idea of a feast is simply to heap mounds of badly cooked meat onto the board and gorge on it until sated, whereupon you are supposed to drink whole butts of their sour beer. And, when everyone is falling-down drunk, they begin wrestling with one another.[2]

You have to remember that the Saxons – always the bad guys in quasi-historical retellings of Arthurian legend – are, of course, the ancestors of the English.

\*

Like Mary Stewart, Rosemary Sutcliffe, Gillian Bradshaw, Marion Bradley, and others,[3] Lawhead situates King Arthur in the immediate post-

Roman period. He runs with the theory that Arthur was a Christian war leader, of a mobile force of semi-disciplined troops, who rallied the Romano-British against the invading Anglo-Saxons, Irish, and Picts (see page 31).

This historicity contrasts with Charis's background in the final years of the fantastic civilisation of Atlantis. The settling of the surviving Atlanteans in Britain as the beautiful, long-lived Fair Folk echoes some cranky theories of links between Atlantis and the Celtic cultures of Western Europe.[4] They're noble and sophisticated; reminiscent of Tolkien's elves or the Tuatha De Danann of old Ireland. This pool of Atlanteans enables Lawhead to demythologise in his fifth-century setting such figures as the Lady of the Lake and the Fisher King.

*

A character cast of stereotypes is not unusual in epic fantasy and is characteristic of the medieval romances ancestral to the modern genre. Lawhead presents a striking polarisation between the Christian characters, who are almost sinless, and their enemies, who are hopelessly evil. The Saxons and Picts are generally depicted as savage brutes, comparable to Tolkien's orcs. Though we know the reason for Morgian's corruption, we see her as so overtaken by hate that her own personality is lost and she becomes little more than a symbol of Satan, as Arthur symbolises Christ. Though archetypes serve important mythopoeic purposes (see page 37), this kind of ethno-religious stereotyping seems troubling in a quasi-historical novel. The idea of an irreconcilable conflict between good and evil is commonly associated with Christianity, but such dualism derives largely from Manichaean influence. In mainstream Christian theology, even the most virtuous people are usually understood to have a dark side and the most wicked to bear in themselves the image of God.

To be fair, there are characters in the Pendragon Cycle, such as Vortigern and Uther, who occupy the middle ground, neither good Christians nor totally evil, but their importance to the story is secondary.

The female characters disappoint. Several women make spirited early appearances but then, generally after marrying, decline into sweet submissiveness. When Gwenhwyfar arrives on the scene, the anxiety of Arthur's advisors about this fiery Irish redhead suggests all manner of drama – which never happens. Most striking is the transformation of Charis, from desperate Atlantean bull dancer to the cold and pure Lady of the Lake. In her case the change is justified by the tragedy of her homeland's destruction and then her beloved Taliesin's death, from which she never really recovers. Morgian's seductive enchantment of

Merlin plays up the opposite stereotype of womanhood. Lawhead thereby rehearses tired old patriarchal values that can do no better than offer women a choice between humble submission and devious sexual manipulation.

Arthur is too good to be real. He is so Christ-like that he functions as a 'type' of Christ in this narrative, and therefore Christ himself – who must historically exist within the same fictional universe – seems distanced as a religious concept that the Christian characters refer to but rarely perceive as a living spiritual presence. One exception is that the angelic stranger who heals Merlin of his torment does leave the impression this was actually an encounter with Christ. Even the biblical types of Christ had big character flaws: David's lust, Joseph's arrogance, Moses' lack of confidence. Only at the end does Arthur evince a minor flaw – of pride. He insists that his wounding by Medraut is negligible, and so resists treatment by Merlin until it's too late. This leads to Arthur's departure and the fall of the Kingdom of Summer. That the kingdom's demise should depend on such a trifle seems to imply – and here idealism yields to realism – that no human political achievement can stand in place of the Kingdom of God, which is not of this world.

*

The trilogy's greatest achievement is the character of Taliesin. Lawhead had more freedom to create a distinctive personality for this less well-known character of Welsh tradition than in the cases of Arthur and Merlin, where both author's and readers' conceptions will inevitably be coloured by scores of other interpretations.

As Taliesin grows up, his poetic and prophetic gifts become increasingly apparent. There's a moving spectacle of the boy desperately trying to express his prophetic insights when he is too young to understand them or find words to match them:

> I was in many shapes before I was born: I was sunlight on a leaf; I was a star's beam; I was a lantern of light on a shepherd's pole.
>
> I was a sound on the wind; I was a word; I was a book of words.
>
> I was a bridge across seven rivers. I was a path in the sea. I was a coracle on the water, a leather boat that ploughed bright waves.
>
> I was a bubble in beer, a fleck of foam in my father's cup.
>
> I was a string in a bard's harp for nine nines of years; I was a melody on a maiden's lips.
>
> I was a spark in fire, a flame in a bonfire at Beltane … a flame … a flame …[5]

The druids who train him in bardic lore discern his greatness. God's Spirit is working in them before they ever hear the gospel, baptising their spirituality, paring out wicked practices from their customs. So when Taliesin hears about Christ it's easy for him to embrace the new faith and find in it the source and fulfilment of his prophetic powers. In his maturity he can speak with tremendous power and authority, yet he never loses his charm as the quintessential silver-tongued poet.

It's Taliesin who conceives the vision of the Kingdom of Summer – a reign of peace and justice – but he dies too soon to see it, leaving it to his son, Merlin, to make the dream become reality. Merlin builds up the expectation of a saviour who will establish the Kingdom of Summer. With the seer's guidance, Arthur fulfils this hope.

*

In Lawhead's world, magic is not morally neutral. It takes the form of either spiritual gifts from God, such as those granted Merlin, or the evil craft of sorcery as practised by Morgian.

Merlin's life begins in wonder: he dies at birth, but his father, inspired by the Holy Spirit, breathes life back into him. Merlin's public image is awesome: berserker, seer, enchanter, healer, bard, and one of the ageless Fair Folk. He lives in submission to God, but his supernatural powers look like sorcery and therefore distress the clergy. There's strong potential here for conflict between Merlin and the clergy, and also within Merlin's soul – the danger he might slip over the edge and use his abilities for his own glory. But Lawhead plays safe and, instead of allowing the conflicts to develop and milking them for drama, portrays the Christian camp as essentially united and Christian characters like Merlin as incorruptible.

Morgian's sorcery is mostly off-stage, though various unhappy events are blamed on her activity. My guess is that the author wishes to avoid glorifying Satan by dwelling on Morgian's satanic activities. However, we do see her power explicitly in an early confrontation with Merlin, which, after some sly attempts at negotiation by Morgian, becomes a direct contest of magical power.

Pelleas's account of Morgian's enchantment of Merlin is also nicely done. Lawhead conjures the eerie mood of the Forest of Broceliande, where Merlin and Pelleas are searching for a Fair Folk settlement, and Pelleas's confusion when Morgian enchants the woods to delay his return to her cottage to rescue Merlin:

Directly ahead, shimmering in the moonlight, stood the house, the light from the hearthfire faintly glowing in the door-way.

Smoke seeped slowly through the roof-thatch, silvery in the moonglow, rising like vapours from a fetid fen.[6]

We don't witness Morgian, disguised as lissom young 'Nimue', cast her spell on Merlin, although her attempt to seduce Pelleas is quite daringly narrated. Whether she actually had her wicked way with Merlin we're not told. Merlin's disgust with himself after this episode might suggest she did, but the tenor of the story makes it more likely he was just annoyed he'd let himself fall into her power.

The most violent confrontation between Merlin and Morgian is not actually described; we see only the aftermath when Bedwyr discovers Merlin blind and exhausted. In sum, the relationship of Merlin and Morgian is a very important thread in the plot but is largely hidden behind the scenes.

*

Lawhead concocts two potent amorous situations. The first is Taliesin's unrequited love for Charis, which begins about the same time as his conversion. For a time Charis is so wounded by her experiences that she cannot respond to either Taliesin's love or Christ's. This generates some impassioned poetry from Taliesin:

Then tell me the word that will win you, and I will speak it. I will speak the stars of heaven into a crown for your head; I will speak the flowers of the field into a cloak; I will speak the racing stream into a melody for your ears and the voices of a thousand larks to sing it; I will speak the softness of the night for your bed and the warmth of summer for your coverlet; I will speak the brightness of flame to light your way and the lustre of gold to shine in your smile; I will speak until the hardness in your melts away and your heart is free once more.[7]

Charis does, soon enough, accept both Taliesin and Christ. Too easily, I felt. The courtship might have been drawn out into a more intense trial for Taliesin.

The other situation is the infatuation of Aurelius's brother, Uther, with Igraine, who becomes Aurelius's queen. Merlin's horror when he spots this source of conflict between the brothers suggests a great drama is about to develop. But this never happens, for Aurelius dies shortly after and we're assured that Uther was in no way responsible.

Merlin's own rather banal delight in his bride reassures us that sex is a fine and wonderful thing in its proper context of marriage. The contrast with the 'Nimue' episode is obvious, but the latter, besides being far more exciting to read, is quite an extreme situation of sexually charged sorcery. Once again, there's a polarisation between good and evil which leaves little middle ground and equates evil with sexiness.

To fortify Arthur's purity, Lawhead has cleaned up the sexual irregularities traditionally associated with him and so deflated much of the power of the myth (see page 34). Medraut is simply Morgian's son; there's no hint of the tale that he was the offspring of Arthur's incest with his half-sister Morgause. (Like *Excalibur*'s Morgana, Lawhead's Morgian is a composite of the traditional characters Morgan, Morgause, and Nimue.) It's also made clear that, contrary to suspicion, Arthur is not Uther's bastard but was begotten in wedlock by Aurelius. Why should the legitimacy of a man's birth be laid to his moral credit? Might it not be consonant with Jesus' blessing of the humble that an illegitimate child should become saviour of his country?

*

The third book of the cycle follows Arthur's escalating campaigns, first against the less cooperative British petty kings, then against the greater menace of the invading barbarians. Lawhead tries to build up the suspense of each struggle against heavy odds, but the suspense fails because we know that Arthur is going to win every time. So the battle scenes become tedious. They're also too clean; they fail to capture the horror of battle, though the second book does include a truly horrific scene in which Merlin finds his pregnant wife's corpse mutilated by Angle raiders. Just as in wartime propaganda, the enemy are so dehumanised that we're not distressed to see them slaughtered in huge numbers.

The British troops' use of prayer and worship to seek victory in battle is no doubt historically realistic, but it disappoints me that the narrative implies no consciousness, on the author's part, that such a practice might be considered a sad corruption of Jesus' teaching of love. At the same time, the very historicity of the setting together with the emphasis on practical military considerations weighs against our interpreting Arthur's battles as primarily symbolic of the spiritual struggle against evil.

Early in his career Arthur makes peace with a few Saxon chieftains by simply demanding peace with such audacity that they are astonished into accepting his terms. This ploy does not succeed for long. The Kingdom of Summer is built upon blood. That is its flaw. Arthur's imitation of Christ is imperfect, for Christ is not a warrior and his kingdom is not established by the sword.

*

In *Taliesin* Stephen Lawhead has written a work of historical fantasy as imaginative and moving as anything in that genre. There is much to admire in *Merlin* too, especially the depiction of Merlin's madness. *Arthur* seems to me less satisfying; even less so the later volumes, *Pendragon* and *Grail*, which I've not examined here. But all three books of the original trilogy fail to exploit fully the dramatic potential of a number of explosive situations – in particular, ones involving sex and sorcery. It's as though Lawhead avoids making the most of them for fear of inciting condemnation from conservative evangelical Christians among his publisher's core market, some of whom regard the whole genre of fantasy – even Lewis's blatantly Christian-allegorical Chronicles of Narnia – as spiritually dangerous.

Yet the books have sold well, and not just to Christians; they have been continuously in print for more than twenty years. Dramatic conflict isn't necessarily the be-all and end-all of imaginative writing. Perhaps, as Stratford Caldecott argues of *The Lord of the Rings*, literature that celebrates genuine goodness can possess an inherent appeal.[8] One can certainly enjoy Lawhead's fresh interpretation of Arthurian and Atlantean legend, and the fine characterisation of Taliesin and Merlin, and some no doubt have enjoyed the military detail of the wargame against the invaders. What troubles me is that, again and again, in the polarisation of good and evil in ethno-religious conflict, in the stereotyping of women, in the indulgent narration of war but avoidance and demonisation of sex, in the suppression of pagan ingredients of Arthurian myth, these books rehearse discredited conservative attitudes that have long been associated with Christianity, that have facilitated that faith's fall from public grace in Britain, and yet have nothing to do with its core message of love and hope.

Christian hope, though, does endure in the trilogy's ending – a hope that is true to Arthurian tradition and also reflects the Celtic-pagan dream of paradise in the west. Arthur has won the crucial battle against the forces of evil, but taken a mortal wound; the Kingdom of Summer crumbles, yet Arthur lives on, somewhere beyond the sea.

---

[1] Stewart, *The Crystal Cave*, *The Hollow Hills*, and *The Last Enchantment*.

[2] Lawhead, *Arthur*, p. 177.

[3] Stewart, *The Crystal Cave*, *The Hollow Hills*, *The Last Enchantment*, and *The Wicked Day*; Sutcliffe, *Sword at Sunset*; Bradshaw, *Down the Long Wind*; Bradley, *Mists of Avalon*.

[4] See, for example, Ó Síocháin, *Ireland*.

[5] Lawhead, *Taliesin*, p. 304.

[6] Lawhead, *Arthur*, p. 85.

[7] Lawhead, *Taliesin*, pp. 424–5.

[8] Stratford Caldecott, *Secret Fire.*

# Storytelling

# Telling Merlin

## Performed by Eric Maddern, Fleur Shorthouse, and Robin Jeffery

For its tenth anniversary, 2001, the Festival at the Edge commissioned Eric Maddern to create a multimedia performance about Merlin. Ambitious in length, range of art forms deployed, and multiplicity of perspectives, *Telling Merlin* presents the changing ways in which stories about Merlin have been told over the centuries. Tales from diverse sources, about apparently quite different Merlins, are mapped on to the life-span of a single individual. The show sparked much discussion afterwards: some people loved it; others didn't get it. To appreciate it fully, you had to understand it was an exploration of the storytelling art and a work of multimedia storytelling theatre, not just a jazzed-up story.

Sam Starmer designed the sets: a backdrop map of ancient Britain; real branches of foliage to one side of the stage and heraldic banners on the other, reflecting Merlin's mediation between civilisation and the wild; and on the front corners of the stage a simulated fire and a spring of running water, which provided an evocative background sound throughout the performance.

Robin Jeffery's music evoked a medieval flavour by means of lute, laouta, and yayli tambour. The opening song had been translated into Welsh by songwriter Gwylim Morus. The performers began this song in Welsh, then seamlessly shifted into English. This imparted the sensation of suddenly discovering that one could understand Welsh and of being magically transported into the ancient British world.

The first act included: the *Mabinogion* tale of Llud and the dragons of Oxford; which set the scene for the young Merlin's part in the saga of Vortigern and the Saxons, from Geoffrey of Monmouth's *History of the Kings of Britain*; and the mature Merlin's madness in the Forest of Celyddon, from Geoffrey's *Life of Merlin*. Eric started off in familiar storytelling style, but this was soon subverted by superb parodies of an ersatz Welsh bard (Eric), complete with broken harp, and a bespectacled academic (Fleur), battling on stage to get their own version of the story heard. Another parody, this time of rustic folk storytellers, came near the end of Act II, relating the Gypsy folktale about Merlin and Trinali. I daresay both these bits of parody may have cut close to the bone for some listeners.

The Vortigern section culminated in a condensed version of the *Prophecies of Merlin*, which Eric delivered with fierce passion, his face transformed by a red spotlight. At a debrief session the next morning, he said that in order to impart a trance-like effect he'd not rehearsed a final script of this speech. This was for me the most powerful part of the show. It was followed by a marvellous fight-dance of two dragons represented by ribbons attached to long sticks, a dance echoed in Act II by a sexy hand-dance signifying the foreplay between Merlin and Nimue.

In the Celyddon section the performance moved from storytelling into drama, Eric playing Merlin, Fleur his sister Ganieda, and Robin pressed into service as King Rodarchus. This sequence included the pig poems attributed to Merlin, which Robin accompanied with the hilarious pig noise of his rumbomba. Later Eric posed cross-legged as Cernunnos from the Gundestrup Cauldron, complete with stag-antlers headdress. It was uncanny to see that iconic image enfleshed as a living man, though the sacred mood was a mite undermined by one or two chuckles from people uncomfortable with that and perhaps by anxiety that the antlers, listing to one side, might fall off his head. This part of the show ended with Eric-Merlin constructing a model of Stonehenge and meeting Taliesin (Fleur).

Act II began with the familiar story of Merlin's part in Arthur's conception and the founding of the Round Table, narrated in conventional storytelling style; Eric deployed the full strength of his charisma to engage with the huge audience packing the Big Top. When the story reached Merlin's romance with Nimue, Fleur suddenly launched into the jazz song 'Lazy Afternoon'. This jolted us in a startling and effective way into a modern setting and a theatre sketch in which Eric and Fleur debated what the philosophy of Merlin stands for today.

At the show's conclusion Eric donned his antlers once more to lead us all in torch-lit procession to 'the Gates of Annwn' – an astonishing spectacle of fireworks and fire sculptures created by David Goff Eveleigh.

Listeners familiar with the source texts had an advantage in making sense of this show's complex structure. The constituent stories were pretty faithful to their separate sources and therefore not necessarily consistent with each other. There was a sense of progression through an individual's life in Act I, but a marked break of continuity going into Act II. It might be more satisfying to be given a stronger indication that the Merlin who appears in the Arthurian sequence represents, in some way, the old age of the Merlin whose youth and midlife are described in Act I. One particular dissonance was that the account of Merlin's attraction to Nimue – feelings we were told he's never felt before – did not acknowledge the first act's mention of him having a wife.

I suspect that the stronger reservations some listeners felt about this remarkable performance are connected not only to any anxieties they may have had about the use of parody and ritual, but to their expectations about what storytelling is. Sometimes, I sense, people want to limit storytelling to a particular 'pure' paradigm of how it should be practised. But there are very different ways of telling stories, and storytelling is not, and need not be, hermetically sealed from other art forms.

*Telling Merlin* is an impressive piece of postmodern storytelling, which foregrounds the slippery identity of a character like Merlin, who's been interpreted in different ways in different periods and places, and at the same time interrogates the ways that storytelling is actually performed, to the extent that the line between 'storytelling' and 'theatre' is repeatedly transgressed. This approach makes its impact more to the intellect and as a spectacle, rather than to the heart, but in doing so expands the possibilities of what storytelling can do and how it can interface with other art forms: not only music and set design, but also theatre, dance, and ritual.

# Writing It and Telling It

After I finished an MA in creative writing at Bath Spa University in 1999 my career took an unexpected turn. I'd previously been a regular contributor at the Storytelling Society that Katy Cawkwell started in Oxford. There was no club of that ilk in Bath, but when, earlier in 1999, I invited Katy to perform a set of *Celtic Tales* with me at Bath Fringe Festival, it became clear that storytelling had potential in this city. The venue was literally packed to overflowing; there were people wedged down the corridor, out of sight but straining to listen. With the encouragement of friends I set up a monthly Storytelling Circle (see pages 68–70), and this opened up diverse opportunities for me to work as a storyteller. In travelling this new path, as both a writer and a storyteller, I discovered exciting synergies between these two arts.

I found that various analyses of story structure could be applied to both writing and storytelling: Aristotle's beginning, middle, and end, elaborated by later writers into three-act structure; Joseph Campbell's hero cycle (see pages 13–14); Vladimir Propp's 'functions' of the folktale (see page 37).[1] However, the folklorist Axel Olrik argues that folktales passed down a purely oral tradition obey certain exacting structural rules: they do not begin with sudden action and do not end abruptly; repetitions occur in threes; no more than two characters in a scene; plot is linear and single-stranded; etc. Deviations from these 'laws' betray some literary influence upon the tradition.[2] Such rules arose naturally from the practical challenges of (a) remembering stories without any possibility of referring to a text, and (b) keeping the story clear enough that listeners, relying entirely on ears and memory, won't lose track of what's happening. In practice, in cultures with a long history of writing – such as Greece – there's been a continuous interweaving between oral and literary tradition as writers have exploited myth and folklore and literate storytellers have taken material from books.[3]

Techniques I learnt from the likes of Hugh Lupton and Ben Haggarty for the preparation of stories for telling have proven useful to me, and my students, in planning stories for writing: the methods, for example, of organising the story as a sequence of 'bones', and visualising each of these bones as if it were a painting or photograph (see page 82), and gabbling through the story at speed to get an arrow-like sense of its momentum. Tim Sheppard's training in story improvisation – based on the theatre teaching of Keith Johnstone[4] – brought home to me the importance, in both storytelling and writing, of finding a natural flow of language, an authentic voice, as opposed to the strained, unnatural voice that novice writers and storytellers alike can easily slip into. Untutored storytellers seem particularly prone to the use of cod medieval turns of phrase. I've also learnt to recognise the hazard, in oral storytelling, of too much wordy detail, which slows the story down and is unnecessary because a storyteller has so many other tools of body language and vocal inflection with which to communicate; and I've learnt why, as a direct corollary, to make a story truly engaging in print requires more detailed and careful wordsmithing, because words are all that a writer has. Nevertheless, intensive practice in the use of oral language, through composing and performing stories extempore, has fed back into my fiction-writing and helped me cultivate a more fluid prose style.

Which is not to say that more formal, or even archaic, patterns of language have no place in either written or told stories. The philologist Tom Shippey has elucidated how, in *The Lord of the Rings*, Tolkien varies the register of language – between 'ironic', 'low' and 'high mimetic', 'romantic', and 'mythic' – according to the characters and situations in play.[5] That's one reason, says Shippey, why some critics are so hostile to Tolkien, since modes other than ironic and low mimetic are unfamiliar in modern English fiction – unlike in modern Greek, say, where a wider range of register is normatively available.[6] It seems to me quite justified for a storyteller to shift into a higher register when telling more mythic stories. What matters is *control*: a conscious mastery of the language you're using so that it remains inflected by your own authentic voice.

In some of my stories I've explored the interplay between writing and storytelling. In 'For Love of Tam Lin' I rewrote the traditional tale of 'Tam Lin', using tricks of pace, repetition, and imagery from my oral telling of the story, but also experimentally applying a pattern of rhythmic progression derived from a dance practice called 'the Five Rhythms'. 'The Waves Never Ceasing' began as a literary short story that conflates several different legends of sinking cities as a single tale presented in the voice of an aged seanachie addressing a young folktale collector. I then adapted the piece for extempore telling, retaining the frame of meeting the seanachie but related from *my* point of view. This I felt uneasy about because the frame is fictional but came across as autobiographically true and therefore claimed a false authenticity for both the story and my supposed encounter with a tradition bearer (see page 119).

The reverse happened with my treatment of 'Phaethon': I started out telling this myth in the frame of meeting in Greece a man who told it to me and who I implied was none other than Apollo, still grieving about the fate of his son; then I incorporated this situation, both frame and myth, within a more expansive literary story, 'The Sun Cafe'. When I adapted for telling my comic-gothic short story 'The White Hoover', I had no choice, because of the way the story ends, but to convert it from first-person to third-person narration. It depends for its effect on sustained innuendo relating to the suction tube of a vacuum cleaner,[7] which I'm afraid I milked for all it was worth at the very bawdy Halloween story session at which I first told it.[8]

One typical difference between storytelling and both fiction and theatre is that storytelling tends to be extempore rather than scripted. Storytellers are rightly proud of the flexibility this gives them to respond to the particularity of what's happening, right here, right now, with this audience in this physical space. But there's no clear-cut line between storytelling and theatre. Some theatre is improvised; some storytelling is scripted. In Euripides' *The Bacchae*, which I saw produced by the Actors of Dionysus, most of the action is offstage and reported by the actors, rather like telling a story; but the fact their speeches were scripted and memorised freed the actors to commit their bodies to superbly sensual and even gymnastic movement. In his performance of *Biowulf*, a poetic cyberpunk adaptation of *Beowulf*, Kevan Manwaring deploys finely wrought wordplay and dancelike movement very different from the more informal use of both language and body in his extempore storytelling. Hugh Lupton's 'praise songs', such as *The Horses* and *The Homing Stone*, are excellent examples of storytelling crafted as narrative poetry, which optimises not so much the physicality of performance as the sculpting of rhythm and image in the spoken word.

Less successful was the Words Allowed initiative in Bristol, which centred on the 'performance reading' of literary short stories. Because they were reading, the performers could not achieve the kind of connection with the audience that a storyteller can.

In church, the 'text-telling' of Bible stories, as promoted by the Telling Place, makes an engaging alternative to the traditional practice of reading the lesson (see pages 65–7). You can make Bible stories more fully your own, of course, by letting go of the text and using your own words and your own imagination, but text-telling does work, and the experience of text-telling scripture inspired me to try text-telling some of my own literary short stories.

I wanted to employ in live performance my prose's more carefully crafted language and more subtle nuances, just as poets do when they recite from memory. The mood and the relationship with the audience proved very different from what I experience in extempore storytelling – the listeners have less scope to influence what you're saying – yet the stories make a powerful impact, and go down well, especially in more

literary or avant-garde contexts. The more stylised energy of performance means that telling 'The Waves Never Ceasing' in this way avoids
the peril I mentioned above of deceiving the audience.

Text-tellings of several of the shorter stories in my book *Exotic Excursions* are now part of my repertoire. That's not to say I'd ever want
text-telling to replace oral composition and extempore delivery as my
principal approach to storytelling. Writing and storytelling are two distinct arts, yet in a literate society they exist in relationship with each
other and there are fertile possibilities of interaction between them.

---

[1] Aristotle, *Poetics*; Campbell, *The Hero with a Thousand Faces*; Propp, *Morphology of the Folktale*.

[2] Olrik, 'Epic Laws of Folk Narrative'.

[3] Alexiou, *After Antiquity*.

[4] Johnstone, *Impro*.

[5] Shippey, *The Road to Middle-Earth*. The five 'modes' he refers to derive from
Northrop Frye's *Anatomy of Criticism*.

[6] Alexiou, *After Antiquity*.

[7] A trope I took from a bawdy song I once heard.

[8] 'The Waves Never Ceasing', 'The Sun Cafe', and 'The White Hoover' are all
included in Nanson, *Exotic Excursions*.

# Listening to Hugh Lupton

Hugh Lupton is one of the culture heroes of the British storytelling revival. As teacher and role model he's been an inspiration to many of us. Much of his more epic performance work has been in collaboration with others, such as his peers in the Company of Storytellers – Ben Haggarty and Pomme Clayton – and latterly the likes of Daniel Morden, Chris Wood, and Nick Hennessey.

## The Iliad

### Performed by Hugh Lupton and Daniel Morden

In a Guildhall packed to the gills – 360 seats, all sold – Hugh Lupton and Daniel Morden premièred for Bath Literature Festival this the prequel to their much acclaimed telling of the *Odyssey*. Most of the audience were not storytelling aficionados, and Hugh began with some introductory remarks to help the listeners get to grips with the large number of characters and the uncanny 'forcefield' qualities of the Greek gods.

Though the action of Homer's *Iliad* did not begin until an hour into this two-and-a-half-hour show, the storytellers were true to Homer in making Achilles – awesome archetype of violence – central to the story. They began with the founding of Troy and then introduced in parallel the early history of Achilles and the man they present as his polar opposite (who also proves to be his nemesis): Paris.

In the opening, and intermittently later, the phrase 'If I could sing I would sing of …' effected jump cuts through time and space and evoked a memory of the generations of epic singers who passed the story down to Homer. This technique was especially potent in the climactic destruction of the city: the cinematic imagery and rapid alternation between speakers brought the story to a swift conclusion.

Symbolic images were repeated in changed circumstances to striking effect: for example, that of a bleeding ring after the deaths of Patroclus and then Hector, and of the shifting balance of Zeus's scales of fortune. Embedded among the imagery and action were some impassioned speeches: especially moving was Achilles' pitying reply to Priam when the Trojan king begs for Hector's body.

The storytellers held the audience all the way through this lengthy epic. Both spoke with tremendous power when the story required it. Daniel's manner was stern, hard, and unsmiling, as befitted much of the material. He's a master of pace – able to switch from rapid runs to stunning pauses. Hugh was more inclined to engage the audience with humour and a smile, but he could be stern too – and ferocious in recounting Achilles' slaughter of Cygnus.

Instead of celebrating warrior values, as the culture of Dark Age Greece did, this telling brought home the awfulness of war. Hector, though noble, appears foolhardy in confronting Achilles after his family have begged him not to. For me the most powerful moment in the show was the description of the night-time no-man's-land that Priam crosses to meet Achilles. The imagery of broken carriages and bloated horse carcasses evoked all the battlefields of history.

For all the valour of the warriors, each significant turn in the war is achieved by the capricious intervention of the gods. Through most of the story the trickster hero of the *Odyssey* plays only a minor role. But when Achilles is killed and the Achaean cause seems lost, Odysseus steps to the fore and now the whole tone of the story changes. Where valour has failed, cunning succeeds. In a few swift sentences, Odysseus and his men are inside the city. The end is fast and terrible. The gods, who for ten years have played a wargame with humans as their pawns, are appalled by the scale and savagery of the Achaeans' destruction of Troy.

Someday, I hope, we may have opportunity to experience the epics of Achilles and of Odysseus told back to back. In Hugh Lupton and Daniel Morden these venerable stories find voices worthy of them.

Hugh and Daniel have followed up their two Homeric epics with further productions based on Greek mythology, such as *Metamorphoses* and *Icarus*. In recent years Hugh has also turned to historical material – with an emphasis on the history of dissent in England …

# On Common Ground

## Performed by Hugh Lupton and Chris Wood

The Bath Literature Festival blurb betrayed no hint that the subject of this show was the poet John Clare. It need not have been so coy. The story of the Peasant Poet is a story that needs to be told. As the opening song, 'One in a Million', hinted, Clare is a unique figure, the poetic genius who happened to be among the many victims of the enclosure of the English commons, who was there to give eloquent testimony to the impact of that catastrophe on not only the economic situation but the very psyche of the common people.

The show began with a prologue of song and anecdote that won the audience's sympathy in preparation for the tragic story that would follow, and posed the question, 'What was happening seven generations ago whose consequences we are now living with today?' Chris introduced a Frank Mansell song about rootedness in the land with an account of the discovery that a Cheddar schoolteacher was genetically related to the Cheddar Man who'd died in the same locality nine thousand years earlier. Such a deep-rooted bloodline does indeed seem something to celebrate, though you wouldn't want to emphasise that kind of thing too much lest you give ammunition to 'blood and earth' xenophobes hostile to immigrants and travellers.

Hugh's telling of Clare's story comprised a series of dramatised snapshots of moments in his life, punctuated by songs from Chris, extracts of Clare's poetry, and a refrain, delivered as if speaking directly to Clare, describing the local landscape that he knew so intimately that it could be equated to the inscape of his own mind. This ecobardic strategy powerfully expressed how – unlike those responsible for enclosure, who saw the land as merely a resource to be utilised – someone who truly inhabits a place experiences the land as an extension of their own being.

The story thread of Clare's doomed romance with Mary Joyce, daughter of a landowning farmer, provided the show's most poignant moment – when they meet for the last time, sundered by an economic shift that has elevated Mr Joyce's fortunes while depressing Clare's. Enclosure undermines Clare's livelihood, destroys his chances with the love of his life, and, in expelling him from the common land that was an extension of his psyche, drives him 'out of his mind' into madness and the lunatic asylum in which he spent his last 23 years.

Chris's melodic singing and delicate guitar- and violin-work deepened the emotional resonance of the story and made the tragic ending easier to bear. After the final song, 'Mad John', the audience applauded loud and long. But the mythic return had yet to be accomplished. In post-applause conversational style, Hugh completed his account of Clare's life and then discharged a scathing indictment of contemporary English society, seven generations on, and what it has done to our land. By his skill, charm, and humility he'd earned the right to do that and we applauded him all the more for saying something that so needs to be said.

Hugh has followed up *On Common Ground* by collaborating with Nick Hennessey on *The Liberty Tree*: a telling of the legend of Robin Hood in which they embed three historical stories about the oppression of dissent among the English common people. Here again Hugh Lupton uses his storytelling to confront us with questions of social and environmental justice that need to be more widely understood – and does so in a way that does not weaken the integrity of his art but, on the contrary, deepens its power to move us.

# The Meeting of Sacred and Secular

From what I've heard about the Network of Biblical Storytellers, and the sheer size of its Festival Gathering, the context of biblical storytelling in the United States is very different from that in Britain. It's largely a matter of scale. Not only are there more people in the USA, but a lot more of them go to church – a large enough population of Christians to sustain a storytelling scene that is independent of the secular storytelling world.

Despite its deep Christian roots, Britain is now in many ways a post-Christian society. Numbers of church members are dwindling. It's arguably one of the most secularised countries in the world. In these circumstances, sacred and secular storytelling tend to be less separate. The Telling Place initiative, the main promoter of biblical storytelling in Britain, draws no strict boundary between sacred and secular storytelling, or between the church and the wider culture.[1] Their events are publicised through secular as well as Christian channels and involve storytellers from both inside and outside the church. The Telling Place was invited to run a session at the 2000 Annual Gathering of the national Society for Storytelling.

Sensitivity is needed, however, in presenting biblical stories in secular contexts. Bible stories are conspicuously absent from most British storytelling events. Many people here are instinctively hostile to Christianity. Such feelings are not so much about God (whom many still believe in in some way) or Jesus (who, as a man, still commands respect, at least among those who've heard of him). They're more to do with the institutional church, perceived as an oppressive and hypocritical social force from whose power people have only recently been liberated. Anti-Christian prejudice is also stoked by Bible-bashing evangelism with which many have been targeted, especially at college. In Britain today the very idea of evangelism is widely viewed as offensive.

All this makes one cautious in telling Bible stories outside the church. The British storyteller Dave Robertson often mixes biblical with other traditional stories. In secular venues he introduces the biblical stories as 'from the "Judaeo-Christian tradition" or something like that – not because I'm trying to hide it but because there's such a negative mindset that as soon as you say "biblical" then people think you want to convert them or be some kind of lunatic'.[2]

The challenge is to make Bible stories presentable to a potentially hostile audience. It seems to me irresponsible to hit an audience with a story that speaks of God's judgment, say, and not to give consideration to how it will be received. Good storytelling practice of drawing in the audience to take an active part in imagining everything that happens in the story (see pages 82–3), and making their own interpretation, is very different from the Calvinist approach of simply preaching a narrow gospel message and expecting the audience to either take it or leave it.

The intimate setting of a storytelling circle, like the one I set up in Bath (see pages 68–70), can nurture a warm sense of fellowship among those who attend regularly. In the case of the Bath Storytelling Circle these include people of diverse persuasions: Christians, agnostics, and also Pagans whose spiritual path is inspired by ancient Celtic spirituality and its perceived emphasis on living in tune with the rhythms of nature. As the indigenous pre-Roman and pre-English inhabitants of Britain, the Celts had an analogous place here to that of Native Americans in North America. The Pagans – in particular the Druids – regard some Celtic myths, especially those in the *Mabinogion*, as sacred stories, whereas other storytellers might approach the same material in a secular way. At a December session of the Storytelling Circle, one of our regulars, Simon Airey, told the Christmas story from the point of view of Balthasar, one of the Wise Men; a few days later, at midnight mass on Christmas Eve, he was telling exactly the same story, in the same way, from the pulpit of Bath Abbey.

In an article in *The Biblical Storyteller*, Sarah Peters has described how storytelling helps to bring together people who are different from each other and to forge among them a sense of loving, accepting community.[3] She was referring to people of different ages and family circumstances within the church. But the same process can work among people from different spiritual traditions. Implicit in this statement, I'm aware, are some deep challenges to the exclusivism to be found in Christian doctrine, and to the way we interpret many biblical stories. If we believe in loving community as the fruit of God's will, we may have to face up to those challenges (see pages 84–5).

---

[1] The Telling Place ceased operations in 2007 (see pages 63–7).
[2] Quoted in Nanson, 'Stories that I Like', p. 5.
[3] Peters, 'From 2 to 102, Storytelling Is for All Generations!'

# The Telling Place

The Telling Place storytelling initiative began in 1998 as a partnership between the Northumbria Community and the Bible Society. During its nine years of existence, it did a great deal of well-received work, attracting large audiences – sometimes numbering several hundred – to many events.

## The Telling Place at Greenbelt

The Telling Place is an initiative to promote storytelling in the church and the wider culture, with a particular, but not exclusive, emphasis on stories from the Judaeo-Christian tradition. Its team run courses, workshops, and gatherings and offer help in setting up story circles and putting on ceilidhs. 'The Telling Place' is also the name of a tent beautifully designed as a storytelling venue for open-air festivals. The creative driving force behind the Telling Place is Angela Knowles, who has been a professional storyteller since 1989 and made her early steps into storytelling under the guidance of Duncan Williamson.

For the past three years, the Telling Place has been a popular feature of Greenbelt, a four-day arts festival at Cheltenham, which in August 2000 attracted 8500 people. Like the Telling Place, Greenbelt has a broad-minded Christian ethos but maintains strong links with mainstream culture and stages performers from both inside and outside church circles.

The Telling Place had a jam-packed programme throughout the festival: two storytelling shows each evening, and daytime sessions on the use of storytelling in education, worship, reconciliation, healing, and community-building. Tracy Radosevic, from the Network of Biblical Storytellers in the USA, ran a workshop on 'text-telling' biblical stories by heart. Chris Sunderland, of Agora, talked about the importance of story in public life (see page 116) and argued the contemporary relevance of retelling the dark and nasty stories in the Old Testament – rarely heard in church – for the insight they give into the fundamentalist mind's quest for purity.

The most spectacular offering was the three-hour epic telling – performed twice – of the whole of Mark's Gospel by a team of twelve storytellers accompanied by two musicians. This was text-telling rather than extempore, but each of the tellers interpreted the text in their own style. In some cases you'd never have guessed they were following a script. Dave Robertson deployed the same hard-edged, no-messing Mancunian voice that characterises his telling of folktales. His storytelling has an electrifying energy and also an earthy humour that sometimes verges on stand-up comedy (see pages 65–7).

Another highlight was a set of wonder tales on the last night by David Campbell, Linda Bandolier, Angela Knowles, and Pam Pott. David spent most of the festival in an MC role, so it was a delight at last to hear a full-length story from him: the tale of the leannán sidhe, told very simply and sparely, every word carefully weighed. Angela sang a lovely bluesy rendition of the ballad 'Lady Margaret'.

The Telling Place audiences were a healthy mix of adults and children. I noticed how closely the children, when outnumbered by adults, attended to storytelling that was pitched for an adult audience. Next to the main tent was a small yurt, where a roster of storytellers encouraged the punters to have a go at telling a story themselves. Some misleading marketing – 'The Tiny Telling Place' – meant that at first the yurt attracted only small children and their parents. Four keen little girls came back again and again, forcing the storytellers to scrape out every last morsel in their child-friendly repertoire. After a change in publicity, adults began to visit the yurt and a few were coaxed into telling jokes and travellers' tales.

Pam Pott's design of the Telling Place tent is a fantastic example of a storytelling venue that is both comfortable and atmospheric. The inner sanctum – walled on three sides with colourful sari material and carpeted with rugs and cushions – was like something out of the Arabian Nights. In the outer area, members of the Northumbria Community and the Bible Society provided continuous hospitality – an important dimension of the Telling Place ethos. Background noise from the festival – including a nearby rock music venue – compelled the storytellers to use clip-on microphones. These worked well, but the background rock music, so incongruous to the stories being told, made for a surreal atmosphere inside the tent.

The Telling Place has been voted the best venue at Greenbelt, and was well attended throughout the festival. It has done a magnificent job of presenting storytelling to a constituency that might not otherwise encounter it. Let me finish with a quote from an email that Susie Minto, the initiative's administrator, received afterwards: 'Thank you for the Telling Place, where my husband, two children, and I relaxed, laughed, cried, and learned so much. The children were telling and singing stories all the way home. Turning on the TV set seemed such an anticlimax. Why do we let it rob us of such rich entertainment hiding deep within ourselves?'

The epic telling of Mark's Gospel was performed elsewhere with a varying line-up of performers, culminating in a theatre tour in 2003 of a more polished production involving a reduced cast and the attentions of a professional director ...

# Mark

## Performed by the Telling Place

Bible stories are rarely heard on the British storytelling circuit. Many anxieties and prejudices surround them, stemming from the church's historical place in our society (see page 61). Now that Christianity has been replaced as dominant religion by market capitalism (see pages 103–9), and conventional churchgoing is fading into oblivion, an opportunity arises to free the Bible stories from their packaging and appreciate them as *stories* – and as much a part of Britain's cultural heritage as any other body of stories.

Enter the Telling Place and an epic telling of the Gospel of Mark, with six storytellers and two musicians, toured to theatres in Swindon, London, and Manchester. Every performance sold out and I was nearly too late to get tickets for Swindon's 600-seat Wyvern Theatre.

*Mark* was, in theory, an unexpurgated text-telling from the Contemporary English Version (CEV) of the Bible, a recent translation into the idiom of contemporary spoken English. Text-telling is premised on the wish to honour the integrity of a text perceived to be sacred. In practice the Telling Place storytellers struck a balance between this aim and the need to play with language to bring the storytelling alive. Dave Robertson peppered his telling with slang you'll never find in the CEV and with comic asides: 'By "Zebedee" I'm not talking about the *Magic Roundabout* character. Remember him?' Simon Airey's smooth delivery had little embellishment of that sort; but, being familiar with the CEV text, I noticed he wasn't following it at all and seemed to be improvising his own translation.

The combination of text-telling and a large theatre venue pushed the telling towards a theatrical style. Gestures and movements around the stage looked controlled and choreographed. Sparing use was made of multiple voices at certain points. Musicians Guy Cowburn and Martin Neil supported the storytelling with bluesy guitar and an exotic array of percussion and wind instruments. For Salome's dance and the beheading of John the Baptist, Dave got the audience clapping to the drums and in moody red light Rebekah Neil danced a sexy Middle Eastern dance to build up the tension to the grisly conclusion of John's head on a plate.

Yet the show was more storytelling than theatre. The house lights stayed on throughout; the communication was eye to eye. Angela Knowles's style was tuned to optimise rapport with the audience. In delivering Jesus' speeches she came across as herself reporting what Jesus had said, though she playfully parodied some other characters. Simon opted for short bursts of character acting. His depiction of the man with an evil spirit hushed the audience as if in the presence of terrible evil. Paul Lancaster used parodic voices to hilarious effect in the Sadducees' pedantic question about marriage in the afterlife. He enunciated his syllables like an actor, with excellent mastery of pace – and the boldest silences I've heard a storyteller dare hold.

Dave ranged the extremes of storytelling and acting modes. His manner was offhand, conversational, his uncompromising Manchester accent matched by a tough, ill-shaven demeanour, yet he combined this with superb timing of voice, gesture, and facial expression and stunning shifts of pace and mood. The comedy when Jesus walks on water brought the house down. Jesus' long prophetic speech shortly before his arrest was probably the most difficult part of the whole story; Dave made it the best, plunging into full-blown acting so powerful that emotionally it overshadowed the climactic sequence of trial and crucifixion that followed. The stage was bathed in blood-red light as Jesus grimly foretells the wars and suffering yet to come. With war then brewing in the Middle East (March 2003), it was scary. As my companion pointed out, its strength came from one's conviction in that moment that Dave *was* Jesus addressing us directly.

One challenge of telling a complete sacred text is that you have to tackle controversial bits you might otherwise avoid. Pam Pott handled Jesus' teaching on divorce by placing the emphasis, in her voice, on the sadness of divorce rather than on condemning it. Some scholars judge the Gospels' relentless critique of the Pharisees to have been an impediment to relations between Jews and Christians ever since.[1] My awareness of this raised a question in my mind about Angela's parody of a nit-picking Pharisee as a feeble-minded old man. It was an expert bit of clowning nevertheless.

Unlike the other Gospels, Mark's ends with the empty tomb. Verses featuring the risen Jesus were appended later. This performance omitted these verses and finished at that liminal moment when Mary Magdalene and friends fearfully leave the tomb. Pam told this in an upbeat tone, the stage flooded with white light; a sense of happy resolution even though Jesus has yet to reappear. Perhaps, though, an opportunity was missed to convey the troubling, otherworldly strangeness of this moment, and the mystery of what exactly happened to Jesus of Nazareth as he passed out of history.

Inevitably, a biblical epic is most likely to attract audiences of church-goers. Which is fine in that it introduces them to storytelling and breathes new life into their sacred stories. But this was as gripping and entertaining a storytelling show as any I've seen. Two-and-a-half hours long and it never dragged. Dave Robertson's performance confirmed that he is a major storytelling talent. There were no prayers, no hymns, no altar call, nothing embarrassing; just quality storytelling. My companion is a die-hard atheist and she loved it.


Owing to differences in organisational culture, in 2004 the Telling Place parted ways with the Bible Society, its main source of funding. It became a members' organisation reliant upon subscriptions. The result was greatly reduced income and a greatly reduced mailing list. Though many churchgoers had been enthused about storytelling by the Telling Place, not enough of them were willing to pay a subscription. The Telling Place closed down in 2007. Its legacy is that it introduced storytelling as a living art to the churches and to thousands of people who might never otherwise have experienced it.

---

[1] Hellig, *The Holocaust and Antisemitism.*

# The Benefits of Amateur Storytelling

The interface between amateur and professional storytelling is a source of tension in the storytelling world. One reason for this, arising from society at large, is the debasement of the word 'amateur' to mean 'inept' and the obsession with 'professionalism' which follows from the contemporary creed that money is the only measure of value. Another reason is intrinsic to the folk nature of storytelling, which blurs the distinction between performer and audience, between trained expertise and the gift of the gab.

I've no intention of writing here about a topic so sensitive! Instead I want to celebrate the Bath Storytelling Circle, which in December 2009 enjoyed its tenth anniversary of continuous monthly meetings, and which throughout that time has operated as a pure folk event: no door charge, no room hire, no paid guests, no grant applications, no committee. When we started, I envisaged the Circle would attract maybe ten people and basically be a space for trying out new stories. But twenty-four people came to that first evening, most of them just to listen, and numbers have remained usually between twenty and forty ever since. I knew that many story clubs invited paid guests, and indeed we had a few approaches from celebrity storytellers looking for a gig, but I was very busy and just didn't have the time to organise a committee or funding; it was simpler just to take personal responsibility for arranging dates with the pub and putting up posters, and rely on willing volunteers to help set up the room and take turns as MC.

I did feel regretful we weren't pulling our weight to provide paid gigs for storytellers from further afield, but the truth is that most nights there wasn't space to fit them in anyway, since there were usually so many people wanting to put their name on the list to perform something – a story, a poem, a song. The quality was variable, of course, and every evening was completely unpredictable. Anything could happen. One night, a tough-looking stranger with a Scouse accent electrified us with his own 'true story' of shoplifting, prison, jealousy about a woman ... and by the end you could have cut the air with a knife because half of us really believed he'd murdered a man over that woman (see page 119). Another time, an entire class of Japanese language students filled every spare seat; only the advanced students stayed for the second half. Just twice over the years, that I recall, we got very bored by an interminable tale from a beginner who'd bitten off more than they could chew.

Mostly it's been great. Nearly every session in those early days, someone would tell a story in public for the first time, and you'd see the moment, halfway through, when their hands stopped shaking, their voice steadied, and they realised, 'I can do this!' Sometimes the sheer authenticity of the beginner's untrained voice can be more compelling than the polished skill of a professional. What has delighted me so much is, not just the diversity of material that's been shared, but the diversity of voice, of individual being, that's shared at the same time. In the early years, especially, I was aware the Circle was bringing together people with very different belief systems – Christians, Pagans, agnostics – to sit in a circle together and share stories that often did convey something of their particular beliefs and values but with none of the antagonism that can arise in open ideological debate. Undergirding the whole experience is a quality of listening that the Circle, despite its shifting membership, has collectively sustained over the years and which conjures a magic in which even the complete beginner can touch people's hearts.

Crucial to the Circle's folk ethic – the peasants entertaining themselves instead of paying to be entertained – has been the absence of any door charge, thanks to the pub's willingness to let us have a room for free. (Sometimes, I might add, we've had to remind the complacent of the importance of buying drinks to keep the landlord sweet.) From the Rising Sun, in the outer darkness of Larkhall, where the Circle spent its first three years or so, Kevan Manwaring – who ran it for the next five years – moved the session via a couple of stop-gap venues to its current home at the Raven, whose city-centre location has brought a steady stream of new faces and also a shift in the kinds of stories told, from a heavy emphasis on traditional stories early on, to a strong component of modern invented stories today. The latter perhaps reflect a connectedness with the many other strands of Bath's literary and spoken-word culture. The Storytelling Circle has preserved its special niche in this ecosystem through its famous 'one rule' – no reading from paper – which has encouraged some of Bath's poets to commit their poems to memory, most notably the amazing Mary Palmer, who was a regular at the Circle before her untimely death in June 2009.

The Circle has nurtured the storytelling scene in the Bath area by promoting forthcoming local performances, workshops, or courses during the customary 'announcements' at the end of the session's first half, which serves also as a pulpit for all manner of counter-cultural shenanigans. It's become part of Bath's civil society. It's also been a meeting ground for many friendships. It provided me with a springboard to working professionally as a storyteller, and it also forged the friendship between the five of us who formed Fire Springs, a professional storytelling team, whose members continue to facilitate regular community events: David Metcalfe now runs the Bath Storytelling Circle and Kirsty Hartsiotis coordinates Stroud Story Circle, while Richard Selby and Kevan Manwaring mastermind two acoustic cabaret nights – respectively, What a Performance! and the Garden of Awen, which do today provide a Bath stage for invited poets, storytellers, and musicians from further afield.

There's one more thing I'll always owe to 'amateur' storytelling. Having been a bit of a Man Who Had No Luck when it came to love, it was at the Bath Storytelling Circle that I met my beloved Kirsty who now shares my life.

# What Does 'Accreditation' Mean?

In an article promoting accreditation in storytelling, Kat Quatermass anticipates certain worries that the prospect of accreditation raises: that it will 'create an unnecessary paper standard without which we won't be allowed to perform', that storytellers 'who don't want to do the qualification won't get bookings anymore', that accreditation will be an expensive extra cost, that accredited storytellers will more readily secure bookings than much more experienced performers.[1] Her dismissal of these 'myths' does not quite put my worries to rest.

I strongly agree with the value of training as well as voice-on experience (and extensive *listening* to other storytellers). When I got serious about storytelling I put myself through as many storytelling courses as I could afford, and, like Kat, harnessed skills from elsewhere in my life, from drama, creative writing, teaching, meditation, dance, the Alexander technique. All that feeds into my storytelling and my own teaching of storytelling. But none of the storytelling courses I took was accredited. So if accreditation comes in – and as I'm not already a household name – will I have to find the time and money to go and be trained all over again in order to be taken seriously?

It may depend what we mean by 'accreditation'. You can have accredited *courses*, such as the degree modules in storytelling at the Universities of Derby and Glamorgan. Or you can demand the accreditation of *practitioners*, as is being imposed in the field of therapy; such accreditation is likely to require, among other things, completion of an accredited course. You see the distinction? The fact I have an MA in creative writing (an accredited course) does not make me an 'accredited writer'.

Kat reassures us that accreditation in storytelling won't exclude anyone from doing anything; but the usual connotations of the word 'accreditation' are exclusive, as in the therapy case. After relating how she was complimented that her first ever volunteer storytelling session for a children's library was as good as or better than the efforts of many professional storytellers they'd had, she says, 'Nice for me, but soul destroying to think that children are not being offered access to truly skilled, well thought out performances ... because people who book storytellers don't know how to recognise that skill.'[2] Implicit in this comment *is* an intention to exclude: those children would not have suffered any sub-standard experience if only accredited storytellers had been chosen to work with them.

Where people's lives or health are at stake, it's hard to deny the value of exclusive accreditation. This is why therapists I've talked with accept (reluctantly) the necessity for accreditation in their field: prioritising ticked boxes over healing talent is the price to be paid to squeeze out the charlatans.

Is storytelling comparable (when it's not being used as a tool of therapy)? What risks are at stake? CRB checks are available to keep out evildoers; that category of risk is taken care of.[3] Are we, then, concerned that incompetent storytellers might cause psychological damage, as an incompetent therapist might? I doubt it. The power dynamic is very different. How much damage can a storyteller really do compared with the sick violence routinely purveyed by Hollywood? No, the risk that really concerns us is that the storyteller might be naff, might fail to entertain, and thereby that the reputation of storytelling as a whole might suffer. You must not *bore* the audience! Storytelling stands or falls by one's power to hold the audience's imagination through the story. The fact that someone has a storytelling NVQ, in which they've studied 'policy and practice', 'cross-cutting issues', and (optionally) 'digital storytelling',[4] will in no way guarantee that they'll entertain the audience; it won't eliminate the risk that the experience may prove unsatisfactory.[5]

The more training and experience you have under your belt, the more confidence a client can have that you can produce the goods. If they want to feel really sure, they'd do better to ask you to tell them a story down the phone than to demand you be accredited. But that would require them to use their own judgement. Which would be at odds with the machine-based ideology from which the vogue for accreditation ultimately derives. Industrial efficiency requires ensuring quality of output and minimising risk to the lowest possible level. This model, facilitated by mechanical, electrical, and now information technologies, has permeated our society. Rather than trust someone's judgement, or take a risk, we're obliged to follow a procedure designed to optimise the desired output. The reason my blood ran cold when I read Kat's article is that the accreditation of storytellers threatens an incursion of this soul-stunting industrial paradigm into a realm that for me is a refuge from it.

In saying this, I feel like the child who remarked on the Emperor's new clothes. I might be accused of being folksy, of not taking a sufficiently 'professional' view of storytelling, because I'm challenging the very assumptions – to be 'professional' is to abide by the industrial model of work – that are understood to be normative. Kat mentions that one benefit of accreditation is that it would help channel resources via the arts funding system into storytelling. The resources would be great. But to get them you have to dance with the Devil. You have to steal the sing-ing harp without waking the Giant. Storytelling is an art. It cannot be controlled by bureaucratic procedure and remain art. It's risky. It exists on the knife-edge of the moment. The client, the audience, the story-teller each takes a risk that the experience may flop. If, in hope of elimi-nating that risk, an NVQ syllabus went beyond 'policy and practice' and taught storytelling skills, to a measurable, nationally agreed standard, its graduates would all sound the same; they'd be so boring that the whole enterprise would defeat itself. It's the willingness to take a risk, to step out on the knife-edge, that ignites the moment and creates the possibility of something special.

Would any kind of accredited storytelling course tend to breed sti-fling homogenisation? From my experience in university-level creative writing, as student and tutor, I'd say, no, not so long as each course, each teacher, each student, is permitted their own idiosyncrasy of approach and there's no expectation that the course's graduates be deemed 'accred-ited storytellers' according to nationally agreed criteria. My vision would be an expanding *diversity* of training opportunities in storytelling. Some, more rigorous, courses might be accredited; others wouldn't be. It's all good stuff to slap on the c.v. to impress potential clients. The real *affir-mation* is not on paper; it's the applause, the look in the audience's eyes, the sound of the silence, the feedback afterwards, the gladness to have you back.

---

[1] Quatermass, 'In Praise of Accreditation'.

[2] Ibid., p. 4.

[3] CRB = Criminal Record Bureau.

[4] Phrases quoted from model syllabus in Quatermass, 'In Praise of Accreditation'.

[5] NVQ = National Vocational Qualification.

# Telling Other Peoples' Stories

At the George Ewart Evans Centre for Storytelling's first annual symposium, in Cardiff in February 2007, there was a talk by Shahrukh Husain on 'Multiculturalism and Cultural Appropriation'. After commenting on India's complex syncretic culture, which cheerfully appropriates stories from diverse sources inside and outside South Asia, Shahrukh examined questions of respect and understanding in some examples of the adaptation of traditional stories for new cultural contexts. Implicit in her talk was an acceptance of the way that stories have historically passed from one setting to another and – whether through folk process or conscious artistic intervention – have transmuted along the way. Nevertheless, she advised against using people's religious stories unless you're strongly in tune with that culture, and also said, in passing, that of course you shouldn't appropriate stories from 'minority cultures'. That last comment begs a big debate that went unexamined on that occasion. Which cultures, for starters, are the 'minority cultures' one may not appropriate stories from? Which are the other cultures from which one may?

Prominent in this arena of debate are the Native American cultures. At the second Tales to Sustain workshop on storytelling and environmental education, held at Bishops Wood Centre, Worcestershire, in April 2007, the Cherokee storyteller Gayle Ross made very clear, in both a session on 'Native Peoples and Earth Heritage' and in an evening performance, her view that only Native Americans have the right to tell their nations' stories. Though this may be a familiar stance to storytelling veterans, it was disturbing news to some environmental educators present who routinely use stories from the world repertoire in their work. For the proscription against telling Native American stories would logically extend to the stories of other 'native' peoples. Where do you draw the line of what, by this reasoning, is out of bounds? May a Cherokee, say, tell Zuni stories? May an Englishman of Nigerian descent tell a Maasai story from Kenya? At a ceilidh I attended on Skye a Scottish storyteller told me he didn't approve of English people telling Scottish stories: I took the hint and when my turn came told a Greek story. He congratulated me on my telling, and I avoided offending him, but on ethnic terms I've probably less right to tell a Greek story than a Scottish one: my mum's maiden name is Kendrick, which I then believed meant I had

Scottish ancestry. (My uncle has since told me that my Kendrick ancestors were Welsh!)

Perhaps, though, the case is special for peoples that historically suffered such an onslaught of colonisation that most of their land was stolen, their population decimated, much of their culture, language, and religion destroyed, and today are disempowered minorities in their own land: the Native Americans, the Australian Aborigines, the San – and let's remember that people in Scotland and Wales suffered similar things in the past, if not quite to such an extreme degree. Perhaps these are the 'minority cultures' Shahrukh had in mind. Such terrible history gives Native American or Aboriginal representatives tremendous moral authority when they speak against the appropriation of their stories. 'This is all we have left. Will you take this from us too?'

The argument goes deeper than that, though. Not only are the stories the treasured possession of the nation in question, but such cultures' conception of what stories are can transgress modern Western assumptions about the function of stories or even about the nature of reality: a story contains power – perhaps certain stories more than others – and if it's told in the wrong way or at the wrong time or without proper understanding, then ill consequence may ensue.[1] This raises questions of whether outsiders are even equipped to *listen* to an indigenous culture's stories, and whether the stories can be authentically told other than in the native language.

The idea that stories can be owned flies against the prevailing sensibility in British storytelling. We speak of 'swapping stories'. We delight in the way the folk process of oral transmission has been revived so vibrantly that we can learn stories by listening to other storytellers as well as by poring over stodgy books of folklore. I was taught to treat the telling of a story as imparting to the audience a precious gift.[2] We feel validated in our art when one of our listeners retells the story to someone else. Much of our pleasure in storytelling may come from the way it leads us to learn about cultures other than our own and discover what things are held in common and what is fascinatingly different. The use of storytelling in multicultural education played a key part in the British storytelling revival.[3]

So when a Native American storyteller precedes the telling of stories to a British audience with a stern command not to retell any of these stories, there's a deep clash of sensibilities. For me as a listener, rapport is undermined. I feel rebuked for something I haven't done, but which secretly I might want to do. The stories do not seem presented to me as a gift. How then am I to receive them? As mere spectacle in the moment? Or as edification, which nevertheless I'm proscribed from passing on – for it's not only storytelling that may be judged as theft of traditional knowledge, but also writing, scholarship, teaching. In stepping outside their own community to tell stories professionally to other audiences, indigenous storytellers step outside their own community's value system into the arena of 'Storytelling as a Spectacle in the Globalised World' so bracingly critiqued by Jack Zipes in his keynote lecture at the Cardiff symposium. In the globalised entertainment industry storytellers compete against each other and other media to seek money and status. You have to exploit whatever capital you have. If you identify as a member of a distinctive ethnic group your capital includes the stock of that people's stories you thereby claim authority to tell. The corollary of this is that storytellers who publicly identify with a particular culture may be expected to tell stories only from that culture.

Ownership of stories stands in opposition to the folk socialism encapsulated by Ben Haggarty's claim, in a workshop some years ago, that 'There's no capital in stories. Anyone can tell any story.' There are moves afoot, in the United States at least, to extend property rights beyond conventional copyright over the particular sequence of words in a text, to encompass the patterns of events which make up stories. These come not only from Native Americans asserting that traditional notions of story ownership constitute a form of copyright, but also from corporate entities aspiring to obtain patents for 'storylines'.[4] The appropriation of stories is sometimes compared to the appropriation of traditional knowledge by pharmaceutical or agricultural companies. When such a company secures a patent over a drug or crop sourced from an indigenous people, in such a way that those people end up having to buy something that was once their own, it seems fair to say that something has been 'stolen' from them. Equivalent 'theft' of stories may be envisaged if stories are deemed property that can be owned exclusively and there's a possibility that corporate entities could secure the rights of ownership. The very idea that stories can be owned makes possible the idea that stories can be lost and thereby makes it imperative for indigenous peoples to protect their stories. But if stories are not owned, then neither can they be lost. If you generously tell me your story and I go away and retell it, you do not lose your story; you still know it and you can still tell it.

Values that strongly emphasise rights of ownership, whether on the part of ethnic groups or capitalist entrepreneurs, seem to me allied to a retreat into right-wing politics in which each individual, company, or nation battens down the hatches and pursues their self-interest in what is assumed to be a grim competitive world. A nation's stories can play a positive role in nourishing community, but to say that only members of the nation have the right to tell those stories prioritises ethnic identity over our common humanity – and that's something twentieth-century history ought to have taught us to be wary of. Slobodan Milosevic's regime, for example, coopted traditional Serbian stories to serve its nationalist project (see page 123).

Yet the position of Gayle Ross and others of like mind is deeply and sincerely held and is taken very seriously by other (non-Native) American storytellers. The scholar Barre Toelken and storyteller Susan Strauss have agonised over moral decisions to stop telling, respectively, Navajo and native Coyote stories and, yet, found it impossible to abide by these decisions because their repertoire had become so deeply part of their own identity. Strauss has also been challenged for telling Jewish stories; as it happens, she actually *is* Jewish but people have assumed she's not on the basis of her physical appearance.[5]

How can we reconcile a strong ethic against telling stories that are 'not yours' with the anarchic tradition of folk and artistic transmission in Britain? How can there be mutual respect between views that are mutually exclusive? Must we choose sides? We may speak of respecting the knowledge and authority of 'native' storytellers, or of the need, before you tell stories from another culture, to thoroughly acquaint yourself with that culture. Well and good; but that's not quite enough when someone's saying, 'If you really respect our culture, you will do as we ask and not tell our stories.' On the other hand, the British storytelling tradition demands respect too. I'd argue that *English* narrative art, like Indian, at its best is fundamentally and gloriously syncretic. How impoverished British storytelling, literature, and theatre would be if everyone felt obliged, whether by law or peer pressure, to limit themselves to personal stories and the tales of their own nation (however one defines one's 'nation'). Shakespeare would be first on the blacklist.

There's a notion in philosophy that advances in thought take place when you hold together one idea with another idea that contradicts it (see page 93). It seems unacceptable to reject out of hand *either* intercultural transmission of stories *or* disempowered indigenous peoples' wish to protect their culture. We have to accept the tension between the two views. That demands trust on one side and, on the other, integrity of heart in deciding which stories to tell. Out of the holding of that tension who can say what synthesis might emerge?

May I suggest one possibility?

Indigenous stories express relationship with the land and are a way in which the land is given voice. For this reason Annie Stewart requests permission of Australia's indigenous peoples to tell some of their stories; it serves the well-being of that country's environment and all its people if those stories are as widely known as possible.[6] You could make the same argument in North America. The immigrant communities there are still strangers in that land; their way of life is destructive of its ecology and has repercussions for the rest of the planet. They might be helped to attune to the ecology they inhabit by knowledge of the land's ancient stories – not merely by hearing those stories, but by internalising them in their souls and society, in other words by telling them. Through this process they, like the Native Americans before them, would be assimilated by the land. The colonisers would be transformed by the colonised.

As for the British, we have transformed our land so intensively that we too are alienated from our own ecology and continue to destroy it. That ecology, in its wild state, had much in common with parts of North America; it was inhabited by many of the same creatures: wolf, bear, fox, beaver, lynx, raven. This is a reason why British storytellers may feel peculiarly drawn to Native American stories: they provide a window into the kind of environmental understanding that people in Britain once possessed but then lost. We too may have a need to be transformed by these stories, even to translocate them into the British mythscape, just as we have begun to reintroduce lost species – the beaver in 2009 – into our physical landscape. If humankind is to stand a chance in grappling with the global ecological crisis now upon us, it will only be through cooperation rather than single-mindedly defending the interests of oneself and one's nation.

---

[1] Toelken, 'The Icebergs of Folktale'.
[2] By Tim Sheppard.
[3] Heywood, *The New Storytelling*.
[4] See Judith Berman, *Vector*, No. 247, 2006
[5] Toelken, 'The Icebergs of Folktale'; Strauss, *The Passionate Fact*.
[6] Stewart, 'Born of This Land'.

# The Storytelling Imagination as Catalyst of Tolerance and Transformation

Live storytelling seems, among the narrative arts, to stand at the opposite pole from cinema. Cinema is the dominant art form of our time: expensive, resource hungry, able to reach huge audiences, produced mainly by big corporations keen to calculate the maximum return on investment, presented on public screens around the world (in exactly the same form each time) and then further reproduced by television, disk, and download. Storytelling, by contrast, is cheap, reaches relatively small audiences, is never the same from one performance to the next, and is so marginalised in modern society that, despite the revival that began in the United States in the 1970s, most people have little awareness of it except as something to entertain young children.

In the spectrum of narrative arts, literature and theatre are intermediate in cost, audience size, and public consciousness. Television is cinema's noisy bedmate, all pervasive, unceasing, mediating cinema and much else that has colonised traditional networks of communication. It's easy to see the relationship between storytelling and television as antagonistic. In many places, the arrival of TV reception spelled the demise of traditional storytelling; in the coffee houses of Cairo TVs blare where storytellers once recited tales from *The Thousand and One Nights*. Storytelling brings people together, stimulates conversation, and thereby helps sustain community. Television inclines people to stay at home and, unlike a live storyteller, it carries on ceaselessly, never tiring, drowning out conversation.

Besides such social factors, though, is there any way that the very presentation of drama on the screen forfeits something of value to be found in live storytelling? The resources of technique available to film seem so much greater: cinematography, sound effects, an orchestra of musicians, a cast of actors, computer-generated imagery. How can storytelling compete with that? One might speak of the charisma and flesh-and-breath vulnerability of the storyteller who is present in person, or the never-to-be-repeated spontaneity of possibility in the unique encounter between speaker, audience, setting, and story. Here, though, I want to explore the ramifications for this question of some thoughts of the poet Ted Hughes – in particular his claim that the dominance of the objectifying scientific perspective has relegated the 'inner world' of metaphysics and myth to the status of superstition and childish make-believe, of no importance to life in the 'outer world' in which we earn our living and grow old.[1] This relegation is injurious to both the individual psyche and to society, says Hughes, because 'our real selves' dwell in this inner world. 'Down there, mixed up among all the madness, is everything that once made life worth living … And whether we like it or not our life is what we are able to make of that collision and struggle' between the inner and outer worlds.[2]

According to the Nigerian playwright Wole Soyinka, in traditional African ritual drama, performances took place in the round and there was no clear distinction between players and audience: the whole community was included within the performance space and took part in the events enacted;[3] in Hughes's terms, there was a fusion of the inner (metaphysical) and outer (physical) worlds. In the classical development of European theatre, with the retreat of the stage behind the proscenium arch, the performance space became physically separated from the audience and partitioned from them by the so-called 'fourth wall' of the stage. Instead of taking part in the drama, the audience watch it from a safe distance.

Cinema takes this objectification of the performed story a step further: the fourth wall is no longer an invisible plane between actors and audience; it is the screen itself, upon which the performance space has been compressed into a two-dimensional pre-recorded picture. Hughes says, 'Reality has been lifted beyond our participation, behind that very tough screen, and into another dimension. Our inner world, of natural impulsive response, is safely in neutral … we are reduced to a state of pure observation.'[4] He describes the camera as 'the perfect mechanism of objective perception', by which the contents of the inner world are evacuated to become an objective spectacle in the outer world, where their moral potency is compromised. 'Scientific objectivity … has its own morality, which has nothing to do with human morality. It is the morality of the camera. And this is the prevailing morality of our time. It is a morality utterly devoid of any awareness of the requirements of the inner world.'[5]

Studies of brain activity seem to support this view. Whereas reading, for example, stimulates brainwave activity, watching TV has the opposite effect, especially in the left hemisphere, where our sense of responsibility is thought to be based.[6] The trancelike state into which television reduces otherwise hyperactive children may be a boon to tired parents, but the very circumstance that young children are trapped inside the home, subdued by TV, is linked to their alienation from the outdoors, thanks to the fencing off of the land and the lethal danger of traffic on the roads. Previous generations were free from an early age to run about outdoors, burning off their energy in make-believe adventures in which inner and outer worlds merged.

So the objectifying quality of film, the passive role it imposes on viewers, limits the medium's capacity to bring together the inner and outer worlds. What we need to foster, says Hughes, 'is a faculty that embraces both worlds simultaneously. A large, flexible grasp, an inner vision which holds wide open, like a great theatre, the arena of contention, and which pays equal respects to both sides.'[7] This faculty is the imagination, which writer and educator Lindsay Clarke pictures as the sacred symbol of the 'mandorla': the eye-shaped area of overlap between two intersecting circles, one representing the outer world and the other the inner; our psychic wholeness, as individuals and as a society, is fuller the greater the degree of overlap between the two circles.[8] Outer and inner healing work together, as in the Arthurian legend of the Holy Grail, in which the greening of the wasteland is tied to the healing of a king who ails both physically and spiritually (see page 38). It is the power of good art, and good stories, to mediate healing transformation through reconciling the inner and outer worlds.[9]

Times of cultural crisis, says Hughes, invoke the need for 'shamans' – great poets – to reforge connection between these two worlds.[10] In some aboriginal societies, in which illness is taken to be spiritual as well as physical, it's the job of the shaman to try to heal sickness by travelling via a trance into the inner world to seek the patient's soul. Hugh Lupton sees storytelling as having something like a 'shamanic' quality: 'The function of the storyteller has always been to straddle two worlds … A storyteller … has one foot in the here-and-now and one foot in the Dreaming, and he (or she) mediates between the two.'[11] Lupton is here extending the Australian Aboriginal concept of the 'Dreaming', the timeless domain in which the Aboriginal myths take place, to refer to the inner world in general. To convey this idea of bridging the two worlds, Lupton tells the tale of 'The Man without a Story' – a man who, unable to contribute anything to a story session, is sent outside, where, crossing a lake in a magic boat, he undergoes a profound transformation (into a woman), lives a whole other life (marriage and children), only to end up back this side of the lake, in the same house, telling the same company the astonishing experience he's undergone.

To express this another way, storytelling breaks down the fourth wall of the stage: the storyteller and the audience share the same physical space in the outer world, and at the same time they imaginatively enter together the inner world. It's a step beyond this *mediation* between the two worlds to proceed into a ritual situation (see page 100), where the two worlds integrate further and audience become congregation and participate physically as well as imaginatively in the drama – as for example when Christians consume the bread and wine in the Eucharist.

The storyteller doesn't transmit a complete imaginative experience as film does. The audience's imagination must be actively engaged in co-creating the experience. What each listener experiences in their own imagination will be unique – and different in detail from what the storyteller is imagining. The essence of a story is not the same thing as the particular narrative embodiment – or 'text' – in which we meet it. Beneath any particular text, the story comprises, in Hughes's terms, two elements: 'its pattern and its images'[12] – what Lupton calls its 'bones' and 'flesh'. The bones are the key events that structure the story. To prepare a story by Lupton's method,[13] you put flesh on the bones by visualising in detail each bone as a picture – what he's described to me as 'dreaming the story' – till you have in your imagination a storyboard of lucidly pictured scenes, which then replay in sequence in your mind's eye as you tell the story. You can deepen this preparation of the story, to the extent of evoking in your imagination an analogue of living memory, by kinaesthetically embodying each scene and by seeking like a method actor to feel the emotions it contains.[14] By doing this imaginative work, the storyteller becomes able, through the magic of the storytelling moment, to stimulate the audience to experience the story in their own imagination. The pattern of scenes determines the inherent significance of the story. 'A simple tale, told at the right moment,' says Hughes, 'transforms a person's life with the order its pattern brings to incoherent energies.'[15]

This method of learning a story has some kinship to another practice that informed Hughes's thought: the 'art of memory', whose history Frances A. Yates has elucidated from its legendary invention by Simonides in the fifth century B.C. up to its use in early modern times. The classical art of memory was a method of organising knowledge in one's mind so it was available for deployment in oratory and scholarship. The practitioner would construct in his imagination a 'palace of memory': this imagined structure, likely modelled on a real building, would contain a large number of 'loci' – places – in each of which was slotted a distinctive image symbolising a particular item of knowledge.[16] Where the classical orator pictures units of argumentation located in the alcoves of a building, the storyteller pictures the scenes of a story located at corresponding points in the geography in which the story takes place – and the Aboriginal maps the myths of the Dreaming along songlines across Australia's actual landscape.

Lupton's visualisation of story scenes also reminds me of St Ignatius of Loyola's method of meditation by visualising (and exploring with the other senses) incidents in the life of Christ. The aim of such meditation is to imagine yourself present in the scene and thereby to gain the spiritual benefit of a deeper sense of connection with Christ. The method can be used either in solitary meditation or in guided meditations in which a leader plays the storyteller-like role of inviting participants to imagine various details of the chosen scene. This overtly spiritual practice illustrates how the active use of the imagination, such as storytelling demands of its audience, can awaken empathy, our sense of connection with others, and thereby has potential to transform us in the depths of our inner world.

Literature must have some capacity to do the same, albeit engaging the imagination in a different, usually solitary way. And film? Hughes's critique of the camera is perhaps hyperbolic. Surely film does activate our imagination in some way. It must have some effect on us. But it leaves so little space for our imagination to work; our emotions are manipulated in a carefully determined way by the combined impact of story, photography, and music. Sometimes, when the actor goes all out to depict the emotional extremity of a situation, and the camera zooms in voyeuristically upon their straining features, even our emotions may be unengaged because nothing is left for them to do.

Whatever the medium, the mere fact a story has transformative power may not necessarily work for the good. The episode of Orpheus losing Eurydice back to the underworld will have a different impact on one's psyche than one of Rambo running around machine-gunning people. The particular transformative effect a story may catalyse depends on what moral qualities its pattern and images mediate.

The Renaissance philosopher Giulio Camillo applied the art of memory to devise a memory theatre – which was actually built, in wood, large enough for people to walk inside. The structure of this memory theatre reverses the usual metaphysics of a theatre: the orchestra, instead of being a performance space looked *into* by spectators seated in the auditorium, is where the user stands to look *out* at a semicircular array of images from classical mythology. These symbolise diverse moral qualities, not merely as units of rhetoric, but as components of the metaphysical cosmos the human soul inhabits. Camillo was a Hermetic Neoplatonist and intended his memory theatre not only to be a means to remember speeches but also to infuse the orator, his speeches, and his listeners with the nuances of virtue associated with the particular knowledge recalled.[17]

Other Neoplatonist thinkers of the Renaissance devised yet more elaborate memory systems, drawing tropes from a blend of mythological traditions, as, in Hughes's words, 'a contrivance for imagining the ordered universe ... a means of organizing the psyche by internalizing the knowable universe'[18] – in which each image is 'a package of precisely folded, multiple meanings, consistent with the meanings of a unified system',[19] and able like contemplation of a Greek Orthodox icon to provide a transformative interface with the metaphysical realm. Robert Fludd envisaged a memory theatre in which the user's point of view is restored to the spectator in the auditorium, looking into an array of loci in the rear of the stage. This design appears to correspond to that of the Globe Theatre in which Shakespeare's plays were originally performed and the mythopoeic patterns they contain were thereby brought to life.[20]

Thinking about mythology in these ways sheds some light on the dissatisfaction I sometimes feel when high mythology is brought down to a mundane level: for example, when someone tells a story about the Greek gods as if they're characters in a comic soap opera. For sure, you can do that, it's amusing, and even Homer does it a bit, but we lose much if we forget that a trope such as, say, 'Aphrodite', contains, folded into it, deeper levels of significance than merely that of a vain beauty who's a bit of a slapper. She is also a great goddess, a major focus of people's religious lives for centuries; she symbolises a profound emotional force that can override reason, the impetus that brings new generations into being. Even more troubling is the exploitation of mythology in films, books, and computer games that prioritise violent action above all else.

Hughes also discusses how some of the Renaissance memory systems point towards the 'idea of a syncretic mythology, in which all archaic mythological figures and events are available as a thesaurus of glyphs ... of all that can be known, of history, of the other world, and of the inner worlds, and in particular of spiritual conditions and moral types'.[21] These figures and events are to be understood as symbolic. Aphrodite, for example, should be regarded not as an objectively existing goddess who actually underwent the stories told about her, but as symbolic of aspects of a spiritual reality that can be engaged with only through symbols wielded by the imagination.

There are reasons why people today may shy away from telling mythological stories in ways that mobilise their deeper levels of significance. The prevailing worldview of secular materialism is wary of those deeper resonances – unless perhaps they be safely packaged in psychoanalytic terms. Moreover, the metaphysical ideas such stories imply can be dearly held by some people and can therefore cause conflict and incomprehension among parties who don't share the same assumptions. This is very obvious when it comes to the myths of living religions, and is a pragmatic reason for excluding metaphysical arguments from academic and political debate.[22] Yet Hughes's analysis of the contemporary neglect of the inner world suggests that we do have psychological or spiritual needs to mobilise the full richness of myth. At the same time, the need for healing of the fractures in society and of the relationship between humankind and the ecosystem urgently demands respectful cooperation between people from different metaphysical traditions.

How can we hold together these conflicting impulses? Let us imagine, as an idea, combining and extending the concept of a syncretic Neoplatonist memory system and the Aboriginal concept of songlines: let us imagine an enormous network of all the important stories of the world's different metaphysical traditions, laid out episode by episode across the earth, like a globe-spanning system of songlines[23] or a memory system emplaced on the earth itself instead of in a palace or theatre of memory. In some places – Jerusalem or Glastonbury, say – the stories of different belief systems will coincide. In the outer world this can be a cause of conflict: people who believe different stories – about history, for one thing, but also about the nature of reality and what that implies for moral values – hold to the truth of their own story and deny the truth of the other's. But if we understand these stories to be work of the imagination, able to symbolically mediate whatever metaphysical reality may exist but not in themselves necessarily *being* that reality, then we have a basis for respect between representatives of competing belief systems: the stories of each tradition can be mutually respected as an *interface* with that (ultimately unknowable) metaphysical reality even when they appear to conflict. Even secular materialists can – with humility about what we can and can't know – find a place in this system, interpreting the inner world in psychoanalytic terms rather than metaphysically.

This essay's line of argument implies the importance of a high view of 'imagination' and the inner world in facilitating respectful conversation among people with different belief systems. Storytelling provides a way of invoking the metaphysical dimensions of people's hopes and needs while avoiding the unhelpful conflict that can ensue when such ideas are presented as explicit statements of faith. In today's context of global ecological crisis such inter-cultural cooperation is vital; stubborn fundamentalism, whether religious or secular, is not a viable option for addressing the global-scale problems we face.

The stories we tell and imbibe cumulatively define who we are and who we're becoming, at the deepest levels of our being, as individuals and collectively. The very way that live storytelling engages the imagination, when performed with skill and mindfulness, may conceivably make this art a more potent catalyst of inner transformation than media like cinema able to reach much larger audiences. But stories, like many aspects of culture, can work for both good and ill. Clarke says, 'if we tell ourselves ethically deficient stories they have a corrupting effect on the imagination, and therefore on the world we manifest around us'.[24] It really does matter which stories we choose to feed our own imagination with and what values they mediate.

1 Hughes, 'Myth and Education'.
2 Ibid., pp. 149–50.
3 Soyinka, *Myth, Literature and the African World.*
4 Hughes, 'Myth and Education', p. 147.
5 Ibid., p. 146.
6 Johnson, 'Strangers in Our Homes'.
7 Hughes, 'Myth and Education', p. 150.
8 Clarke, *Imagining Otherwise.*
9 Hughes, 'Myth and Education'.
10 Hughes, 'The Poetic Self'.
11 Lupton, 'Betsy Whyte and the Dreaming', p. 33.
12 Hughes, 'Myth and Education', p. 152.
13 Developed through his collaboration with Ben Haggarty and Pomme Clayton in the Company of Storytellers.
14 For this perspective I'm indebted to Shonaleigh Cumbers.
15 Hughes, 'Myth and Education', p. 153.
16 Yates, *The Art of Memory.*
17 Ibid.
18 Hughes, 'Shakespeare and Occult Neoplatonism', p. 295.
19 Ibid., p. 309.
20 Yates, *The Art of Memory*; Hughes, *Shakespeare and the Goddess of Complete Being.*
21 Ibid., p. 308.
22 I'm indebted to Mika Lassander for this observation.
23 As imagined by Bruce Chatwin in *Songlines.*
24 Clarke, 'Fiction and Mystery'.

# Ecobardic

# Tales to Sustain

In the spring of 2005, Eric Maddern invited a number of concerned storytellers to Cae Mabon, his retreat centre in Snowdonia, to spend a weekend exploring how storytelling might be applied to the challenge we today face to make our society ecologically sustainable. Eric thought this was the first time in Britain a group of professional storytellers had gathered for this specific purpose. The group, numbering sixteen, included jobbing storytellers and environmental educators, ecobards and an ecowarrior, creativity coaches, and, I fancy, at least one elemental spirit in human disguise.

Though Jon Cree, Malcolm Green, and Eric took on the job of coordinating our activities, the weekend was deliberately not pre-planned. The first third of our time together was devoted – through dialogue in pairs, small groups, and plenary – to constructing an agenda. That might not sound an efficient use of time, but it was soon clear we were at the start of a process that would extend way beyond this weekend: we were in effect setting a provisional agenda for this larger-scale process. I say 'provisional' because it was a rolling agenda that kept morphing throughout the weekend and will continue to do so as storytellers respond to the ever unpredictable unfolding of the ecological crisis.

Our agenda divided loosely into 'challenges' and 'practice'. The latter was explored through a series of mini-workshops in which people shared some of the practical expertise they employ in their own work. Alasdair Taylor and Mel McCree offered indoor and outdoor bodywork exercises, based on the premise that a gentle and sensual relationship with one's own body facilitates a similar relationship with the earth. Chris Holland taught us how to stalk light-footed like a fox. Jane Flood had us confront the shadowy 'underbelly' of our psyche to empower us to handle the dark side, the bad news, so integral to many ecological stories. Pat Bowen, Jon, and Malcolm engaged our senses and imagination with physical details of the woods around us, both to inspire poetry and storymaking and to interface our storytelling with the outdoor setting. Shando Varda ran imaginative games in which we envisioned the characteristics of desirable futures and the processes by which such futures might be reached. Esyllt Harker and Jane explored the interplay between story, language, and place in their work within geographical communities.

The 'challenges' were examined by discussion: What do we mean by 'sustainability' in the present context of ecological crisis? What should be the role of the storyteller in furthering a sustainability agenda? How do we construct stories that provoke questions about sustainability? How might storytelling be used to raise issues of sustainability with influential decision-makers? The question about the storyteller's role stirred debate about the desirability of loading stories with any kind of agenda. David Metcalfe articulated the point that everyone's storytelling is inevitably coloured by the values they hold – some kind of agenda will be implicit, whether or not you're conscious of it – yet, in delicate tension with this, stories don't need to be didactic, or even *about* sustainability, to convey through metaphor the values associated with sustainability. In one team's effort to construct a story that raises questions of sustainability, Malcolm was keen that we should fashion a story that was directly challenging to ourselves, and people like ourselves, rather than one that pointed a finger at people who were, for us, 'other', such as youths or corporate shareholders.

The sharing of actual stories, many but not all with ecological themes, took place during evening sessions in the roundhouse. One night Eric invited us to contribute true stories, fortunate and unfortunate, about the state of the earth. The most heart-rending tale that night – Chris Smith's account of an Arab family's suffering in Israel – might, at first, seem unconnected with sustainability, but, when you think about it, Israeli–Palestinian conflict has ecological roots in the competition for fertile land. The third night, Eric compèred a cracking session in which nearly everyone performed and then we sang old songs while David and Eric took turns on guitar. There was a wonderful feeling of togetherness, the kind of collective experience that, so long as it doesn't become exclusive, people need more of to strengthen us to grapple with the ecological crisis in a civilised, cooperative way.

The need for fellowship in the face of that challenge was one reason I valued this gathering. Most of us were keen to remain in touch and to meet again a year hence to exchange more stories and more theory and practice. Some felt inspired to enhance the green dimension of their storytelling. Others began to hatch plans for a larger sustainability-centred event open to the public.

The venue of Cae Mabon – the trees and rushing stream so powerful a presence and the centre's hand-built accommodation and compost loo providing practical insight into what a more sustainable way of life might be like – conferred some consistency between what we were talking about and our lived experience that weekend. The enfolding woods dispelled one's sense of the normality of urban life. When we walked in pairs to share deep thoughts, a gentle snowfall through the trees transported us into a kind of otherworld. My own thoughts turned to the finitude of mortal life and a dawning realisation that our secular response to the ecological crisis, though vital, may be futile without some spiritual source of hope. In the shifting sands of that bigger picture, stories are our guide (see pages 165–9).

One dusk at the lakeshore, standing on the remains of the old railway wharf, now overgrown and crumbling away, David and I watched the snow smoking off Snowdon into the slate grey sky and tried to make out, across the lake, the swallows that Malcolm assured us were feeding low above the water, a shimmer of movement that only his far-seeing eyes could detect.

'Things can't be too bad,' he said. 'At least the swallows are back.'

Since this first meeting in 2005, there has been a Tales to Sustain gathering every year (except 2006), at a different location each time and articulating a different intention for our activities. These events have brought into being a loose but growing network of practitioners in the application of storytelling to environmental education and activism.

I'm grateful to David Metcalfe for his input into this article.

# What Do You Mean, 'Ecobardic'?

Fire Springs conceived the idea of writing an artistic manifesto in 2005, in the aftermath of producing *Return to Arcadia*, our third major story-telling epic rooted in environmental themes, at a time when I had just published a monograph on *Storytelling and Ecology* and Kevan Manwaring was working on *The Bardic Handbook*. We had a sense that, both in the bardic arts – storytelling, poetry, music – and in the arts more generally, a great deal of work had engaged with issues of environment and sustainability, but that this effort remained fragmentary and marginalised. The arts, we felt, weren't pulling their weight as much as they might to address the challenge of global ecological crisis.

There are various reasons for this. First, there's the commercial prejudice against work that has radical implications. It's hard to say whether this reflects the fear that such work won't sell well enough to reap much profit, or a deeper fear of radical social and economic transformation actually coming about. Perhaps it's a mixture of the two.

A television producer told me a few years ago, 'The environmental thing is the kiss of death to getting a project into production. Nobody will want to touch it because they know it just won't get the audience.' When I mentioned David Attenborough, he said, 'Attenborough's very careful not to harangue people too much about environmental problems. He keeps the focus on enjoying the wildlife.'

I pointed out that Attenborough's 2000 series *The State of the Planet* uncompromisingly describes how human activities are destroying biodiversity and explains what needs to be done to halt that trend.

'That', said the producer, 'was the one series of his that flopped. Got very poor ratings, I recall.'

It's an encouraging sign that since then media such as the BBC, *The Independent*, and certain film-makers and novelists have helped to greatly raise the profile of climate change, albeit at peril of implying that climate change is the only environmental crisis we face, whereas in fact it's but one component of a much more comprehensive crisis in the way human beings inhabit the earth.

Another force that works against environmentally committed art is the hegemony of postmodernist criticism, which has stalled the arts in a cultural doldrums in which it's difficult to evaluate anything as more worthwhile than anything else. When I mooted the idea of this manifesto to one artist friend, she said, 'You can't have artistic manifestos any more. The very idea of them is seen as obsolete. No one's going to accept that anyone has any right to say *this* is the kind of thing you ought to do.' The irony of such postmodernist freedom is that, in withholding judgement of aesthetic quality and moral salience, it valorises work of tedious predictability, whether that be formulaic Hollywood blockbusters or the high art of blank pieces of paper pinned to the wall.

Even the bardic arts are vulnerable, as Jack Zipes warns,[1] to the commercial pressure to conform to proven styles of performance: the slam poet in black leather ranting about bad sex; the slick humour of the storyteller who knows how to make the audience laugh and to avoid challenging their complacency.

The premise of what Fire Springs call an 'ecobardic' approach to the arts is that the global ecological crisis through which we're now living challenges postmodernism's refusal to judge the worth of art in other than monetary terms. The question of whether such a crisis actually exists is not the manifesto's task to prove. This we take as given, but not simplistically. It's impossible to know what exactly the future will bring, especially in a subject like climate change, understanding of which hinges upon complex and rather abstract science. More tangible are the escalating human population, the visible degradation of habitats, the conflicts for diminishing resources. One of the capacities of the arts is to address emotional and existential aspects of the crisis, of which science, politics, and economics tend to be oblivious.

One problem that arises when art-making is brought together with some purpose that is not in itself artistic is that the art may be so compromised by that purpose that it ceases to be good art. I had first-hand experience of this through my involvement, at a national level, in the Christian arts scene. In this milieu many people believed that art was of value only to the extent that it promoted Christian teaching. Many people with a strong artistic calling underwent a protracted struggle within themselves to accept that their work could have intrinsic worth without directly promoting the gospel. Discussions were hijacked by enthusiastic believers, often young in their faith, who'd not yet gone through this struggle and needed to hear the arguments for art trotted out by those who had successfully integrated their art and their faith. Much standard work was put forward as worthy of a public simply because, in its clumsy, unsubtle way, it presented a Christian message.

Environmentally committed art could easily be vulnerable to the same pitfalls, all the more so as the puritan impulse in British culture begins to transfer its allegiance from Christianity to environmentalism – something I believe we already see (and this may not in itself be a bad thing) in attitudes towards recycling and transport. A way around this conflict between art and agenda is to reconceive the conflict as a *tension*, in other words to stop thinking about things in terms of mutually exclusive alternatives. This kind of binary thinking is endemic; you see it on breakfast TV whenever they tackle some controversial topic by wheeling in two experts with diametrically opposed views. Such polarisation of problems is unlikely to prove constructive. Better, if you can, to have your cake and eat it; to accept the tension between competing impulses – making great art and applying art to the purpose of social transformation – and see what creative possibilities emerge. And accept too that different pieces of work may arise from different points on a continuum. In my own storytelling repertoire are stories with a hard-hitting ecological message and others that don't speak to environmental issues at all – but I'd choose not to tell stories that actually conflict with my ecobardic principles, such as a story that implies it's heroic to use violence against other people to secure resources for your own loved ones.

Suzi Gablik's *The Reenchantment of Art*, an extended manifesto for a new approach to art, especially the visual arts, falls into that trap of making art subordinate to purpose. Gablik says that the circumstance of environmental crisis requires that any art, to be worthwhile, must serve some instrumental purpose of social transformation. She dismisses the whole tradition of aesthetics, and thereby places art in the position of starting all over again from scratch, to produce work whose functioning *as art* is debatable. An example she gives is Dominique Mazeaud's 'art project' of clearing rubbish out of the Rio Grande. Okay, it's an excellent thing to do, I did something similar on a beach where I lived in Greece, and the experience may inspire some writing or other creative outcome, but what may be lost in holding up such activities as a model of the art we need is any comprehension of the particular qualities, beyond those of other kinds of endeavour, that art can contribute to our grappling with the challenges of our time.

It's those qualities that Fire Springs' *Ecobardic Manifesto* attempts to elucidate. The crisis we face requires action in diverse fields – political, social, scientific, economic, religious, educational – but what characterises the distinctive contribution that art can make, *as art*, applying the resources of theory and practice that have evolved over the centuries? Upon the core premise of responsiveness to the strained relationship between human beings and the rest of the ecosystem, the manifesto elaborates five key principles: (1) connecting with one's roots in time and place and at the same time celebrating the diversity of other traditions; (2) daring to discern and critique in order to offer cultural leadership; (3) respecting and engaging with one's audience as a creative partner; (4) cultivating the appreciation of beauty by means of well-wrought craft;

(5) re-enchanting nature and existence as filled with significance (see pages 95–7).

These principles take inspiration from certain qualities of bardic tradition, in both its ancient and modern manifestations; hence the name 'ecobardic'. Owing to Fire Springs' particular circumstances as a British storytelling group inspired by the notion there's a spiritual dimension to people's relationship with the land, the bardic tradition is our chosen entry point into this terrain of ideas. Other artists, in other disciplines and other cultures, may have different entry points into the same territory. They may not accept the label 'ecobardic'. That's fine. More important is that there should be a creative exchange of ideas and the exhilaration of an evolving movement. We don't expect people to agree with everything our manifesto says. There's a tension to be held between accepting diversity of opinion and sharing a collective spirit. The last thing we want to see is anyone ticking off a list of criteria to see whether they check out as a bona-fide ecobardic practitioner.

Some who've read the manifesto have queried the lack of a conclusion telling the reader 'this then is what you should do'. My feeling is that it may be important to the spirit of the manifesto, and to the scale of cultural shift the ecological crisis demands, that we do not put forward a prescriptive programme. If we did so, I can imagine that many otherwise sympathetic artists would say, 'That's all very well, but I have my own ideas what I want to do in response to this challenge.' Again the tension needs to be held: between artistic freedom and moral purpose. Better perhaps, in the manner of a good story, to provoke thought and the question, 'So what am *I* going to do?' The manifesto finishes with a selective list of ecobardic exemplars in diverse disciplines. Their work fills out the picture of an emergent movement. We may seek out others like them, take inspiration from their work, and stand on their shoulders to see what we can add that, cumulatively, will help to change the course of our culture and make a difference to the future of our planet.

---

[1] Zipes, 'Storytelling and Spectacle in the Globalised World'.

# Age of Enchantment

As any green festival or any issue of *Resurgence* will make obvious, there are vibrant and growing currents of art that celebrate the earth and reflect upon humankind's relationship with the rest of nature. As yet, these currents are fragmentary, marginalised from mainstream culture, and vulnerable to the dictates of economics and to reactionary political forces. The postmodernist paradigm that still governs the arts implies that any bit of artistic expression is as valid as any other if it can secure an audience. Time, then, for a paradigm shift in the arts – as part and parcel of the paradigm shift the green movement seeks in society and consciousness as a whole.

I'm not talking about a narrow prescriptive movement, of which there have been many in the history of the arts, but about a broader sea change in the sequence from Renaissance to Enlightenment to romantic to modern to postmodern. Fire Springs' *An Ecobardic Manifesto* speaks the coming of the next paradigm: one in which postmodern respect for diversity is coupled with responsiveness to the critically strained relationship between human beings and the ecosystem we inhabit; a paradigm to whose gradual emergence over the past century countless artists – from D. H. Lawrence to Ursula Le Guin, Paul Nash to Werner Herzog, Ted Hughes to Te Vaka – have already contributed. The manifesto offers not a prescriptive programme but a set of provocative principles, inviting each artist to consider how their work might respond, with integrity, to the needs of our age of ecological crisis.

At the heart of this bold aim is a paradoxical tension between expecting art to serve an agenda and valuing art for its own intrinsic value. There's a puritan spirit afoot in the green movement, which, taken to the extreme, would reduce art to an instrumental tool of social change and ecological survival (see pages 92–3). The way forward into the new paradigm is to embrace the paradox: to accept both that art should serve a sense of responsibility *and* that art is a fundamental part of the fullness of human life.

The arts can help us orientate ourselves in time and space: to understand the geography we inhabit and the history that brought us where we are, to comprehend what's happening here and now, and to contemplate the possibilities of where we may be heading – whether they be hopeful trajectories, as in Kim Stanley Robinson's green-socialist science fiction, or bleak warnings, as in the cyberpunk dystopia of *Blade Runner*. In the face of a relentless bombardment of information, most of it of no consequence to us and working to smokescreen the self-interests of the powerful, the arts can also provide cultural leadership: to help people to distinguish what matters and what doesn't matter, to make sense of what's going on in the world and what they ought to do, and to sculpt meaning in their lives. Here again, there's that tension to embrace: between the provocation of action that one could plausibly undertake, and consolation in the shadow of problems that seem too awesome for the ordinary person to do anything about. In Barry Lopez's story collection *Light Action in the Caribbean*, for example, one story viciously exposing the ruthless Darwinian logic of neoliberal economics is preceded by another delivering a heart-lifting vision of fulfilment after long years of seemingly futile commitment.[1]

For many people today who stand outside any spiritual tradition, the arts are the main connection to spiritual territory. They have incantatory, visionary, and ritual power to re-enchant the world, its creatures, and our lives with significance beyond the material utility that science and economics acknowledge. Such enchantment has intrinsic value; it helps us live with joy in the face of a deepening crisis that, even if we do all the right things starting from today, may not upcurve into recovery till after we who are alive today have gone (see pages 164–5). But it also shifts our perceptions in ways that may influence our values and choices. For example, if a story or a painting causes us to perceive members of another species – wolves, say, or beech trees – as inspirited beings, then we may feel less inclined to let them be destroyed.

Allied to this enchantment is the arts' power to cultivate our capacity to perceive beauty, be it in other people, in the world around us, in moments of being. Such aesthetic sensitivity to what is around us seems to me crucial to the aim of making us care about the state of the environment; beauty and ugliness are so much more tangible than parts per million of polluting chemicals, important though such data may be. For art to nurture the appreciation of beauty, it needs itself to be finely wrought. Laurie Lee's beautiful writing, in re-enchanting the Slad Valley in Gloucestershire and helping people appreciate its beauty, has helped to protect that landscape from development. Architects and makers influenced by the Arts and Crafts movement have sought to directly craft beauty in the built environment in harmony with the surrounding landscape.

Finally, if audiences are to be engaged, stirred up, transformed, motivated to do something, it matters that art should be in some way relational. It should treat its audience with respect – and compassion. It should invite some kind of agency from us, the response of our intellect, our emotions, our action. Barry Lopez's story 'Apologia', about wildlife roadkill, so moved me that I made a resolution not to drive above fifty miles per hour after dark. Yet again there's a tension between provocation and consolation. The intention of some work may be highly polemic. Other work may be purely contemplative of beauty. Art located between these extremes may inspire the imagination to effect some kind of transformation – a healing transformation within our heart perhaps, and perhaps also in the way we live and, let's hope, in the world we manifest around us.

We ought not expect every work of art to elicit the same kind of effect or pursue the same kind of intention. If a new phase in the history of the arts does indeed cohere into being, it will be a great ecosystem of different artists doing different things, impacting on audiences in different ways, eliciting different kinds of transformation. Such is the richness and diversity of a new paradigm in the arts – just as in the political arena the green movement can increasingly be seen as not the caucus of a single issue but the beginning of a whole new pattern of civil society. The diverse streams of 'ecobardic' art that have already sprung into being will flow together into a wide river of creativity and imagination, to transform the collective consciousness of our civilisation.

---

[1] Lopez, 'Light Action in the Caribbean' and 'The Construction of the *Rachel*.

# Mapping the Ecobardic Territory

In response to Fire Springs' publication of *An Ecobardic Manifesto*, Eric Maddern convened at Cae Mabon an 'Ecobardic Mini-Fest' over the Beltane weekend in 2009. Although the manifesto addresses the arts as a whole (see pages 91–7), the weekend was focused on the bardic arts of storytelling, poetry, and music. The aim was to share lots of ecobardic work, develop the ideas in the manifesto, and give each delegate feedback on a current ecobardic project. Rather than simply report how the event went, I'll try here to summarise the potion of thought that we collectively brewed. 'Mapping the Ecobardic Territory' was a heading Eric coined that nicely connects the imaginative exploration of ideas with understanding the physical world in which we live.

We started and ended with simple outdoor rituals that invested us with the fertile ambience of the springtime woods, bright with bluebells, and enabled us to declare our intentions of what we wanted from the weekend and that its fruit should nourish our work in the months afterwards. The symbolism of Beltane, a time of new growth, well expressed this wish that what we did, here and now, should be transformative and have consequence, for ourselves and the world, beyond our immediate experiences in this remote Snowdonian fastness. The island utopia Aldous Huxley depicts in *Island* is ultimately vulnerable to external forces, Kevan Manwaring pointed out, and the same is true of any idyllic counter-cultural enclave – witness the heavy-handed closure of the Big Green Gathering later in the year. You can seek to reverse this dynamic: to take the revolutionary spirit of the 'island' out to transform the world beyond, just as a spiritual retreat is undertaken not to escape the world but to strengthen yourself in order to have an effect in the world.

One aspect of the ecobardic territory we explored was to apply the idea of 'ecosystem' to human culture. Just as nature's complexity is organised as an ecosystem, so people's diverse creative endeavours comprise an 'ecosystem', in which not only artists but all of us would do well to express in our lives qualities of community and symbiosis, as do exist in nature, and not just the competitiveness of Darwinian (and Thatcherite) survival of the fittest. We discussed the metaphor of 'mosaic' – a pattern of shards, each beautiful in itself, making up a whole whose beauty exceeds the sum of its parts – as nicely conveying the value of diversity, in society, nature, landscape, and the 'ecosystem' of creative work. There's a tension to be acknowledged between self-interest and coopera-tion. If you want to challenge people to change the way they live you need to comprehend their motivations, recognising that most of us are strongly driven to secure our own livelihood and yet at the same time we do feel compassion for others and many of us have a deep-seated feeling for nature – a capacity that has been nurtured by the art of the past. So you have to ask the questions: Why should people want to change their lives? How can they be helped to do so?

Another part of the territory is 'the big picture': sharing stories of place, history, science, and society so people may understand how they are connected to things beyond their own immediate concerns. There's need for healing of things that happened long ago, the healing of the ancestors as well as ourselves, as sought in the peace ceremony at Dyrham in 2007 in remembrance of the battle in 577 by which the in-vading Saxons sundered Wales from the West Country;[1] and there's need to envision the future – positive images as well as negative ones – and stories of how to get there. The idea of utopia nowadays connotes stasis and even tyranny (see page 136). We need positive visions of the future that accommodate a continuing dynamic of change. The ecological con-cept of a 'climax community' is a promising aim for humankind's pres-ence on the earth – if we note that the idea of climax as a static end point has been replaced in contemporary ecology by an understanding that climax involves an unceasing flux of change in a mosaic of local habitats.

In the landscape of our mortality, hard ecological reality meets a maelstrom of emotions and spiritual purposes. Consciousness of mortal-ity drives some people to behave in irresponsibly destructive ways and others to try to make a difference to the world. Some, Gwyn Edwards explained to us, construct a 'hero project' for their life, a quest that might, in some way, make one immortal but that if frustrated may leave one disconsolate. Many people approaching the end of their lives become keen to leave some kind of legacy for the well-being of others. Such im-pulses can strongly drive both the impetus to creativity and the kind of work we choose to make. They also condition what value we find in the art we imbibe.

To accept mortality, we agreed, people need to discover meaning and values, and especially love. Here the arts have a vital role, having for many people in Britain taken the place of religion. The realm of meaning and values is, of course, highly contested territory. What values do we mean to promote in our work? What values are implicit in it, and in the stories we choose to tell or that we imbibe and (as consumers) promote? An ecobardic approach will promote respect for the other (whoever or whatever that might be) and for oneself, and a sense of being part of something larger (Earth, Cosmos, God), and also courage and hope. We're up against the anomie in which many people today live, 'on the thin line of sensation between no future and no past',[2] propelled from one sensation to the next without stopping to think about what they're doing. There's need for art that will make people think and help them be real instead of being defined by the commodities they consume.

In modern consumer society many people have little sense of relationship with the land they live on or the people they live among. We discussed the role of art in the challenge of learning to become 'native' in the place you live. You need to learn its history, customs, ecology, its stories about the way people have inhabited the land. Each of us shared our personal story of our sense of belonging to place and culture. Even in a small group there was a radical diversity of experience: in one person a deep sense of rootedness in one land and its native culture; in another a sense of alienation from one's birthplace and a discovery of belonging in a different culture; in yet another a sense of assimilating elements from different places and cultures.

In the bardic arts it's the element of 'ritual' – eliciting the audience's active participation – that perhaps has more immediate power than anything else to transform us and thereby the world we manifest around us. Techniques of ritual that Kevan covered in a presentation on this topic included: movement; sacred space; costume; music, drumming, and incantation; rhythm, pause, and repetition; 'magic numbers' (threes, fours, fives); the points of the compass; giving offerings; the audience having opportunity to speak; and the performer's ability to 'cast an invisible net' of connectedness around the listeners. In the enclosing space of Cae Mabon's 'Dragon Snug', Kevan then recited his long bardic poem *Dragon Dance*, which elaborates the mythopoeic qualities of the five 'quarters' of the British Isles – four mapped on to the cardinal directions, and concluding with Cambria, 'the centre'. In light of Eric's earlier remark that in Snowdonia we were at the geographical centre of the British Isles, I experienced during this performance a moving sense of the intricate, sacred beauty of these islands arrayed around me and of my own sense of emplacement in them.

Another quasi-religious element of bardic art we discussed, which works in a quite different way, is 'preaching'. That word has acquired negative connotations, partly because of the reaction against the church, partly in expression of the postmodern zeitgeist that everyone should feel free to do what they want. Artists are afraid of seeming preachy and it's actually quite rare, outside the obvious contexts, to encounter preaching, certainly in storytelling. There's a boundary to be pushed here. There is a need for leadership, for someone to say things that need to be said, to spell out why some things are no longer acceptable though the momentum of our culture assures us we needn't worry about them (see pages 113–14). Why not preach a bit if you can do it well, if your content is sound, if you make sense and treat your audience with respect? Oratory is one of the traditional bardic arts; it speaks directly where storytelling and poetry make their point indirectly. But art forms can be combined in innovative ways. Eric shared with us preview extracts from his show *What the Bees Know* which fluidly moved between storytelling and oratory to put across an assertive ecobardic message. 'Not pure storytelling,' you might say, but his skill and charisma make it work, so you really sit up and listen to what he's saying.[3]

Even more assertive is what Kevan calls 'commando bardism': the revolutionary tactic of seizing the moment, even when you're not invited, even when it's against the rules, to speak some poetry, story, oratory, to organise an event, a stunt, to get the word out somehow. Strong forces of self-interest defend the status quo and try to silence dissenting voices. Risks must sometimes be taken to defy their claim to authority.

In any cause you might want to promote, Angharad Wynne explained, there's a chain of consequence from knowledge, to interest, to action, to adoption, to sharing it to involve others. At some points in this chain the live spoken word really makes a difference because it's more likely to be believed than other media. People can be averse to listening to depressing stories; they need encouragement as well as warning. Without sledgehammering people into paralysis and denial, we need to touch their hearts enough to make them think and then act; to suggest creative alternatives; to follow up the word with opportunity for action – as when a lecture in Stroud about peak oil by Richard Heinberg was followed at the same event by the launch of Transition Stroud. But we shouldn't expect there to be a single sure-fire approach. More extreme strategies have their place too. Kevan recalled the Greek masks of tragedy and comedy: if people got too self-satisfied the playwright would remind them of pain; if they got too desolate he tried to cheer them up.

On the final morning we applied some of this theory to construct a 'songline' through the woods around Cae Mabon. Each person selected a spot in which to present a story, poem, or song that connected in some way with that spot. To furnish a mood of ritual concentration, we perambulated from one locality to the next in silence except for Eric slowly beating the bodhrán. This simple group activity deepened my consciousness of the particularities of that landscape and enchanted the area with significance – exactly the effects that can strengthen people's love for place and thereby their willingness to look after it.

Eric told the story of Brân's rescue of Branwen in the presence of a rock outcrop in which he pointed out the shape of Brân's fabled head and alongside it that of his troublemaking brother, Efnisien. Kevan

commented how the presence of Efnisien beside his lordly brother symbolises the need for ecobardic art to accommodate the voice of dissent,
even within the green movement, to maintain a dynamic dialogue and
prevent green policy solidifying into a new tyranny. The trickster speaks
also to the need to dance with the devil to get things done: to play the
game of publicity, networking, commerce, to achieve what Angharad
called a 'quilting' of the ecobardic idea in the public mind – while taking
care not to sell out your principles. Our closing ritual crystallised for me
that it is part of an artist's work not only to make the work but also to
devise ways for it to reach a public.

---

[1] Manwaring, 'Hill of the Seven Healing Winds'.
[2] MacIver, *The Ramparts We Guard*, p. 84.
[3] In Eric's subsequent development of this show, he has deployed something of
the style of a stand-up comic to sweeten the preaching element (see page 153).

I'm grateful to Kevan Manwaring for his input into this article.

# Faith, Freedom, and the Fast-Capitalist Commodification of Story

The myth that needs contestation is no longer the myth of Greco-Roman religion, feudalism, Christianity, or Communism, it is much more nefarious. It is the myth of freedom in societies dominated by a capitalist market system that creates enormous barriers for the free exchange of experience.[1]

The publication of stories, like every endeavour these days, is compromised by the sacrosanct assumptions of market economics: that people's reason for existence is to consume products, and that the only proper motive for any enterprise is to make money to purchase those products. But stories, whether of real experience or of the imagination, are one of the most important ways that society's prevailing assumptions and dynamics can be questioned. If stories become controlled by commercial forces that are heedless of people's and planet's authentic well-being, how can we hope to challenge the operation of those forces? The critic Steven Connor notes how sadly ironic it would be if the puissance of the novel, in particular, should be smothered by its commercial homogenisation, for 'the novel, more than any other form, preserves the possibility of that intensity and organic complexity of human experience which is increasingly under threat by the monstrous impersonality of industrial and economic forces in modern life'.[2]

The technological acceleration of capitalism has today produced a condition of 'fast capitalism',[3] in which economic change is implemented so rapidly and under such a dense smokescreen of media imagery that it cannot be critiqued until it has already happened. This has facilitated the prioritisation of market values over social, spiritual, aesthetic, and even moral values. It is presumed that the liberal market economy represents the best of all possible worlds, 'the end of history'.[4] Everything has been commodified; everyone is on the make. People's most heartfelt concerns are exploited by the provision of products catering to them. Their fears have been commodified by the insurance industry, their spiritual longings by a smorgasbord of 'New Age' merchandise and services. Their impulse to exercise their own creativity and imagination, says Jack Zipes, is

blocked as they 'stumble against those market forces that make commodities out of our lives, the market forces that create a new myth of
freedom which actually conceals our daily alienating experiences'.[5]

In this essay I write from a Christian perspective – to confront the
complicity of Christian tradition with this situation, and to mobilise a
Christian basis for challenging it. For Christians are swept along by market dogma like everyone else, often failing to question economic principles that, as 'common sense', 'the way things are' in 'the real world',
seem to stand beyond ethical debate. The attempt is made to hype Christ
with the methods of the marketplace. But the Christ so hyped lacks authenticity; he is not the Christ who transforms people's hearts, or the
Christ daily crucified in the slums and war zones of destitute countries.
The Christian voice rebounds back inside the bunker of church membership, its energies wasted struggling to preserve arcane doctrines that no
one else comprehends.

The supremacy of market doctrine has spiritual as well as moral consequences that Christians should care about. I believe that it can, and
should, be challenged from the standpoint that the gospel offers the liberation of people's hearts and minds from bondage to the zeitgeist. There
is scope for an alliance of artistic and Christian values. Might a Christian
notion of risk-taking faith, coupled with artistic integrity and critical
insight into the tyranny of fast capitalism, provide a basis for the art of
story to continue to nourish our souls?

*

The gentleman publishers of an earlier age published books that accorded with their own literary vision. They used income from bestselling
titles to subsidise work they thought worthy of a public but less certain
to make a profit. In the early decades of the twentieth century, my distant cousin Edward Garnett, reader to a succession of London publishers,
applied an uncompromising vision for literary quality and originality –
against the commercial pressure to 'give the public what they want' – to
nurture a generation of remarkable writers, including the likes of Joseph
Conrad, Edward Thomas, D. H. Lawrence, Liam O'Flaherty, H. E. Bates,
Henry Green, John Cowper Powys, and Naomi Mitchison.[6] That time has
gone. Publishing has become big business. The old publishing houses
have coalesced into large conglomerates. With the sale of Reed Consumer Books to Random House in 1997 a large proportion of London's
celebrated literary publishers, including ones that Garnett helped to
build up, became imprints of a single company. The conglomerates are
themselves mere divisions of multinational media corporations which
demand large profit margins from each of their business units. Thus fic-

tion publishing is expected to deliver profits on the same scale as TV, cinema, and mass-circulation magazines. Every book has to make money. The corporate strategists try to apply the same principles to selling books as for selling other mass-produced products. In 1932, Q. D. Leavis predicted that 'Publishers would come to depend more and more upon low-quality formula fiction, designed to produce maximum sales in the shortest possible time, sales maintained by the crass stimulation and manufacture of markets by advertising and promotion.'[7] That is exactly what's happened. The aim is to predict the demand for each product as accurately as possible, produce that quantity, and then promote the product sufficiently to make the sales match the prediction. For this to work smoothly you need products for which the demand is easily predicted.[8] Products that are 'safe', says Ursula Le Guin; that don't take risks, that don't try anything new, that won't unsettle the consumers, or change them, or make them think.

> If art is seen as having moral, intellectual, and social content, if real statement is considered possible, then ... the middlemen begin to fret. The publishers, the gallery owners, the entrepreneurs, the producers, the marketers, become uneasy. In so far as they are in the business for money, they are happier if art is not taken seriously.[9]

Publishers' efforts to control the interaction between consumer and product, to match production with demand as tightly as possible, have led to the assertive marketing of genre categories for which a measurable readership exists. The segmentation of the fiction market into categories may appear to encourage diversity, but in fact promotes imitative surrender to formula within each category, impedes the dynamic exchange of themes and innovations between genres, and excludes work that does not neatly fit any category.

Hence the preference to recycle the tried and trusted. When market values are supreme, success is inevitably judged in commercial terms. Michael Crichton, Jeffrey Archer, Dan Brown are seen as successful novelists because their books have sold in great numbers. Who are we to judge the quality of their work? Aggressive promotion of brand names can achieve massive sales in spite of stale recycled content and feeble prose. The same logic drives the publication of ghostwritten novels under the names of celebrities, and of bland novelisations of films and TV series. *Star Trek* and *Star Wars* have spawned so many spinoff books that at times they have taken up half the bookshop space allotted to the entire science fiction genre.

The quest to access the largest possible audience has driven down the quality of fiction in pursuit of a progressively more facile lowest common denominator. The publishers, distributors, booksellers, newspaper critics – all those who make a living out of writers and who gatekeeper what the public reads – are so conditioned by this commercial imperative that they underestimate the reading public's intelligence and sensibility. Richard Addis, former editor of the *Daily Express*, admitted 'that when he thought of his average reader he pictured the uncouth, simple-minded boyfriend of a former secretary from somewhere up north'.[10] Not only is this kind of attitude patronising and cynical; it may over time become self-fulfilling: if you keep feeding people stories that make limited demands on their intellectual and emotional faculties then eventually those faculties will atrophy. Yet, every now and again a book of great quality and originality gets through and its popularity spreads like wildfire by a chaotic effect of word-of-mouth recommendation over which publishers and distributors have no control.

Live storytelling is not, as yet, gatekeepered by big business. But, Zipes points out, storytellers too compete within the globalised culture industry, and market forces therefore constrain what they can do. If you want to keep getting bookings, the pressure is to deliver the kinds of stories you're sure will go down well, will put bums on seats, and won't disturb whoever's paying the bill. That can mean not telling the stories that people actually need to hear.[11] It can mean surrendering your personal authenticity – the quality that gives storytelling its unique moral authority – into a stage persona that is a caricature of who you truly are.[12] Greater commodification of storytelling, as seen in the United States, means more emphasis on merchandise and more possessive claims to the ownership of stories (see pages 74–6).

Writers and storytellers committed to their vocation have to scratch a living from the opportunities available to them. A few achieve celebrity. Lucrative opportunities may then arrive – and with them deeper temptations to compromise the integrity of their work. Ernest Hemingway wrote, 'our writers when they have made some money increase their standard of living and they are caught. They have to write to keep up their establishments, their wives, and so on, and they write slop. It is slop not on purpose but because it is hurried. Because they write when there is nothing to say or no water in the well.'[13] When a small press dedicated to some cause and/or to publishing high-quality work achieves commercial success, its priorities may change and it may attract takeover bids from larger companies.

Thanks to advances in technology and the deregulation of finance by a neoliberal political economy that has favoured their interests, big multinational companies have dramatically extended both their production and their marketing throughout the world. In each country they operate in, they compete against each other and against local businesses, thus sharpening the intensity of competition everywhere. They minimise costs by exploiting workers in different countries, who are in effect made to compete against each other in a worldwide labour market, and in doing so they kill local businesses that cannot minimise costs in the same way. The conglomeration of publishing houses is one manifestation of such globalisation. Another is the use of low-cost printers in the Far East and the wasteful squandering of fuel to ship the printed books to markets on the other side of the globe – and the equally wasteful pulping of unsold books because it's cheaper to do so than either to store them in hope of backlist sales or to underestimate sales and have to reprint.

In fast capitalism, products are produced and sold as rapidly as possible to reap as much profit as possible as fast as possible. Short-term profit margins are pursued at the expense of product quality. Novelists are often expected to write each new book within twelve months so it can be promoted alongside the paperback of last year's book. Never mind the time required for ideas to develop or for prose to be refined. The hype becomes more important than the product itself, merging in consumers' minds the product with the slogans and images used to promote it, and so blinding them to the reality of the product and the ethics of the way it has been produced and distributed.[14] In their pursuit of maximum profit the corporate media forge a conformity of thought and fashion, a homogenising blandness that is destroying traditional culture around the world and that sanctions mediocrity and ignorance.[15] The political nature of decision-making sinks out of view. The ideology of market economics is not seriously questioned outside the polders of academia and counterculture; it is simply accepted as the way the world is. The supremacy of that ideology thereby undermines the possibility of ethical debate about its social, environmental, and spiritual consequences.

*

Must we accept this state of affairs as all-powerful and inexorably able to neutralise any resistance? Must audiences inevitably succumb to the hype of 'bestsellers', 'blockbusters', and 'big names'? Or could people be helped to discover in themselves the wit to choose cultural products – including stories – they can truly value for their intrinsic quality and interest? What about the writers, the storytellers, the auteurs? What difference can they make if they really try? And what difference can faith make? How can we liberate ourselves from complicity with fast capitalism's ruthless economic imperatives? Geoffrey Shacklock says we can begin by asking honest questions about what is going on – to connect the realities we experience to 'the lessons of the past and the prospect for a better future'.[16]

Let us ask who really benefits from the supremacy of market doctrine. Certainly not the workers. A large organisation has an immensely stronger bargaining position than the individual employee, who generally is expendable and can be replaced from the pool of unemployed. Consumers do not really benefit either, since the quality of the products we purchase is impaired, as I've explained, by the emphasis on speed and cost-cutting.

The only people who really benefit from untrammelled market economics are those with capital to invest. To those who have shall more be given. Capitalism has always been like this, but since the 1980s market doctrine has been elevated to such a lofty status in public discourse that it has come to seem beyond serious challenge. The managers of a public limited company are said to have a 'moral duty' to do everything they can to maximise the profits of the company's shareholders. Who defines this morality? Not God, that's for sure. What kind of morality prioritises the enhancement of the wealth of those with surplus cash over the interests of workers, the needs of society, or the health of the environment? The law of the market is the law of the jungle – the survival of the strongest – but we shy away from acknowledging this. Not just corporate shareholders but all citizens of rich nations benefit from the international economy's exploitation of poorer countries. Boycotting a few companies deemed guilty of some particular excess will not absolve us from the collective guilt that accrues from the interconnectedness of the global economy.

People who believe in ideals of justice and truth should question not only the ethic of market economics but also the intellectual capitulation to the idea that its underlying assumptions represent an irrefutable truth. Otto Maduro points out two problems the Christian community faces here.[17] The first is Christianity's historical association with the development of capitalism, especially the early Protestants' trust in commerce – anticipating Adam Smith's 'invisible hand' of the market – to shape the best earthly society that can be hoped for, given the corruption of human motivations by sin. The second is epistemological. Throughout its history Christendom has conceived of knowledge as consisting of things being either true or false. Despite the collapse of belief in religious truth and the impasse of contemporary philosophy in the never-never-land of postmodernism, a covert belief in the idea of unchallengeable truth has covertly endured in the Western mind and is now embodied not in Christian doctrine but in the doctrine of market economics. To put this in blunt religious terms, one might say that the lordship of God has been replaced by the lordship of Mammon (i.e. money).

The gospel preaches liberation from whatever holds one in bondage. It is radically defiant of worldly values of self-interest. That's why, during the centuries when Christianity possessed worldly power, there was always a moral need for 'heretics' to challenge the discourse of authority. The challenge today is to liberate our culture from unquestioned ways of thinking, and in particular from the holy writ of market economics. I do not believe that the relentless advance of fast capitalism has to be inevitable, but it will require great creativity to picture alternative pathways that honour Jesus' teaching of compassion for the weak and cherish the beauty of creation. For believers, the price of finding them may be to accept uncertainty in what we can know to be true (see pages 84–5).

\*

There remain pathways of freedom in the creative industries. Some writers and even some film-makers have won sufficient celebrity to tell whatever stories they choose. While the large publishers and retail giants do battle to maximise shareholder value, small independent publishers and bookshops have found specialised niches to offer quality fiction they believe in for the discerning reader. Beneath them is a whole underground of small-press publications produced more for love than money, and most likely encountered through networks of literary and performance events. The same counter-cultural networks provide storytellers with opportunities to tell whatever stories their hearts move them to tell.

Advances in information technology, which have facilitated the freer, faster movement of capital, also make possible 'changes from mass production to flexible specialisation',[18] facilitating the activities of the small press – not only in production but also in marketing, using the internet to bypass the middlemen and reach the public directly. Even the individual writer can post samples of their work on the web and then print and supply books to customers upon demand.

The globalising of the world's economy is often said to encourage beneficial exchange between countries. The problem is that it's much more beneficial to richer countries, and richer people, than to poorer ones. It is worth making a distinction here between multinational globalisation and the smaller-scale international trade in locally distinctive creative work.[19] The latter kind of trade may sometimes have involved unfair exploitation of local artists, but it does mediate genuine cultural exchange, not the imposition of a dominant, homogenising culture on a weaker one. Small publishers who are motivated by more than commercial imperatives will benefit from networking with their counterparts in other countries, as Dedalus, for example, have done in publishing English translations of contemporary European fiction. In storytelling, such international cultural exchange happens face to face whenever people from different countries meet together to listen to each other's stories, whether that happens informally or through storytellers being invited from overseas to take part in festivals or tours.

The fate of narrative art in our brave new world truly matters. Salman Rushdie says that literature is for many in secular society a means of connecting to the transcendent – 'that flight of the human spirit outside the confines of its material, physical existence which all of us, secular or religious, experience on at least a few occasions'.[20] C. S. Lewis describes literature's enlargement of one's being to see the world from new perspectives: 'Like the night sky in the Greek poem, I see with a myriad eyes, but it is still I who see. Here, as in worship, in love, in moral action, and in knowing, I transcend myself; and am never more myself than when I do.'[21] Both fiction and storytelling can be more than a pleasing composition of words, more than a good story; at their best, they transcend the economics of pleasure and in doing so may transform their audience and thereby transform the world. Ben Okri's says, 'Art wants to pass into life, to lift it; art wants to enchant, to transform, to make life more meaningful or bearable in its own small and mysterious way.'[22]

Commercially driven design of products to exploit known markets cannot be expected to produce work that will do that. Lewis Hyde makes a compelling argument that, although artists must earn a living somehow and although art must be bought and sold through networks of trade, the quality that really makes something *art*, that gives it that transformative potency, has nothing to do with commercial logic. It is a priceless gift, which the artist does not own but instead receives from beyond: through inspiration from the world around them, from other people and other works of art … and, a believer would say, from God.[23] Despite the economic constraints upon its publication, the writing of fiction remains freer from external control than more costly art forms such as film.[24] It is composed by one person in private and requires no expensive equipment, only the investment of time. Storytelling allows yet freer individual expression, in that it's not only composed but also reaches its audience without incurring industrial costs. In exhilarating contrast to Zipes's critique of the myth of freedom, Ursula Le Guin cries, 'See, the thing is, as a writer you are free. You are about the freest person that ever was. Your freedom is what you have bought with your solitude, your loneliness.'[25]

Writers and storytellers can exercise the freedom to tell the stories their heart moves them to *if* they take the risk, the step of faith, that the work may not win them wealth or recognition. Central to the gospel, to the religious impulse in general, including secular manifestations such as the green movement, are the vision of a better world, or a better way of living and being, and the struggle to bring this into being (see pages 135–7). Each generation needs storymakers inspired by such visions who have

faith to put them into well-crafted words and images, artists with pene-
trating insight into the reality of their times and an ability to plumb so
deep within their souls that they touch the divine wellspring beyond.
Ben Okri calls us to 'return to pure contemplation, to sweet meditation,
to the peace of silent loving, the serenity of deep faith, to the stillness of
deep waters. We should sit still in our deep selves and dream good new
things for humanity.'[26] The great visionaries, the great storytellers, mediate between the numinous and the human. They speak honestly and daringly from the heart, offering 'a singular vision', as Mike Riddell puts it,
dragged 'wet and wild and pumping from the creative womb'.[27]

Hopeful and meaningful envisioning of pathways – narratives – into
the future will draw upon prophetic insights into the way the world is
(see page 163). It will challenge the present order and question our certainties and imagine creative alternatives. In this way, narrative art –
when it dares to be true to its inspiration, to be free – can help to undermine the oppressive assumptions of market doctrine and liberate us
from the tyranny of fast capitalism.

> The storyteller must realize that he/she is *not* free to tell stories
> but has the power to liberate himself/herself and others through a
> genuine exchange of experience. The storyteller provokes thought
> and action through story, awakens the storyteller in others, lis-
> tens, and seeks an opportunity to tell another story that subverts
> the myth of freedom.[28]

---

1 Zipes, *Revisiting the Storyteller*, p. 10.
2 Connor, *The English Novel in History*, pp. 18–19.
3 Agger, *Fast Capitalism*.
4 Fukuyama, *The End of History*.
5 Zipes, *Revisiting the Storyteller*, p. 12.
6 Jefferson, *Edward Garnett*.
7 Paraphrased in Connor, *The English Novel in History*, p. 18.
8 Radway, *Reading the Romance*, p. 29.
9 Le Guin, 'Stalin in the Soul', p. 206.
10 Pinchen, 'And Now the Good News', p. 11.
11 Zipes, 'Storytelling and Spectacle in the Globalised World'.
12 I'm indebted to Jack Zipes for this insight.
13 Hemingway, *Green Hills of Africa*, p. 28.
14 Shacklock, 'Fast Capitalist Educational Change', pp. 78–80; Reymers, 'Growth
   and Fast Capitalism'.
15 Mayer, 'The Post-modern World'.
16 Shacklock, 'Fast Capitalist Educational Change', p. 81.
17 Maduro, 'Globalization and Christianity in the 21st Century'.

[18] Begbie, 'Postmodernism and the Arts', p. 17.

[19] Lorimer and O'Donnell, 'Globalization and Internationalization in Publishing'.

[20] Rushdie, 'Is Nothing Sacred?', p. 103.

[21] Lewis, *An Experiment in Criticism*, p. 141.

[22] Okri, 'Beyond Words', p. 89.

[23] Hyde, *The Gift*.

[24] Rushdie, 'Is Nothing Sacred?', pp. 107–8.

[25] Le Guin, 'Talking about Writing', p. 190.

[26] Okri, 'Beyond Words', p. 94.

[27] Riddell, 'Art for Art's Sake', p. 4.

[28] Zipes, *Revisiting the Storyteller*, p. 12.

# Telling Stories from the Big Picture of Ecological History

In my formative years I absorbed, from my education, from the media, a grand narrative about humankind's relationship with the ecosystem. It's a story of progress: the invention of tools, the taming of fire, the domestication of crops and animals, the carving of farmland from wilderness, the building of cities. Nested in the larger story are countless discrete episodes that stand alone as stories we tell: the domestication of wheat in Mesopotamia; Columbus's discovery of the New World; the invention of the steam engine to power Britain's industrial revolution. All these things enabled an accelerating expansion of the human population as part and parcel of an ongoing 'conquest' of nature. In essence, this story and its constituent episodes are true; these things did happen.

But they're not the whole story.

History has traditionally been narrated by the powerful. Their experience, their perspective have been taken as normative. Stories told from white or upper-class or male viewpoints have tended to shield from critique the privileges of these typically dominant parties. The stories of less powerful people have tended to be silenced. Instrumental in the women's, labour, and civil-rights movements of recent times has been the telling of stories that expose the price paid by the disadvantaged to serve the interests of the powerful. Testimonies of real-life experience played an important part in the campaign to end the slave trade.[1]

In a comparable way, the grand narrative of our conquest of nature presents as normative the perspective of *humankind* as the dominant party with respect to non-human nature – and particularly the perspective of the elites of historically expansionist nations. What it omits are the stories of the losers: many non-human components of the ecosystem, and people adversely affected by environmental change, diminishing resources, and increasing population density; stories that add up to an alternative grand narrative, now escalating into global ecological crisis.

It therefore seems important to balance the stories of progress with the stories of the price of that progress. Both upbeat and downbeat stories fall within the scope of this essay about telling true-life stories from the history of human interaction with the ecosystem, but it's often the downbeat ones that pack a stronger punch, that make us question our social order, and therefore require special care in the telling. Such stories are very diverse and involve a wide range of timescales, from incidents during a single day to processes that unfolded over the course of years, centuries, even millennia. Some examples I've worked with include: the collapse of the Maya civilisation when its soil was exhausted; Alfred Russel Wallace's independent discovery of the origin of species by natural selection; the genocide of Tasmanian Aborigines at the hands of British colonists (see page 144); the salvation from extinction of Père David's deer (see pages 130–2); the problems that Maasai pastoralists have faced since the appropriation of much of their land for agriculture and game reserves (see pages 129–30); the beating up of conservation officials by wildcat loggers in the Mayan Biosphere Reserve in 1992.[2] Another good example is the fate of Sir John Franklin's expedition in search of the Northwest Passage, which David Metcalfe tells as a prologue to performing the folk song 'Franklin'.

Stories of this kind present many of the same challenges as true-life stories from history in general. One additional challenge they can pose is to elicit compassion towards non-human entities as well as humans.

## THE PASSENGER PIGEON

In the basement of a museum in Bath I once saw, in a glass case, a stuffed bird about eighteen inches long with handsome plumage – blue above and a wine red breast. The caption said this specimen came from the eastern woods of North America. It's name was *Ectopistes migratorius*, otherwise known as the 'passenger pigeon'.

The passenger pigeon was once the most abundant bird on earth. It's possible that forty per cent of all the birds in North America were passenger pigeons. The early European settlers were amazed to see such enormous flocks, hundreds of kilometres long and containing literally thousands of millions of birds. The naturalist John James Audubon saw one such flock in Kentucky in 1813. He said the sky was literally full of birds and the noonday sun was darkened as if by an eclipse. Their droppings fell from the sky like snow and the noise of so many beating wings overwhelmed his senses. He dared to venture inside a wood where the passenger pigeons were nesting. The smell in there was incredible and the droppings lay so deep on the ground that at first he thought they were snow. When the birds returned to their nests, the sound as they landed in the trees was like thunder, their wooing calls were like the ringing of bells, and branches snapped off, whole trees collapsed, under the weight of so many birds.

The native people had always hunted the passenger pigeon. The flesh was tasty and the birds were easy to kill: you could just knock them down with a pole. But for the European settlers, struggling to make a new life in a new land, the passenger pigeons were like manna from heaven. They killed them for food. They killed them for sport. They organised mass hunts, after which each man took as many birds as he wanted and the rest were left for the pigs.

After 1800 the industrial revolution was underway and in the fast-growing cities there was a lucrative market for game, and passenger pigeon became a fashionable delicacy. Now the hunting became commercialised. It became mechanised. The birds were killed with guns, with nets, with fire, by pulling down trees, and even with a primitive kind of machinegun. The new railways were used to transport the carcasses to market and the telegraph brought the latest information to help the hunters track the movements of the flocks.

The passenger pigeons were killed in enormous numbers. In one year a thousand million were killed in the state of Michigan alone. In the 1850s a single New York agent was selling eighteen thousand carcasses per day. The native people protested against this scale of slaughter. They were ignored. People said the passenger pigeon needed no legal protection because they were just so numerous.

But they were becoming less numerous. On top of the hunting, rapid deforestation to make space for farmland was destroying the food supply they needed of beechmast and acorns. In 1878 the last really big flock of one thousand million passenger pigeons nested near Petoskey, Michigan. The hunters came – and destroyed that flock. In one month they took three hundred tons of pigeons. Every day of that month there were five freight cars packed full with their carcasses.

Now the passenger pigeon was in trouble. Their population fragmented and dwindled. Their breeding cycle was disrupted. Their nesting sites were destroyed. Each pair of birds was able to produce only one chick per year. They just couldn't breed fast enough to replace their losses.

The last flock of any size – 250,000 – nested in a wood on the Green River, Ohio, in 1896. The hunters got word by the telegraph. From every direction they converged by railway upon that wood. And they obliterated those birds. Of the 250,000 just five thousand escaped. The hundred thousand newborn chicks, of no commercial value, were left to the predators. The carcasses of the adult birds were loaded on to a freight train and sent to market. But a derailment further down the line brought the train to a halt. In the hot sun the carcasses tightly packed in the freight cars soon began to putrefy. The whole lot went to waste and were dumped in a ravine nearby.

After that, sightings of passenger pigeons were few and far between. In 1902 a flock of 140 was reported in Arkansas. Most of them were shot down. In 1904 one was seen in Vermont. Someone shot it down. In 1906 one more bird in Arkansas. It was shot down. In 1907 one was sighted in Quebec. Again it was shot down. And that was the last time anyone shot – or saw – a wild passenger pigeon.

There were still a few in zoos. But they didn't breed well in captivity, and one by one the captive birds died.

Until there was just one left.

They called her Martha. She was born in Cincinnati Zoo in 1885. People came from all over the United States to see her – the last of the passenger pigeons. She lived on to the age of twenty-nine. She died on 1 September 1914 at 1.00 p.m. With her death, the passenger pigeon, which had once been the most abundant bird on earth, became extinct.

Martha's body was taken at once to the Smithsonian Institution in Washington, to be stuffed and put on display in a glass case. She remains in the collections of the National Museum of Natural History to this day.[3]

'Why did you tell that story?' people sometimes ask after I've told 'The Passenger Pigeon'. Like all stories I tell, it's one I feel moved in my heart to tell. I read about the passenger pigeon in Robert Silverberg's *The Dodo, the Auk and the Oryx* when I was eleven. The story helped inculcate in me a concern about endangered species. To tell a story like this one raises consciousness and, I hope, evokes empathy for the creatures in question (see pages 143–4). If people know what happened in the past, the mistakes that were made, then perhaps that will affect their opinions and actions today. Some years ago Chris Sunderland, whose runs a consultancy called Agora promoting forums for quality conversation about public life, persuaded me that storytelling could be a more engaged element of civil society if it included more true-life stories, environmental and otherwise. Many traditional stories do indeed convey moral teaching, but their imaginative distance from the real world makes it relatively easy for the listener, if so inclined, to ignore their applicability to real-world situations, unless one provides a way for this to be unpacked.

The mere telling of a true-life story, on the other hand, can automatically, without any comment, make a moral or political impact.

Of course, the selection of which side of the story to tell, which details to include, may crucially determine the particular impact a story makes. The privileged and powerful may put a spin on events which protects their own interests. The disadvantaged, when they get a platform to tell their stories, may exaggerate things to favour theirs. Activists may misrepresent the facts as a result of inadequate knowledge or a propagandising zeal that assumes ends justify means. Michael Hanlon's science articles in the *Daily Mail* are sometimes slanted to endorse a complacency about the ecological crisis which is consonant with that newspaper's right-wing politics. In one piece about species extinctions – a topic I happen to know something about – I noticed that every statement Hanlon made was factually correct, yet these carefully selected statements added up to the implication that human action is a negligible cause of extinctions – the reverse of the prevailing scientific interpretation of the research he was citing.

If your listeners catch you misrepresenting known facts, the credibility of your story will be undermined. But there's a deeper moral issue. The impact of a story presented as true history is strongly conditioned by the audience's assumption that these events actually happened. When you proceed during a performance from a traditional story to a serious, perhaps hard-hitting, historical story there's a striking shift in the audience's mood, a new gravity of attention as they realise that what they're now listening to is something that really happened.

All of this begs questions about the nature of 'truth' and how much we can really know about the past. Some might throw up their hands and say, 'We cannot know anything for sure about past events. All we have are stories, texts. Who is to say which are really true? How can we make any distinction between so-called "true-life stories" and other kinds of stories? Why regard the former as any "truer" than mythic stories?' There's an important point here, which leads into deep philosophical waters. Many stories do blend myth and history. Myth may well be a conduit to profound truths about existence. But we run into trouble when stories that cannot be factually substantiated – tales of 'blood libel' against the Jews, to take an extreme example – are promoted as factual truth. The converse problem arises when people deny the reality of events there's strong reason to believe did take place – for example, the Turkish government's stance towards the Armenian genocide. If we discard the particular significance of true-life stories, then we discard moral responsibility towards the real world.

That the impact of these stories can be so strong, and can so readily be abused, makes certain demands on the storyteller's integrity – in their respect for the audience, for the real people the stories concern, and for some notion of truth. To render the absolute and whole truth about past events is impossible. There will be selectivity; there will be interpretation; there will be judgements between conflicting accounts, which may themselves be biased in various ways. But science and historiography offer us a paradigm for seeking the facts of a matter as honestly as they may be gleaned from the available evidence.

When researching a true-life story, it's useful to distinguish which facts seem beyond dispute, which remain contested, and where there are blanks of knowledge. Someone once challenged me how I can be sure that vast passenger pigeon flocks ever existed or were hunted. This strikes me as a metaphysical question that leads nowhere except escape from reality. There's no dispute among historians that passenger pigeons flocked in enormous numbers. The exact numbers can only be estimated, the precise mechanism by which the species became extinct is conjectural, but it's beyond dispute that hunting and habitat destruction were the primary causes. I've chosen to use the latest of the dates given by different sources for the last shooting of a wild passenger pigeon. That a few wild birds might have survived in remote places after Martha's death is theoretically possible, but there's no evidence any did. So far as the sum of human knowledge can demonstrate, it seems fair to present her as the last of her species.

However, in telling the story of the American bison, which was almost exterminated like the passenger pigeon but was saved at the brink, I have to deal with factual uncertainty about one rather important factor. Some accounts say that the United States government deliberately promoted the massacre of bison to undermine the livelihood of the Plains Indians who were resisting the USA's westward colonisation. Other accounts imply the hunting was entirely commercial. Unable to pin down the truth of this, but suspecting such government complicity to be likely – though unofficial – and that it therefore should be mentioned, I explicitly acknowledge my uncertainty on this point as I tell the story.

The need for integrity means researching the facts as thoroughly as you can, using multiple sources if you can find them. It means respecting your sense of what actually happened when you make decisions about what to include and how to shape the story. Since an oral story, unlike a film or a book, is never ossified in a final form, you can modify it in the light of new information.

Not only political motives but also the demands of effective story structure may tempt us to make free with the facts. Real life doesn't come with the neat structure of a folktale. The storyteller has to sculpt a storyline out of history's tangled complexity. Film-makers routinely and grossly misrepresent history – to satisfy the strict story structure believed necessary to please a mass audience and recoup the money invested – at the same time as they evoke the frisson of 'This is a true story' by prefacing the film with a few lines of historical context. Storytelling, because it hinges so much on the teller's rapport with the audience, allows more structural freedom but at the same time focuses the ethics of the situation: how meaningful is the relationship I've cultivated with my audience if I'm misleading them about events I'm presenting as real history?

My feelings about this were crystallised by an incident at a storytelling club years ago. A man none of us knew came to the club and told what appeared to be a true story from his own life. He was a powerfully built man and spoke with a Merseyside accent. His story was about growing up in working-class Liverpool, getting involved in petty crime, which escalated into serious crime and a prison sentence. It culminated in his killing his erstwhile partner in crime. Even when he'd finished, many people there still believed it was a true confession and were frightened what the man might do next. It was in fact a skilful wind-up. Although the truth of the situation was admitted before we all went home, some felt they'd been abused by this story's being presented (by a live storyteller) as true. On reflection, I felt they were right and modified my own practice in consequence (see page 54).

I like to tell the passenger pigeon's story in a stark 'history lesson' manner in order to maximise its impact as something that actually happened. I include selected dates and statistics to reinforce its authority as history and to convey how events developed over the course of a century. Depending on your taste as a storyteller and the context in which you want to tell the story, there are other ways in which you could put across this story. You might blend history and fiction by, for example, telling things from the point of view of Martha, or of a man who hunted the passenger pigeon flocks in his youth but lives long enough to visit Martha in the zoo. Such an approach, though it makes liberal use of the imagination to fill out characters, scenes, and plot, can yet honour the facts of history as you understand them.

Even the history lesson style can use evocative images. A set of key images can help to define an *emotional* structure that, to some extent, takes the place of the structure of *action* in a good folktale. Three images in my mind's eye structure my telling of 'The Passenger Pigeon': (1) the mind-boggling scale of the flock witnessed by Audubon; (2) the putrefying carcasses in the stalled train from the Green River nesting site; (3) Martha, alone in the zoo, watched by visitors. Of these the third is for me the story's emotional centre of gravity: the crucial moment of empathy when the whole species has become personified in a single individual, the last of her kind. When I'm rehearsing the story, this moment still commonly takes me close to tears.

When I'm telling the story to an audience, though, I try to suppress my own stronger feelings. My intention is that, yes, I'm sharing something that's important to me, but I want the audience to have space to supply their own feelings in response. Moreover, respect for the audience means not only honesty but also compassion. When you're telling a true-life story of injustice or senseless destruction, there's a risk your own moral judgement may spill over into a sanctimonious or ranting tone in which it's as if you're rebuking the audience for the deeds that were done. I try to hold an intention of compassionate restraint and thereby maintain rapport.

Care also needs to be taken in deciding when and where to tell especially the more shocking true-life stories. As the storyteller-naturalist Malcolm Green impressed on me, people can't take too much bad news.[4] In a public performance situation, where an audience have paid to be entertained, Fire Springs may embed one story of this kind as an anchor of real-life gravity amidst a set of more intentionally entertaining material. In educational, political, religious, or avant-garde contexts bolder use of challenging historical stories may be justified.

One strength of live storytelling is the way it facilitates a 'return' from the story into the here and now of our own lives, like the return of the mythic hero from the realm of adventure (see page 14). The storyteller is there in person to guide the audience into the story and then guide them back. By sustaining a cohesive rapport, you help this group of people share the impact of the story together. The way you shape the story's conclusion, too, contributes to this quality of return. Be aware, though, that a normalising ending – a reassurance that everything's all right now – may compromise the intention the story should challenge people; many fairy tales may be judged politically conservative because their ending implicitly endorses the existing social order. Music is an excellent tool to facilitate the return. David Holt tells the story of the sinking of the *Titanic* – that iconic clash between human artifice and non-human nature – as he heard it from one of the last extant survivors. The story ends very downbeat: the people in the half-filled lifeboats keep their distance, lest the boats get swamped, till the people struggling in the water have all died. The audience are appalled. Holt brings them back by playing the blues on his guitar.

Where, finally, can we source stories of ecological history? The publications and websites of conservation organisations are one port of call. Natural history museums and documentaries may provide some ideas. Most fruitful for me are erudite semi-popular books in the fields of popular science, natural history, ethnography, and exploration, backed up by forays into encyclopaedias, specialist journals, and the web to ferret out particular details. If you keep your eyes peeled, you may also spot insightful stories about the environment lurking in general history and travel writing and the broadsheet press. Rarely can you take stories of ecological history straight off the shelf, ready to run, as you often can traditional stories. You have to do the work of gathering information and then shaping it into a form that both honours what actually happened *and* makes a good story.

---

[1] Stearns, *Global Outrage*.

[2] Nabhan, *Cultures of Habitat*.

[3] Anthony Nanson, 2002. Principal sources: Day, *The Doomsday Book of Animals*; Paul, *Dinosaurs of the Air*; Silverberg, *The Dodo, the Auk and the Oryx*.

[4] Nanson, *Storytelling and Ecology*.

# Two Sides to a Story: storytelling as a tool of the imagination in conflicts over environmental resources

## Imaginative thought

In a training context you might well expect the focus to be on learning practical skills you can use, rather than on theoretical thinking. But the importance of thinking about things carefully is a crucial part of the practical question of how storytelling can help us apply our imagination to situations of conflict among people – and between people and wildlife – who are competing for natural resources.

The trend of government policy in Britain, and of the zeitgeist generally, is to emphasise skills over thinking. The implicit aim is to fashion citizens who will serve the economy as skilled worker-consumers but will not disrupt its smooth running by thinking too much (see page 105). Such policy seems blind to the need, in our age of environmental crisis, for people to think intelligently and imaginatively so they can understand what's happening and respond creatively and cooperatively to the challenges, instead of stubbornly pursuing short-term self-interest and blaming problems on 'immigrants' or 'rogue nations'.

Notice, for example, the unmindful reactions to global warming now it's become the main focus of environmental concern: climate change caused by burning fossil fuels, we're told, is the biggest single challenge to human security; therefore we must invest in a massive expansion of nuclear power, we must dam the Severn estuary, we must build a million wind turbines. At a presentation about global warming at Cheltenham Science Festival in 2005, Sir David King, the government's Chief Scientific Advisor, said in reply to a question about the plan to build half a million new houses in the counties around London, 'The question, to me, is a no-brainer. If people need houses, you've got to build 'em.' The assumptions that lie unacknowledged behind that statement! What about population growth? What about second homes that are empty most of the year? What about derelict areas elsewhere in the country? Why should each adult or couple expect to live in a separate house rather than communally with others? Why do we accept that domestic housing should be a massive capital market milked by the rich at the expense of the poor?

We can't afford to dismiss complex political questions as 'no-brainers'. Skills, though important, can't by themselves resolve conflicts. You need to know not only how to do something, but also whether to do it, why you should do it, the pitfalls of doing it. Things like 'story' and 'tradition' are not inherently good. Like science and technology, they can be used for good or for ill. The Nazis coopted the Germanic myths. The battle of Kosovo in 1389, a great theme of Serbian legend ever since, became a cornerstone of extreme nationalism in the 1990s. The honoured place of hunting in national traditions – and featuring in many stories – is used to justify practices such as the continued hunting of whales by the Japanese and Norwegians, despite the fact that the contemporary situation – much diminished populations of whales and greater understanding of these animals' intelligence and capacity to feel pain – is very different from that in which the traditions originated. So we need to question the values of the traditional stories we tell: to ask whether a story needs to be rewoven so that as we harness whatever wisdom it continues to bear we can make it speak to the realities and heightened ethical knowledge of our time.

The thinking we need is not merely intellectual cogitation, but imaginative thinking about real people and real situations: in particular, to imagine how a conflict situation may seem to some party other than yourself or your own group; and to imagine the possibilities, for good or ill, of how the situation might change.

## The instinct to pursue self-interest

As a child grows up they have to learn to 'decentre', that is, to imagine things viewed from a different perspective than one's own present perspective. The simplest kind of decentring is spatial: right now you can't see the fox that's just run behind the shed, but you can imagine that if you moved to a new position where you could see behind the shed then you would be able to see the fox again. Later we learn to imagine how things might *feel* from someone else's point of view: 'How would *you* like it if someone stole *your* lollipop?' To empathise like this is not always easy even for adults, especially when the problem at hand concerns not people you know and love, but strangers, or people of a kind (immigrants, cyclists, managers, your tribe's ancestral enemy) from whom you're alienated, or even creatures of another species. Which is why it's a radical step to generalise your mum's injunction 'How would *you* like it if … ?' into the so-called Golden Rule: 'So always treat others as you would like them to treat you.'[1]

Working against that noble ethic, however, is the strong instinct most of us have to pursue our own self-interest. According to the theory of evolution, far more individual organisms are born than, given the available resources, can survive to adulthood and reproduce. There is thus a struggle for existence, which Darwin called 'natural selection', whereby weaker individuals are weeded out and more able ones survive and reproduce. Human beings possess such adaptability and technology that we've now vastly outcompeted other species of large animals, so that our population has exponentially increased and the populations of other animals, except our livestock, have declined. But the struggle for existence applies among humans too – think of the countries devastated by famine, war, and disease – and continues to buttress our instinct to serve our own interests.

As we're a social species, the pursuit of self-interest applies not only to individuals but also to groups, each member of which may gain from the group's collective pursuit of its members' interests. The logic of natural selection was consciously applied to politics in twentieth-century fascism, most dramatically by the Nazis, who tried to advance one ethnic nation's collective interests – including access to natural resources such as land – by exterminating other ethnic groups. In our own day, the economic doctrine of neoliberalism has institutionalised the struggle for existence in a more individualised – and superficially more civilised – form in which owning capital is the key factor that favours one's chances of flourishing. Yet the fascist brute-force approach often still prevails, as happened in Kenya in 2008: in a situation where population growth was outpacing available land resources – and the rich and powerful had taken the best land – youths without prospects allied with ambitious local leaders to try to implement by genocidal force the 'majimbo' doctrine of driving out people of other tribes to create ethnically homogenised regions in which the landless would occupy vacated property.

Those who defend such politics of natural selection demonstrate a failure of imagination: they fail to imagine how it must feel to be one of the losers in the struggle for resources. Failure to comprehend that the other is a conscious being like yourself leads to the exploitation or abuse of human beings – and animals – as if they were inanimate objects. I had an insight into this when, long ago, I took part in a business simulation game: 'labour' was merely a cost you had to minimise as much as you could without triggering industrial action.

Sometimes, as in Milton Friedman's economic principle of sustaining a large pool of the unemployed in order to keep down the cost of labour, people wilfully shut down their sensitivity to the other's plight. Other times they simply may not understand the effects of power and economics. In discourse about human endurance during times of crisis, you sometimes hear people say, 'We're an adaptable species. We've been through hard times before, but, each time, we've managed to survive and we've flourished once again.' When it comes to humankind's catastrophic impact on the global ecosystem, you may hear a similar heroic narrative about life as a whole: 'Each time that life on earth has suffered a mass extinction, there's been an amazing radiation of new species. Even if we destroy ourselves and most of the species on the planet, life will find a way to carry on.' The problem with this kind of thinking is that it's too macro. It fails to take seriously the enormous significance of suffering and death to the individual conscious being. Again there's a need to extend one's imagination. Each human being – and, I suspect, each individual of many other species with which we share the earth – is a whole universe of consciousness, infinitely precious to themself and to those who love them. The philosopher Philip Goodchild says,

A child has died of diarrhoea. A lover has vanished without trace ... A people has been subjected to genocide. A city has suffered intensive fire bombing ... Let us not count occasions and figures, though the occasions are too numerous and the figures too immense to count. Each event, in its own significance, outweighs the counting of numbers.[2]

If we hold to the ethics of the Golden Rule and wish to resolve conflicts peacefully, our natural instinct to pursue self-interest needs to be balanced by other kinds of impulse – compassion, charity, love – that transcend biological logic. That human beings are capable of this there's ample evidence. Some animals are too. A man may transcend the biological instinct to inseminate as many healthy women as possible. A couple may transcend the biological impulse to raise as many children as they can. People selflessly give of themselves in many different ways for the sake of others. What the global ecological crisis – and each local environmental conflict within that bigger picture – seems to demand is a *collective* transcending of our biological instincts: collective but humane choices to limit population growth and to limit the resources we consume. It's unfortunate that many forces in the world today – the globalised capitalist economy, the breakdown of community it's causing, the intensifying competition and cutbacks as we approach the limits of growth – seem to be driving us the other way, towards more selfish and not more altruistic behaviour.

## False consciousness

My personal feeling is that the need to transcend biological logic may, ultimately, require some form of metaphysical inspiration (see pages 155–6), but in this essay I shall try to address the challenge within a secular framework. Let's begin with the Marxist idea of 'false consciousness': that in blindly pursuing what appears to be their self-interest people may not actually act in their own interest – for example, the working man who votes for a conservative party because he thinks they'll keep out immigrants, whereas his interests would be better served by voting for a socialist party that would tax the rich more and spend the takings on public services. Someone very engaged with the plight of the poor in Africa asserted to me that 'in Africa right now environmental concerns are a luxury'. Okay, people on the edge of starvation may have no choice but to exploit whatever resources are available, however much damage such action (felling the trees from a watershed, killing the last game) may do to the environment and their own long-term prospects; but for the rest of us there's a kind of false consciousness when we express the absolute necessity of some activity (maintaining a company's profitability, buying a house big enough for more children) that in fact helps to undermine our collective environmental security, and our children's.

Such false consciousness is understandable, since humans didn't evolve in circumstances that required them to contemplate problems on scales beyond the family group's immediate needs (see pages 164–5). Edward O. Wilson says,

It was necessary for survival for the ancestral human beings to throw everything they had against the wilderness in an attempt to conquer it, to utilise it … to expand the population, to gain security, to control, to alter, and for millions of years that paid off without undue damage. But … we succeeded too well and at long last we broke nature and now, almost too late, we're waking up to the fact that we've overdone it.

Wilson optimistically goes on to express his belief that, 'given enough education, enough awareness, enough sensitivity to problems presented to them, people have the capacity to do amazing things and change their attitude'.[3] Can we redirect the cleverness with which we've advanced our self-interest and procreation – towards now restraining these instincts in order to assure the collective well-being of ourselves, our environment, and our descendants, both globally and in each local situation of environmental conflict?

## The other's point of view

Let's return to the Golden Rule and the importance of imagining how things seem from someone else's point of view. This is one of the things that stories do well. Told or written, they can take us inside perspectives different from our own. C. S. Lewis says,

> Those of us who have been true readers all our lives seldom fully realise the enormous extension of our being that we owe to authors … My own eyes are not enough for me, I will see through those of others … I regret that brutes cannot write books. Very gladly would I learn what face things present to a mouse or a bee; more gladly still would I perceive the olfactory world charged with all the information and emotion it carries for a dog.[4]

If you know someone's story you'll understand their motivation. Stories are propelled by specific desires their protagonists pursue. They end – in classical story structure – when the protagonist either achieves their desire or conclusively fails to do so.

### THE TWO CHAMPIONS

There were two kingdoms that shared a common border. In one country they worshipped the sun and in the other they worshipped the moon. The two kingdoms quarrelled over the strips of territory either side of the border. They used their religious differences to drum up hatred of each other, and then they went to war. Each gathered an army and the two armies met at the frontier. Row upon row of warriors, sunlight glinting on their war gear, faced each other across the no man's land.

It was agreed that each army should send forward a champion to fight in single combat. The strongest, most skilful warrior in each army was selected. The two men advanced towards each other, grim faced beneath their helmets, with a sword in one hand and a shield in the other. On the chest of one was emblazoned an image of the sun; on the chest of the other an image of the moon.

When they met, they fought like demons. They fought all morning long as the sun rose higher in the sky. They fought through the midday heat when the sun was at the zenith. They fought on and on as the sun descended towards the west. They were both such strong and skilful fighters that neither man could gain the advantage. They were still fighting, nose to nose, locked in each other's arms, when at last the sun went down and it grew too dark for them to see their own swords in front of their faces.

By then they were exhausted. They both collapsed on the ground, too weak and battered even to crawl back to the camps their respective armies had made for the night.

'I hate you!' groaned the Champion of the Sun.

'I hate you!' replied the Champion of the Moon.

'I have to kill you,' said the Champion of the Sun. 'Back home I have a wife who loves me and a little boy who wants to be a warrior like me. I have to kill you to protect them from the likes of you.'

'I had a wife,' said the Champion of the Moon. 'Your people killed her in the last war. That's why I have to kill you.'

There was a long silence. The moon rose into the night sky. Presently, the Champion of the Sun asked the other man, 'What was she like, your wife?'

'She was lovely. We'd been sweethearts since we were children. I used to play with her in the woods not far from here.'

'Sounds like you had a happy childhood,' said the Champion of the Sun. 'Not like mine. My father made us work all day in the fields and he'd beat us if we complained.'

'I'm sorry to hear that,' said the Champion of the Moon.

And so they talked, about their childhood and the other things they had done in their lives. They talked and talked as the moon rose higher in the sky. Still they talked as the moon descended towards the west. Only for the last hour or two of the night did they sleep. Side by side they lay, their swords and shields and helmets scattered around them.

The sky turned grey, then pink in the east. Sounds and smells of breakfast-making emanated from the two camps. The two sleeping champions were woken by the warmth of sunshine on their faces. Wearily, painfully, they creaked to their feet. They put on their helmets. They picked up their swords and shields. They looked into each other's eyes.

Then they dropped their swords and their shields and they embraced.

Finally they turned and walked away, each back to their own army, leaving their swords and shields behind them. They could not fight each other any more ... because you cannot hate someone when you know their story.[5]

The storyteller Simon Airey once told this story – originally devised by Dan Keding – to two Dinka soldiers of the Sudan People's Liberation Army (SPLA) who'd been assigned to protect him during his visit to war-torn southern Sudan. The SPLA had for years been fighting for that re-gion's independence from the Khartoum government in the north. In Simon's version, the two enemy nations in the story were 'the people of the North' and 'the people of the South'. He found it an eerie experience to be telling that story in the gloom of a little hut, in bush country that every year was scoured by government troops, to a pair of scar-faced warriors whose automatic rifles were propped against the mud wall. When he'd finished, there was a long pause; then one of the soldiers said, 'That is an interesting story. I shall have to think about this story.'[6]

Not an easy task for those men, who were fighting for their people's lives and freedom against a ruthless and powerful enemy. The point I want to emphasise is that when you know both sides of the story you often can't make a simple distinction between goodies and baddies. Few people actually consider themselves evil. From their own point of view, most people are just trying to get through the day, or to 'get the job done'. Which is not, of course, to dismiss the necessity of moral judge-ment in the many conflicts where there is an asymmetry of blame, often attached to an asymmetry of power. But sometimes there's a grave sense of injustice on both sides of a conflict. I once read a history of the Pales-tine–Israel conflict which consisted of two narratives, one by an Israeli scholar and one by a Palestinian.[7] The two narratives were so different – and so sympathetic – that it was hard to believe they both dealt with the same place and period.

At a Survival International meeting I attended, three representatives of the Maasai – an elder, a moran (young man of warrior age), and a woman – explained how the Maasai, a cattle-herding people, had been driven from their traditional pastures by farmers settling the land and by the establishment of game reserves. You might expect that campaigns defending the environment and tribal peoples would share the same po-litical constituency, but in this context wildlife and tribal interests were set against each other and the prevailing mood of the meeting was of belligerent defence of Maasai interests. Quite an edgy atmosphere. It felt as though many of the Brits present had as much at stake as the Maasai, in jockeying for status in their careers as researchers and campaigners. At one point a retired biologist said he'd studied the ecology of East Africa for forty years and observed a clear degradation of the savannah and de-cline in its biodiversity as the population of Maasai livestock increased. He was immediately hissed down by people outraged he'd defied the norm of opinion in the room. Later, a soft-spoken young man asked whether the Maasai had always lived in the lands where they live now.

'No,' replied the moran. 'Many years ago our forefathers came south from the Nile valley. They discovered our land and brought cattle there.'

'Was the land empty, then, when they first arrived?'

'No, there were wild animals of many kinds.'

'Just animals? There weren't any people?'

'No, there were people also.' The moran made a dramatic gesture with his arms. 'But we Maasai drove them away – for we are a warrior people!'

'I see,' said the young man.

There was an embarrassing silence – no hissing this time – as everyone clocked this admission that the Maasai have pursued their own interest as strenuously as anyone else. Today, as disempowered victims of circumstance, they can do that by seeking sympathy for their plight, but in the nineteenth century, before they were stymied by British colonisation, the Maasai were the most feared military force in East Africa. The meeting's MC quickly called for another question and the rupture of consensus was smoothed over.

## Telling true-life stories

When we tell stories about real-life conflicts, then, the purposes of peace and justice, of speaking truth to power, may demand that we present both sides of the story and also that we expose any asymmetry of blame. The challenge is that the truth is complex. The novel is well suited to narrating such complexity. Not only can a novel be as long as it needs to be, but it can readily tell the story through multiple voices that cast different perspectives on the situation. The oral story, by contrast, needs to be simple and snappy enough for a live audience to follow; yet it offers peculiar strengths in the connections it forges between teller, listeners, setting, and the story's content (see pages 145–6).

## PÈRE DAVID'S DEER

In 1861 a young priest by the name of Father Armand David travelled to China as a missionary. He had a passionate interest in natural history and while he was in China he undertook a number of expeditions into remote places and discovered many creatures that at that time were unknown to Western science. The most famous of those creatures is the giant panda, but the discovery that's today most linked with Father David's name took place in the Imperial Park, not far from the city of Beijing.

He heard rumours of some kind of sacred animal that was said to live inside this imperial hunting park – and nowhere else. The park was enclosed by a high wall and Europeans were forbidden from going inside or even peeping over the wall. But Father David was determined to find out what this mystery creature might be. So one night he bribed one of the guards and climbed over the wall. By the starlight he saw among the shadowy trees a herd of strange deer of a kind quite unlike any other deer. They had broad spreading hooves, large antlers, and a long shaggy tail.

This species of deer, known in China as 'milu', had been extinct in the wild for more than three thousand years, since the time their swampy habitat was all converted into paddy fields to grow rice. Ever since then they had lived only in the Imperial Park. Father David knew that this unusual species of deer would be of great interest to scientists in Europe. So he persuaded the French Ambassador to ask the Chinese authorities for a few specimens to send to Europe. At first the authorities refused, but David kept up the pressure and in the end they relented and allowed a small number of milu to be sent to European zoos.

Slowly they began to breed. The zoos sold the excess offspring to other zoos, usually keeping just one breeding pair in each zoo. A wealthy English collector of rare animals, the Duke of Bedford, bought some of these spare offspring and assembled a herd of eighteen head on his estate at Woburn Abbey. The Chinese deer seemed to flourish in the cool, damp English climate, perhaps not so different from their original habitat.

Back in China, in 1896, disaster struck. The walls of the Imperial Park were breached by a flood. Many of the deer were drowned and the rest escaped into the surrounding countryside, there to be killed and eaten by hungry peasants. The keepers managed to round up thirty survivors and bring them back into the park. Then in 1900 the Boxer Rebellion rose against the growing European influence in China. A coalition of European powers sent an army to crush the rebellion. The Imperial Park was occupied by European soldiers, who killed the remaining milu and sold the meat. Only two individuals survived.

Meanwhile the specimens in European zoos were in trouble too. They seemed unable to thrive as isolated pairs. One by one they began to die. By 1920 they were all dead; and in that same year the last survivor in the Imperial Park died as well.

At this point the milu would have become extinct – had it not been for the Duke of Bedford, who, aware of the problems in China, had been carefully managing his herd and, despite big losses during the First World War, still had a herd of fifty head at Woburn Abbey. Carefully maintaining the size of his own herd, he began to sell surplus animals to zoos. The numbers slowly increased. In 1964 London Zoo sent four milu back to China, to Beijing Zoo. In the 1980s the species was reintroduced into the wild for the first time in three thousand years. Today there are several hundred at Woburn Abbey, breeding herds in many zoos, and a wild population of more than two thousand of these animals that are known in the West as 'Père David's deer'.[8]

I tell this story as a stark true-history account, with little imaginative adornment, delivered in a single authoritative voice and presenting a particular set of values: sympathetic to the plight of the milu and celebratory of the efforts that saved it. I quite like to tell stories from history this way, to maximise the moral impact of communicating something that actually happened and ought to be remembered (see page 119). But I'm aware this approach is rather didactic, makes big demands on the storyteller's knowledge and integrity, and excludes alternative perspectives.

## Incorporating fact in fiction

A different strategy is to compose a fictional story around a real-world situation. This widens the narrative possibilities, at the price of reducing the authority and impact of the story as 'something that really happened'. Let me present an example, which I wrote as a literary short story but have often since told from memory. Since I first read about the fate of the passenger pigeon (see pages 114–16), I have always felt deeply moved by the thought of an animal species reaching the very cusp of extinction, the point in history when the entire species has been reduced to a single individual. Some years ago I read in a newspaper that the coelacanth, a 'living fossil' crossopterygian fish closely related to the first land vertebrates – a fish that had been thought extinct since the time of the dinosaurs until it was discovered alive and well in the Indian Ocean in 1938 – was now in danger of extermination from illegal collecting. I decided to extrapolate the situation into the future to the very moment when the coelacanth's doom is sealed:

### THE LAST COELACANTH

Dr Sheperd regarded the scaly, steel-blue features of the coelacanth. Her watch would soon be over. Life-support monitors flickered on the console by the tank. The fish was doing fine, though it looked so ugly and old.

Dr Sheperd reflected that she too was getting old. Too old to be at sea in the small hours of the night.

The radio crackled into life. The sub had caught the other one, would get back to the *Kobi* in two hours' time. The crew weren't sure whether it was a male. Dr Sheperd typed on the intercom to summon Dr Hiroto. She knew that if she had been in the sub she could have confirmed the gender at once. Ten years ago she would have been in the sub.

Hiroto came in, a smile on his smooth young face. Young enough to be my son, Dr Sheperd thought. He sat at the computer and set to work – a well-trained component of Professor Tatsui's team. Once again Dr Sheperd felt a pang of guilt that she had not joined Tatsui's effort sooner. She had been so determined to try to conserve the coelacanth in the wild; every effort to keep them alive in captivity had seemed futile. By the time she had joined forces with the Japanese and helped them build an accurate simulation of the coelacanth's habitat, the trade in dead specimens had taken its toll. It was more than a year since the last one had turned up on the black market; Dr Sheperd had seen it – sickly brown in its tub of formaldehyde.

Tatsui's latest survey had been incredibly rigorous, had tagged the entire population of coelacanths. Both of them.

When the sub arrived, the fish was quickly brought up to the lab. Dr Sheperd and Dr Hiroto locked the transport tank into the aquarium prepared for it. The coelacanth was flushed into view, metallic blue and as ugly and primeval as you would expect of a creature that had been thought extinct for sixty million years.

Dr Sheperd applied her expert gaze to its anatomy.

'It's a male, Mako.'

Hiroto grinned and came to stand by her as they watched the two coelacanths squaring up to each other across the space between their tanks.

'Do you think she likes him?' said Hiroto.

'She doesn't have much choice.'

Then something started bleeping on the console by the male coelacanth's tank. A light started flashing. They hurried to check the monitors. Both pressure and temperature were shifting way off optimum. Hiroto dived to the computer. His fingers danced across the keyboard.

'I don't understand. The computer —'

'Manual override!' ordered Dr Sheperd.

Already she was twisting controls on the console. The coelacanth's vital indicators had gone erratic. Its motion in the tank was becoming unsteady.

It took two minutes to restore the conditions to optimum. By then the male coelacanth was drifting on its side and the monitors were showing flatlines. Dr Sheperd didn't stop working. She hooked up electrodes on the tank, selected the voltage, and shot a current through the water. She did this three times. The fish did not respond. Its blueness was beginning to fade.

Dr Sheperd sank on to her chair, suddenly exhausted.

Hiroto was almost in tears. 'I'm so sorry. I don't know what happen to the computer.'

He looked like a child with a broken toy. Dr Sheperd reached forward and touched his elbow. She didn't know what to say.

'I ... I could do with a coffee, Mako.'

Hiroto made a quick bow of the head and hurried out. Dr Sheperd cupped her chin in her hands and regarded the two tanks. The body of the male was now quite brown. The female came to the front of her tank and looked back at Dr Sheperd with ancient, tired eyes.[9]

This story is told essentially from a single viewpoint, Dr Sheperd's, but actually contains three different voices: those of Dr Sheperd, Dr Hiroto, and the narrator; the last of which faintly invokes at the end the perspective of the coelacanth itself. In storytelling, as in popular cinema, it's common to focus the story around one central character with whom the audience are invited to identify. This tends to simplify the ethics of the story: anyone antagonistic to the hero is likely to be tarred a baddie. The oral story, moreover, is inevitably dominated by the voice of the storyteller. One way you can widen the narrative perspective in storytelling is to open an ironic distance – by tone of voice, by 'comment', by a look in the eye – between protagonist and storyteller. Another, more theatrical, approach is to assertively voice the perspectives of different characters in the story, either by acting them or by deploying multiple storytellers to narrate different story strands.

## Pathways of consequence and change

Whether you want to tell a true-life story or a fictional tale incorporating historical fact, you have to grapple with the amorphous complexity of real life and real history. Secondary sources may usefully predigest the information for you, but you have to judge how far you can trust them.

The more knowledge you can glean about a real-life situation, the better placed you'll be to tell its story. The storymaker's task is – with respect for the truth as you understand it, with as much respect for the competing parties as they deserve – to shape a compelling storyline out of an inchoate mass of information (see pages 118–19). Think of Michelangelo sculpting the statue he's envisioned within the block of stone.

A story consists of a causally connected sequence of events. Something stories do well is to demonstrate the pathway of consequence by which one thing leads to another. I once helped at a storytelling workshop for a big conservation charity, in which each of several teams was asked to fashion a story from a set of data about a real-life conservation problem. Owing to lack of more structured guidance, the outcome in pretty much every case was neither storytelling nor a story: instead the groups presented theatre sketches in which one or other character expounded the problems and possible solutions. To present a real-life conflict as a story, you have to construct a chain of events – propelled by the needs and desires of the competing parties (or representative characters) – that reflects what's happened in the real situation. Or might happen.

For the storymaker can apply their imagination to try to imagine how the situation might change. You can, of course, imagine future scenarios in which things get worse, as I did in 'The Last Coelacanth'. This is the easier option; it requires less creative toil and lends itself to conflict-driven adventure, as in most contemporary science fiction. Prophecies of doom have an important part to play in warning us away from the paths of folly we might blunder down. But if we desire to help ameliorate conflict and suffering, we need also to imagine how things might conceivably change for the better. In the science fiction anthology *Shine*, Jetse de Vries has solicited a set of stories that try to do exactly that. Some of them put a naive faith in the capacity of technological innovation to solve the problems of our time, but de Vries acknowledges that positive change must be 'hard fought'.[10]

The more intractable the situation, the greater the imaginative challenge. Consider, for example, the Gir Forest in India, refuge of the last three hundred Asian lions, surrounded by open land, that's grazed to the bone, where a dense and impoverished human population press up against the protected area and run into conflict with the lions as the people and their livestock snatch resources from the marches of the forest.[11] Imagining positive change in such a situation of conflict involves extrapolating the consequences of present trends into the future and examining the desires of the competing parties and asking the question, 'What would have to happen – what decisions, what effort, what compromises, what restraint of desire – for change to happen in a way that would meet the most vital needs of *all* the competing parties?' In the case of the Gir

Forest, this might well require expanding the scale of consideration to include economic and demographic policymaking on a national or even international level.

It's not just about imagining an idealised end point, but also, and more importantly, about imagining the steps along the way, the process that converges towards reconciliation. At a meeting I attended in Bristol about envisioning the cities of the future, the Muslim academic and publisher Masoud Yazdani pointed out that the problem with any prescriptive vision for the future is that what may seem a utopia to one person may seem a repressive imposition to someone else with a different set of needs or desires. Agora consultant Chris Sunderland replied that what matters more than the content of any vision is the quality of relationship – including, vitally, the quality of conversation – between the partners negotiating the process of change.

Storytelling is a highly relational form of communication, involving the willing cooperation of teller and listener. So it offers, firstly, a promising way that the parties in a problematic situation can each share their own experience of the story of what has actually happened. A storyteller who has no vested interest in the situation, but is thoroughly acquainted with its complexities, might then attempt the more challenging task of constructing a story that advances the situation into the future in a positive way. If they have the necessary facilitation skills, they may involve the stakeholders in this creative process. The telling of such a transformational story face to face with people involved in the situation is a charged exercise, whose success will hinge on the teller sustaining the respect of everyone listening.[12] This is the front line where storytelling merges into conciliation work. Few modern storytellers, yet, have the expertise to do this down there in the nitty-gritty of real-world conflict.[13] But I would suggest that storymakers of all kinds can exercise their imagination, like the some of the contributors to *Shine*, to devise stories responsive to real-world environmental conflicts, yet fictionally distanced from them, with the aim not necessarily of directly transforming those conflicts but at least of seeding our imaginative culture with reconciliatory story patterns.

The use of stories to imagine possibilities for change is not a scientific process that can be expected to accurately predict the future outcome of present action. It's an intuitive exercise of the imagination. It engages with the visceral needs and desires that drive people's actions. Our imaginative culture is saturated with the story pattern in which the hero must win his deepest desire by defeating, often violently, an antagonist whose face is set implacably against him. The scenario is win or lose – and if you lose you may die. It's the same old dualist – or duellist – game as natural selection or market competition. But the game need not be a zero-sum game; there may be win–win possibilities if we have the imagination to envisage them. That's why we need stories, lots of them, speaking to all manner of problematic situations, in which interests on all sides, including those of nature, are respected; in which conflict is transformed through parties mutually accepting the compromise of self-interest, of consumption, of gain, of procreation, of tradition, even of freedom; in which, against the logic of biology, fascism, capitalism, and so much of history, the degree of compromise is greater for the stronger than the weaker.

------

[1] Matthew 7:12.

[2] Goodchild, *Capitalism and Religion*, p. 212.

[3] Edward O. Wilson, interviewed in Attenborough, *State of the Planet*.

[4] Lewis, *An Experiment in Criticism*, p. 140.

[5] Retelling by Anthony Nanson (1998) of a story heard from Richard Walker, and subsequently Simon Airey and Amy Douglas, but originally devised (as 'The Two Warriors') by Dan Keding, based on a saying of his grandmother's.

[6] Simon Airey, personal communication, 2002.

[7] Cohn-Sherbok and El-Alami, *The Palestine–Israeli Conflict*.

[8] Anthony Nanson, 2002. Principal sources: James et al., *The Red Book*; Silverberg, *The Dodo, the Auk and the Oryx*.

[9] Reprinted from Nanson, *Exotic Excursions*.

[10] De Vries, *Shine*, p. 9.

[11] Quammen, *Monster of God*.

[12] I'm indebted to Alida Gersie for pointing this out.

[13] Again I'm indebted to Gersie for this observation.

# How Can Storytelling Re-enchant the Natural World in an Electronic Age?

As human populations expand, colonise territory, and exploit resources, so the populations of other species tend to diminish, some to extinction, and living habitats are transformed into deserts of concrete, tarmac, monoculture, and bare earth. In England, where the industrial revolution began, this process continues despite a vigorous conservation movement; for example, the intensification of agriculture over the past thirty years has dramatically reduced the populations of many bird species.[1] Some will ask whether such things matter. Are not human interests more important than non-human ones? Does not economics trump ecology? Is not the conservation of wild creatures and landscapes merely a preference of leisured classes conditioned by nineteenth-century romanticism? It's not my aim here to counter these arguments. I shall assume that the vital priority of conserving 'nature' can be persuasively argued on multiple bases: that human existence depends on a complex interconnected ecosystem; that nature nourishes our psychic well-being; that it's intrinsically beautiful and interesting; that non-human entities have their own right to exist; that nature is a divine creation; that long-held assumptions that its bounty is inexhaustible are invalidated by today's global ecological crisis.

In *Storytelling and Ecology* I surveyed the gamut of ways that live storytelling can interface with ecological concerns. Here I shall address the particular question of how storytelling can help to foster love for nature; for surely people need to care about the well-being of nature before they will be willing to pay the price of protecting it. Taking inspiration from traditional cultures' 'enchantment' of nature, I shall consider – in terms of empathy, connection, significance, and sacredness – how storytelling may help to 're-enchant' people's perception of wild creatures and places. Finally, I shall subject the above premise to a realist scepticism that, paradoxically, invites a metaphysical response in which the mythic imagination has a vital role.

## Alienation

The critiques of environmentalism I listed above imply an opposition between mutually exclusive alternatives: civilisation or nature; human or non-human. The Greek island of Zakynthos has seen head-on conflict between conservationists keen to protect the nesting sites of the endangered loggerhead turtle and local people angered by restrictions of their freedom to develop tourism facilities on their land.[2] In England, nature conservation areas, where development is curtailed, are segregated from land zoned for human residence or food production where wildlife tends to be eliminated. To experience much nature other than the opportunist species able to survive in urban areas, city dwellers must travel to protected or remote areas where biodiverse nature is allowed to flourish. Children, unable to simply run into the fields to play, watch TV instead.

The way forward lies in reconciling this opposition between nature and culture, in our thinking, in our hearts, in the way we inhabit the land. The mythic idyll of 'Arcadia' is an idealised vision of people and nature flourishing together in the same landscape. Whether or not such an ecotopia ever existed, it's a far cry from the combative attitude to nature which Dimitrios Theodossopoulos observes in Zakynthiot countryfolk struggling against weeds, pests, and climate to eke a living from their land.[3] Some attribute this antagonistic relationship to Christianity's historical assertion of human dominion over nature.[4] David Abram traces Western culture's alienation from the earth to the Greek invention of an alphabet that divorced thought from sensual reality.[5] Others look back to the rise of organised agriculture which consigned to a 'golden age' memory the ancestral hunter-gatherer's wild freedom as one 'link in the long chain of creation'.[6]

Do we find, then, an Edenic ecotopia among hunter-gatherer societies? Colin Turnbull observed in the Mbuti people of the Congo a profound love for the Ituri Forest they inhabit, and indeed worship, yet also observed them heartlessly mocking animals they'd speared.[7] The myth of the noble savage, though sometimes truer than sceptics credit, has never been true to a perfect degree. The Eskimo hunting life entails much hardship and fear, Barry Lopez observes:

They are afraid because they accept fully what is violent and tragic in nature. It is a fear tied to their knowledge that sudden, cataclysmic events are as much a part of life, of really living, as are the moments when one pauses to look at something beautiful.[8]

The power over nature that science and technology have given modern civilisation poses a grave threat to the ecosystem but also offers us the possibility, if we choose it, of working towards new kinds of participation in nature's complexity, which might both promote nature's flourishing *and* enhance the joy of human existence. To do that requires an alliance, instead of the traditional antagonism, between scientific understanding and forms of sensibility – romantic, deep ecology, creation spirituality, Pagan – that extend the scope of respect for the 'other' to encompass the non-human.

## Enchantment

Traditional societies perceive the landscape as permeated and animated by a coextensive mythscape of stories, songs, spirits, and other aspects of what I shall call 'enchantment'. Of the Gloucestershire valley in which he grew up in the 1920s, Laurie Lee writes,

> There were ghosts in the stones, in the trees, and the walls, and each field and hill had several. The elder people knew about these things and would refer to them in personal terms, and there were certain landmarks about the valley – tree-clumps, corners in woods – that bore separate, antique, half-muttered names that were certainly older than Christian.[9]

This enchantment of nature grants an awareness that one's livelihood depends on nature's fertility; knowledge how to sustainably extract its resources; fear of its power to inflict harm; remembrance of where ancestors have done deeds and been laid to rest; a moral code mapped upon places and creatures; and communion with the divine.

Such perceptions have been dismissed as superstitions from which people may be liberated by Christian – later, materialist – 'truth'. 'The spirits *in* natural objects, which formerly had protected nature from man, evaporated,' says Lynn White. 'Man's effective monopoly on spirit in this world was confirmed, and the old inhibitions to the exploitation of nature crumbled.'[10] The tide of modernisation has swept away nature's enchantment at the same time as it has swept away much of nature.

In describing nature as 'enchanted' I have in mind Tolkien's use of the word 'enchantment' to denote a storymaker's 'subcreation' of a 'secondary world' that imaginatively reflects truths about the 'primary world' we inhabit (see page 15).[11] The mythscape is not susceptible to scientific observation. It exists in the imagination; whatever 'truth' it mediates is not the same as verifiable, scientific 'truth'. Yet, if such enchantment has mediated respect for nature in traditional societies, might some 're-enchantment' of nature help to instigate more respect of that kind today? Not to reconstruct the mindset of past societies. Not to abandon scientific understanding that has liberated people from unnecessary fears and harmful ignorance. Not to cleave to non-rational belief systems held to be incontrovertible truth. I mean a re-enchantment of nature in that faculty we acknowledge to be our imagination – the storyteller's, the listener's, the collective imagination of the people who share the stories and the land – but which nevertheless shapes who we are and what we value (see page 81).

In examining how storytelling can help to re-enchant nature, I shall address both the *content* of the stories we choose to tell and the *process* of storytelling as an activity. Lest this sound like a masterclass in brainwashing techniques, let me acknowledge that, yes, the promotion of respect for nature is in part a political mission and, yes, one could try to use storytelling in a cynically manipulative way; but it's also a mission of relationship, and means should be in harmony with ends: if we aim to foster more respectful relationships with something other – non-human nature – then our storytelling must be respectful of the other – the listener – as an autonomous being, whose imagination will respond in ways we can't expect to control. If storytelling takes place outdoors, in nature, we must respect too the autonomous power of nature to contribute to the experience in unpredictable ways.

## Empathy

### THE GOLDEN TOAD

In 1963 a herpetologist – an expert on reptiles and amphibians – by the name of Jay Savage heard reports of a some kind of brightly orange-coloured toad, unknown to science, that lived high in the cloud forest near Monteverde in Costa Rica. There were stories about this toad. It was said to be very hard to find because it was so shy, but that if you did see one you would be astounded by its beauty, you would experience fear, and you would find happiness. There was a story about a man who did find one of these toads, and caught it, but then he let it go because he didn't recognise happiness when he had it. And about another man who also caught one of the toads and who, again, let it go, because he found happiness too painful to bear.

In April 1965 Jay Savage travelled to Costa Rica and climbed up high into the cloud forest. At that altitude the clouds formed low among the trees – that's why it's called the 'cloud forest' – and so the forest was filled with mist, and everything was moist, and there were many pools of water. There he found the toads, hundreds of them, gathering around the pools to breed. The females were a dull mottled colour, but the males were a brilliant golden orange. Amidst the lush green vegetation they looked like jewels.

Jay studied these animals, described them, and named them for science: *Bufo periglenes* – the 'golden toad'. He observed that the males greatly outnumbered the females. So the males would fight each other and even jump on mating pairs to try to get a go at fertilising the female's eggs. Sometimes there'd be so many males they would form a so-called 'toad ball': a writhing mass of males all trying to get at the single female in the centre. The tadpoles took four or five weeks to metamorphose into adults. Throughout that time they depended on the pools neither drying out nor flooding over. For the rest of the year the toads completely disappeared till the next breeding season. They're believed to have secreted themselves in damp places underground.

The golden toad inhabited an area of just ten square kilometres of the cloud forest, where many other amazing creatures lived as well. So in 1972 the Monteverde Cloud Forest Reserve was declared, to protect thirty square kilometres of pristine cloud forest, including the entire range of the golden toad.

Moving on to April 1987 … when another herpetologist, Martha Crump, visited the cloud forest to study the golden toad. She found the forest oddly dry for that time of year. There was an exaggerated El Niño event that year: unusually intense heating of the Pacific Ocean had driven a mass of hot air over Costa Rica, which meant that clouds could form only at a great height above the treetops and not down among the trees as they normally would. There were few pools on the forest floor, and those few were shrivelled in size. But there were plenty of golden toads. On one day Martha counted fifteen hundred of them crowded in the shrunken pools. In one pool no bigger than a kitchen sink there were 133, most of them males besieging a handful of females.

Five days later, the pools began to dry out. Martha watched the jelly masses of eggs desiccate and turn mouldy. In May the toads made a second attempt to breed. The same thing happened: the pools dried out and the eggs were wasted. Out of more than forty thousand eggs, Martha saw only twenty-nine tadpoles that lasted longer than a week.

The following year, in April 1988, she returned to the cloud forest. The forest was again very dry. This time it seemed sterile too. There was no sign of any golden toads. And it wasn't just the golden toads that had disappeared after the extreme El Niño of the year before. Of fifty species of frogs and toads that lived in the Monteverde Cloud Forest Reserve, thirty species had disappeared; but whereas the other ones had more extensive ranges and could be found elsewhere, outside the reserve, the golden toad lived nowhere else. Not only had the frogs and toads failed to breed, but something had happened to the adults too. It's thought that because there were so few moist places left underground where they could live they'd had to crowd closely together and that this facilitated the transmission of a fungal disease.

Martha searched and searched, for day after day. She was about to give up when on 21 May she spotted a single male golden toad sitting by a pool, waiting for a mate. At another spot the same day, someone else spotted another nine toads: seven males and two females.

The next year, April 1989 Martha Crump returned yet again to the cloud forest. Things were much the same. Again she failed to see any golden toads, until 15 May, when she spotted a solitary male sitting not three metres from the very spot where she'd seen one the year before. She was almost certain it was the same one, still waiting for a mate.

No other golden toads were seen that year. The following year, there were none at all. Over the next few years the scientists searched and searched and searched. Jay Savage, who'd discovered the species back in the sixties, came to help in the search. At last, in 2004, the golden toad was formally declared extinct. The zoologist Tim Flannery claims it to be the first documented species extinction caused by modern climate change.

The golden toad was known to Western science for just twenty-five years, from its discovery in 1964 to its last sighting in 1989. I wonder whether Jay Savage thought about those stories he'd been told: about the man who found a golden toad, and let it go because he didn't recognise happiness when he had it – and about the other man, who also caught a golden toad, and let it go because he found happiness too painful to bear.[12]

A typical property of a good story is that it elicits empathy for the characters, especially the main protagonist, so that we care what happens to them. In my telling of 'The Golden Toad', the protagonist may appear initially to be Jay Savage and later Martha Crump, but the real protagonist of the story is the golden toad as a species. The 'desire' of that species-protagonist is to survive, in which purpose it conclusively fails. Near the end of the story the empathy we feel for the plight of these animals becomes focused in the single individual who now embodies the entire species: this is the story's emotional centre of gravity, exactly as in the story of the passenger pigeon, which too was reduced to one known individual before it became extinct (see pages 114–16). We empathise with this individual as we might with a human being in some tragic situation. Indeed the story of the genocide inflicted by British colonists on the Tasmanian Aborigines, which I also tell, has the same structure: the Tasmanian race, so it was believed, was reduced to a single individual, a woman called Trugernanner, who'd made a heroic but ultimately doomed attempt to save her people.[13]

Other true-life stories, that focus entirely upon an individual animal, may extend our compassion towards its species by evoking empathy for that individual. A moving example is the story of the Currumpaw Wolf of New Mexico, who cleverly evaded many traps set for him, until his mate Bianca was caught and killed, whereupon he allowed himself to be caught and chained, and then died during the night without sustaining any wound.[14]

Many traditional stories too – the fables and some wonder tales in Europe, and much of the mythology of Africa, the Americas, and Australasia – make an animal the protagonist and thereby elicit empathy for that animal, though the fact these stories tend to overtly anthropomorphise the animals does colour the quality of empathy we're prompted to feel for the species in question. The same is true of the 'just so' stories written by Rudyard Kipling and Ted Hughes.

In these different ways, then, both true-life and imaginative stories can begin to 're-enchant' nature by eliciting empathy for that which is 'other': not just the human other – of different gender, ethnicity, class – but the non-human. In Greek stories since antiquity the trope of metamorphosis has suggested a fundamental reciprocity between human and non-human;[15] it's sometimes coupled with the hero doing a kindness to animals, as in 'The Mother of the Sea' – in which the fisherman Yiankos gains the power to change form into eagle, lion, and ant through having aided representatives of each of these species.[16]

To feel empathy for animals takes not so vast a stretch of the imagination. To feel it for plants requires rather more. To experience empathy for the non-living elements of nature – mountains, rocks, caves, lakes, streams, seas, even the planet as a whole – may require one to attribute to even these things some notion of spirit or consciousness. Important about the *process* of storytelling is that it engages the audience's imagination in an active way. The listener, like the reader, actively perceives experiences from the point of view of people, or beings, other than themself (see page 127). This active imagining creates in the mind an experience akin to a memory; and this experience, including our empathy with the story's protagonists, becomes part of who we are.

Audiovisual media such as film do not engage the creative imagination in so active a way. The imaginative work is done for us and presented to us as a spectacle. From a remote citadel the film-maker manipulates us to empathise with the hero, to feel strong emotions; but when the film is over we leave the screen behind and walk away (see pages 80–1). Al Gore's documentary about global warming, *An Inconvenient Truth*, dissonantly subverts our normal experience of cinema. We watch the spectacle of Gore addressing, like a storyteller, a live audience. We're stirred by a momentous story that bears the gravity of something that's actually happened and is still happening; a story whose ending, for good or ill, depends on what collectively we will do. But then we walk away. In my case, alone. I left the cinema in tears, needy to share in company the challenge of receiving that story. My feeling of isolation in that moment points towards the second way storytelling can re-enchant nature: by making a connection.

## Connection

The beauty and educational value of nature documentaries are undeniable; yet the uplifting sense of wonder to be had from watching, say, the BBC's *Planet Earth* can become an end in itself, not so different an experience from watching fantasy-scapes created entirely from computer graphics. Many people's knowledge of nature derives more from TV than the real thing; watching such programmes in the comfort of your own home can be a substitute for going outdoors to experience nature directly. Moreover, the selection of uplifting footage – typically from unspoilt places like nature reserves – conveys a false impression of nature's well-being. Once sufficient footage of creatures and habitats is archived to provide samples for computer animation, the audience's desire for images of nature might in theory be satisfied without the real thing needing to exist – as already demonstrated by TV series like *Extinct* and *Monsters We Met*, which reconstruct species of animals that humans have exterminated.

Audiovisual media, and other communication technologies like the internet and mobile phones, tend to distance people from what is physically around them. Abram argues that writing too is guilty of this effect.[17] Where storytelling scores over all these media is in the way that, at the same time as it engages the listener's imagination, it also confronts them with the physical presence of the storyteller and also the other members of the audience and the environment in which the storytelling is taking place. It makes a connection between the actual and the imagined, between the primary world we inhabit and the secondary world of the story (see pages 81–3).

In England, at least – where the combination of omnipresent communication technologies and entrenched neoliberal political economy has exacerbated people's alienation not only from nature but from society too – the confrontation with a live storyteller can pose a radical challenge. Some listeners new to storytelling don't at first realise that storytelling is a relationship, that the storyteller, not being a TV screen, cannot tell the story well unless the audience actively listens; you have to work to win their attention, to the story, to the whole situation of you telling the story to them in this place. This eliciting of responsiveness to a stranger – the storyteller – is one tiny step, against the grain of late modern society, towards a more general sense of responsibility to the reality around us: other people, other species, the physical environment. The story is experienced collectively. In situations that permit it, the telling of one story may trigger discussion or the telling of other stories by other speakers. In Africa, Cynthia Ward explains, 'the value of the oral tale to the oral culture lies not entirely in the tale itself, but, perhaps more significantly, in the discussion it generates after it is told'.[18]

In the storytelling moment a web of connections is woven between the storyteller and the audience, and among the audience, and between them and the place where they are. If this place is outdoors, then a connection is made with whatever aspects of nature are manifest there. The connection is deepened if the storyteller incorporates qualities of that place into the storytelling, or chooses stories that pertain to the local ecology – or, as Hugh Lupton describes, are set in that very place:

> This knowledge of the place informs the telling, so that when a story is told 'in situ' what the mind's eye is seeing (the invisible world) locks in with and corresponds to what is actually there. The teller becomes a medium through which the landscape can speak.[19]

This kind of connection can readily be sought with landscapes, habitats, plants. It's trickier to persuade a wild animal to stand still while you tell a story in its presence. But telling stories about places and creatures, whether in situ or not, leads us to the third way storytelling can reenchant nature: by according places and creatures a unique significance.

## Significance

Trees are a good example. They're a key element of many habitats and – in attaining ages that plumb beyond the human lifespan into the past, and in their branching form – they are rather like stories in themselves, as Tolkien implies in his allegory 'Leaf by Niggle'. Once people have learnt to distinguish different kinds of trees, imaginative significance can be imparted to particular species by the telling of stories in which those species feature, most potently when this is done in the presence of living specimens.[20] The trick is to find not stories that mention trees as scenery, but ones in which the tree is a major character, such as 'The Girl in the Bay-Tree',[21] from Greece, or 'The Green Ladies of One Tree Hill'[22] (about beeches), from the British Isles.

In both those tales the tree's spirit manifests as a dryad-like female being. In the Welsh tale 'The Woman of Llyn-y-Fan'[23] the spirit of a *lake* similarly takes womanly form. Such anthropomorphism is not essential. The protagonist of the Estonian tale 'The Lake that Flew Away'[24] is a lake, Lake Eim, which retains the form of a lake throughout.[25]

From a modern materialist perspective, such stories are of course make-believe. How are we to understand the significance they bestow on non-human entities? The tree spirits are a metaphor, the materialist will say. A metaphor of what? Of some archetype in the human psyche? No doubt. But must we be so anthropocentric? What does the metaphor signify about the trees themselves. In Tolkien's theory of 'mythopoeia' the metaphors of fantasy reveal 'the "living light" within each thing. He claimed that it was through fairy tales that he first understood the real wonder of basic things: of stones and iron and trees and fire and wine and bread.'[26] Through our imagination and the power of words, Tolkien believed, we see inklings of a greater reality – something like Plato's world of 'forms' – in which the true being of all of nature resides.[27]

This heightened vision of the significance of creatures, things, and places chimes with the Australian Aboriginal concept of the Dreaming: a vision of mythical beings, some pictured as archetypes of wildlife, creating the topography along 'songlines' that criss-cross the land. It's a vision that transcends time: not merely a memory of a golden age, but an eternal coming into being which continues to take place so long as the landscape remains intact and people keep singing the songs that narrate this creative process. It bestows immense significance on the landscape and thereby resists, to the extent the colonised Aborigines are actually able to resist, the damaging of land and ecology by modern development.[28]

Every country has its own mythscape of stories: ranging from personal anecdote, through history, legend, folktale, to the myths of the land's creation. For the storyteller, there's a tension between well-structured, well-travelled *folktales* (to be precise, 'märchen'), which often have lost any specific mooring in the landscape – but are very entertaining – and *local legends* that are more anecdotal, less satisfying purely as stories, but gain meaning from their location in the landscape. The Aboriginal songs of the Dreaming are an extreme case of the latter. But there's plenty of middle ground. Many episodes in the story of King Arthur map on to the British landscape. Localities in Scotland, Wales, England, and Brittany make competing claims for some of the same events; something that need not vex us unless we be determined that the stories represent historically true events (see pages 31–8).

Uther Pendragon, the High King of Britain, conceived an insatiable desire for the most beautiful woman in all Britain. Her name was Ygerne. But Ygerne was married, to Gorlois, the Lord of Cornwall. Uther Pendragon, he had to have her! He led his armies sweeping into Cornwall and besieged Gorlois in the castle of Dimilioc. Meanwhile Ygerne took refuge in the castle of Tintagel. Perhaps you've been there – and seen how it's defended on all sides by cliffs that fall sheer into the waves and is joined to the mainland by an isthmus so narrow that a single warrior could hold off an army.[29]

As I tell this I picture my own memory of Tintagel and seek complicity with those in the audience who've been there too. The castle is long ruined and, thanks to its fame as the place of Arthur's conception and birth, the peninsula it defended is today managed by English Heritage to conserve both its archaeology and its ecology. In this kind of way many archaeological sites, their rubble of stones made significant by stories, are protected as de facto nature reserves. In Greece, think of the anemones and pines of Olympia, or the soundscape of crickets, frogs, and rushing wind in the trees at Epidaurus. Pedro Olalla's *Mythological Atlas of Greece* enables one to track the stories of the ancient gods and heroes across the landscape.[30] With stout boots, plenty of water, and a stick to fend off psychotic sheepdogs, you can try to follow Greek 'songlines'.

But small nature reserves are vulnerable to climatic change. Sustainable populations of larger animals need freedom to roam. If people are to be reconciled with nature they need to be able to coexist with wildlife in the same territory. This suggests a need to enchant with significance not just points in the landscape but geographical space on a larger scale. Olalla's atlas labels whole rivers and mountains implicated in mythic events: the story of Atalanta's youth ranges across the whole of Mount Parthenio; who knows at what spot on the Eurotas river Zeus impregnated Leda with Helen and Polydeuces? (See page 7.)

E. W. Soja's notion of 'thirdspace' is an attempt to break down the binary opposition between objective and imagined perceptions of geographical space.[31] Catherine Parker has applied this concept to examine holistically the human inhabitation of the Mantinean Plain, in Arcadia, during antiquity and found that it was affected by a combination of economic, social ... and also sacred factors.[32] Let us consider now the fourth and most radical way in which storytelling can re-enchant nature: by evoking a sense of the sacred.

## Sacredness

### ERYSICHTHON

Long ago, when gods still walked the earth, the land of Dotium was greatly blessed by corn-haired Demeter, the goddess of all growing things. Its forests teemed with game. Its orchards hung heavy with fruit. Its deep, dark soil gave rich harvests of grain.

But Erysichthon, the King of Dotium, had no fear of Demeter or any other of the gods and often spoke of them with scorn.

'Is not the land mine, to do with as I choose?'

So he killed the game and cut down the trees howsoever he pleased. He even began to cut down the sacred grove of Demeter. But when he commanded his men to cut down the huge, ancient oak that stood in the very centre of the grove, they all cowered back in fear. This tree was so sacred, so precious to Demeter; its branches were festooned with ribbons and garlands and on warm spring nights the dryads, lithe and lovely, would dance around it.

But King Erysichthon had no fear of the goddess. He raised his axe, took aim – and as the blade bit into the bark, sap red like blood spurted from the wound, and a voice from inside the tree cried out in pain, the voice of the dryad who dwelt in that tree.

King Erysichthon did not hear – or if he heard he did not care – and he raised his axe to strike again. Then one of his men ran forward to protest against this attack on the sacred tree. The King whirled around – and with one blow of his axe he sliced off the man's head. Now the rest of his men were more afraid of the King than of anything else and they came forward with their axes and together they hacked and they hacked – and with every blow the dryad in the tree screamed in pain. They hacked and they hacked and they hacked, all day long they worked, till the tree began to teeter and to totter and with a creaking and a groaning and a crunching and a cracking the huge, ancient oak crashed to the earth.

With her dying breath the dryad cried out from the tree, 'May the curse of my Lady Demeter fall as heavy on you, King Erysichthon, as this my tree falls upon the earth!'

Corn-haired Demeter, the goddess of all growing things, heard the dryad's dying words. And all the kindness and warmth and generosity in her heart was transmuted into anger.

She summoned one of her oreads, the mountain nymphs, and commanded her, 'Go to the land of Hunger and tell my sister, Hunger, to punish King Erysichthon for what he has done, to put in his belly a hunger that shall never be satisfied!'

The oread did as her mistress commanded and flew away to the east, across the sea, across the mountains, into the night, to the cold, barren desert where Hunger dwells. There she was: Hunger! Like a living skeleton she seemed, with her leathery skin sucked tight against her bones, with her long, clawed fingers and hollowed eyes, as she stooped down to gnaw the dry lichen from the rocks with her bleeding teeth.

From a safe distance high in the sky the messenger called down, 'Your sister the Lady Demeter asks you to punish Erysichthon the King of Dotium because he felled the sacred oak; to put in his belly a hunger that shall never be satisfied.'

Hunger reared up and looked down with her hollowed, far-seeing eyes, down across the mountains, across the starlit sea, to the fertile land of Dotium, to the flickering candlelight of the royal palace, to the open window of the chamber where King Erysichthon slept.

Down she flew, swifter than wind, across the mountains, across the sea, and in through that palace window. For a few moments she hovered above the King's sleeping body. Then she stretched out a clawed hand and peeled back the coverlet, and clamped her bony arms around him, and pressed her bleeding teeth against his lips, and breathed into him, deeply.

Then she left him.

And in his dreams King Erysichthon beheld a vast banquet of all manner of luxurious foods. Yet in his dream, however much of this food he ate, it did not satisfy him; he still felt hungry.

In the morning he awoke and he was hungry, so he called for breakfast. The servants brought his breakfast and he ate it. But when he'd finished he was still hungry. So they brought him more food, they brought him all the food in the palace, and he ate it all.

But he was still hungry. So they brought him food from throughout the kingdom, they gathered all the fruit and grain and slaughtered all the livestock and game, and he ate all this food.

But he was still hungry. So they emptied the treasury, they stripped the palace of its fine furnishings, to buy food from abroad. They felled all the trees to sell the timber, they sold everything of value in the kingdom, to buy yet more food. And the King ate all this food.

But he was still hungry. So he commanded that the common people be sold into slavery abroad to get more money to buy yet more food. Then the rest of the people fled in fear that they too might be sold into slavery. Even his own servants abandoned him ... till there was no one left but his own daughter, who loved him.

But he was still hungry. So in the night he entered the room where his daughter slept and he killed his own daughter and he ate her. The next morning he sat alone in the ruins of what had once been his fine palace, surrounded by what had once been his lovely, fertile land and was now a barren desert with nothing but dust and stones and piles of his own turds.

And he was still hungry. He tried to eat his own turds, but that was no good. So he bent down and lifted his foot up to his mouth, and began to chew, and he ate himself.[33]

To tell this story in the presence of an oak or near Mount Ossa, where ancient Dotium is believed to have been,[34] might evoke feelings of empathy, connection, and significance towards oak trees or that locality. But it's also a potent ecological parable for today's world. Its motif of 'the fairy's revenge' is widespread in folklore, including in the modern Kosian tale 'Myrmidonia and Pharaonia'[35] which appears to derive from the Erysichthon myth. To amplify the ecological resonance I've added some description of the land before and after Erysichthon lays it waste. I've also replaced his selling his daughter into slavery with his eating her[36] – to intensify the story's impact and as a metaphor of the way that overconsumption of resources today is destroying the livelihood of our descendants.

The story bespeaks the awesome power that nature can unleash. In the aftermath of the Indian Ocean tsunami and the flooding of New Orleans, Richard Mabey commented, 'From the planet's point of view, humans are a pest species – and it's trying to cull us.'[37] These forces greater than ourselves can be understood in scientific terms. We may also contemplate nature's scale and complexity with a romantic sense of the sublime. But venerable stories that depict nature as inspirited by gods present us with a quality that demands we treat nature as respectfully as we ought to treat our fellow humans; that curtails the exploitation of re-

sources; that invites our worship. This quality, anathema to the materialist zeitgeist, is the sacred.

Among the gods and exotika (see pages 16–17), it's quintessentially
the nymphs – elemental beings in womanly form – who inspirit the
Greek landscape, as the Orphic hymn 'To the Nymphs' sings:

cave loving, who delight in caves, air haunting,
you of the springs, quick running, dew clad, light stepping,
visible, invisible, you of the ravines, many-flowered,
who dance together with Pan in the mountains, shouting out.[38]

The strong association of nymphs – in modern Greek folklore called 'ne-
reids' – with water sources, and the perception of such places as sacred,[39]
seems pertinent to the environmental peril that unrestrained use of water for irrigation poses in some areas of Greece today, including the area
where Erysichthon lived.[40] Rather similar are the 'well maidens' in the
Arthurian romance 'The Elucidation' – whose rape causes the wells to
dry up and the land to be laid waste.[41]

In Britain it's typically the fairies, the old gods, and the saints that
have sanctified hills, springs, trees, and caves. The sacredness of Glastonbury's landscape is even today upheld by tales of St Collen, who dwelt on
the Tor; Gwyn ap Nudd, lord of the underworld, who dwelt within it;
King Arthur, who either was buried under Glastonbury Abbey or still
sleeps within the Tor; and Joseph of Arimathea, who brought Christ's
chalice, now deposited in the Chalice Well, and planted a thorn tree
from the Holy Land on Wearyall Hill.

Of course, we no longer perceive the spirits of nature as real ... do
we? As we discuss these things, here at the foot of Mount Olympus, we
don't think the gods are actually up there listening ... do we? Yet how
can we be sure they're not? There are people in Britain – Druids and
other Pagans – who do honour the spirits of nature, the ancestors, the
gods, as if they're real. Their sharing of native myths and wonder tales
nourishes their sense of nature as sacred. A comparable movement is
underway in Greece.[42] For those who believe in the one God, meanwhile, the re-enchantment of nature as sacred can diversify the ways one
sees divine creativity revealed. Whatever exactly the 'sacred' may mean
to us, surely Lupton is right when he declares,

The land we inhabit is wounded, it has been desecrated as never
before ... and it will not recover until it has become, in some way,
sacred again. Part of the process of re-sacrilisation must involve
telling the myths of landscape, re-storying and re-dreaming the
land, using word and song to make numinous once again the mys-

terious ground that is the grandfather of all grandfathers, the grandmother of all grandmothers.[43]

## Repertoire

When stories become elevated in status, people can get anxious that the purity of tradition be preserved. They might object to my amending the story of Erysichthon. I would reply that stories do change, and need to. Ovid's account of Erysichthon differs from that of Callimachus.[44] The world keeps changing. Some values promoted in traditional stories need today to be critiqued – the celebration of hunting, for example (see page 123), as well as war. From a modern perspective the labours of Heracles might be judged a rampage of ecocidal destruction. Many European folktales deploy animals in a symbolic way that disrespects their real nature. Wolves, for example, have been stigmatised as a symbol of evil in a way that has catalysed their persecution out of all proportion to the threat they pose and without regard for the ecological services they provide.[45]

So, besides sourcing pertinent stories from tradition, there is work to do to develop new repertoire that responds to present circumstances in ways that will re-enchant nature. Such 'ecobardic' repertoire may draw upon history and science, experience and invention, and may need to blend elements from different traditions, including indigenous traditions that contain more authentic and respectful knowledge of nature than has survived in European folklore (see page 78).

In their storytelling epic *I Become Part of It*, the Company of Storytellers devised a conjectural mythology for Mesolithic England using insights from archaeology and anthropology and motifs 'translocated' from the mythologies of hunter-gatherer peoples – in North America and Siberia – who've faced similar environmental conditions.[46] Eric Maddern's one-man show *What the Bees Know* brings together traditional wisdom stories (including 'Erysichthon'), original songs, and stand-up-comedy-style commentary to communicate the environmental crisis and the kinds of qualities we need to cultivate in order to live sustainably on the earth. Hugh Lupton and Chris Wood's *On Common Ground* links the treatment of the English landscape, in consequence of the enclosure of the commons, to questions of social justice and people's access to the land (see pages 59–60).

In *Robin of the Wildwood*, Fire Springs reinvent the legendary forest outlaw Robin Hood as a mythic guardian of the woods. We augment the medieval ballad material with ecology's account of the evolution of the British wildwood, the English folktale of 'Herne the Hunter', the real-life sabotage of road-building by ecopagan protestors in the 1990s, and motifs from Celtic, Germanic, and Greek myth. Erysichthon's felling of Demeter's oak is translocated as Guy of Gisborne's felling of Sherwood Forest's great oak, sacred to Urswick, Lady of the Wild Things.[47]

## Mythopoeia

By re-enchanting nature, storytelling may aspire – alongside diverse other efforts – to help foster a collective sensibility that constrains the exploitation of the earth's resources and seeks the mutual flourishing of humankind and nature. However, this lofty ambition flies against the biological instinct of human nature to pursue short-term self-interest above all else (see page 125). Christ's teaching of agape (selfless love) radically challenged that impulse, yet history offers sparse evidence that voluntary suppression of self-interest has ever characterised whole societies. This is why I feel a degree of scepticism about the premise on which this lecture is based: that if people's hearts can be transformed then the ecological crisis can be solved. Eloquent warnings about the impact of industrial development have been voiced by sensitive souls, such as William Blake, since the industrial revolution began. They are louder now than ever, yet the rates of economic development, human population growth, and ecological destruction are greater than ever. A gap yawns between talk and action. Regulations are imposed, nature reserves are set up, but such Noah's-ark exercises in damage limitation seem overwhelmed by the deluge of frantic exploitation pushing the other way.

In studying the global ecological crisis, I've experienced, like others,[48] an existential crisis of hope. I desire a hopeful vision of the future – for present and future generations, for the earth's biodiversity – yet I find it hard to evade the conclusion that, whatever I and like-minded people might do, the crisis is likely to worsen, with dire consequences for much of nature and humankind. How is one to cope with this knowledge and live one's life with joy? Even if we do eventually find a way to reconcile our biological instincts with the well-being of the ecosystem, it seems unlikely that the state of the global ecosystem will cease to deteriorate within the lifetime of anyone around today. If that's so, the secular vision of ecotopia may be seen as a myth of a golden age located, not in the past, but in a future beyond our own death – much like the Christian hope of 'a new heaven and a new earth'[49] (see page 18).

By challenging my own premise, have I undermined everything else I've said? Not necessarily. Hope should not surrender to 'Götterdämmerung', as novelist Kim Stanley Robinson calls the hard right-wing stance of defiantly behaving in selfish destructive ways in expectation that eco-catastrophe cannot be averted.[50] Pessimism must not yield to despair,

Tolkien believed, because we cannot know for sure what the future will hold (see page 166).

Here I shall breach the bounds of rationalist materialism. To take seriously the work of storytellers, must we not take seriously the realm of the imagination, where that which is possible is not limited by that which is observable in the material world? Margaret Alexiou points out that the prefix 'para-' in many Greek folk genres – 'paradosi' (tradition), 'paramythi' (wonder tale), 'paralogi' (ballad) – 'signifies going outside the normal frontiers'; in these genres, 'meaning lies precisely in the gap between "true" and "not-true" – that is, between past experience and potential future'.[51] If we indulge this freedom, if we refrain from reducing the imagination to neuropsychology, then stories' enchantment of nature in our imagination may perhaps be more than a tool to foster ecological compassion; it may, let us imagine, contribute to something that extends beyond our mortal existence, beyond distinction between past and future. Tolkien suggests that the subcreative art of enchantment – like the Aborigines' singing the land into eternal becoming – 'may actually assist in the effoliation and multiple enrichment of creation':[52]

Blessed are the legend-makers with their rhyme
of things not found within recorded time.
It is not they that have forgot the Night,
or bid us flee to organised delight,
in lotus-isles of economic bliss ...

They have seen Death and ultimate defeat,
and yet they would not in despair retreat,
but oft to victory have turned the lyre
and kindled hearts with legendary fire,
illuminating Now and Hath-been
with light of suns as yet by no man seen.[53]

In this vision the meaning of myth is not merely as metaphor of something in the world we know, but also as shadowy intimation of a greater reality outside Plato's cave. Through the lens of the imagination both storymaker and audience engage metaphysically with this other world. Of course, if we seek an entirely otherworldly hope, we may well neglect the moral imperatives of the material world. King Arthur's utopian kingdom falls apart when his knights depart to quest for the Holy Grail. It's not a case of either/or – but of both/and. The binary opposition of ideas must, paradoxically, be transcended: the 'actual' and the 'imagined', history and myth, flesh and word; to seek, against our biological instincts, a sustainable peace with nature, and at the same time to find via our imagination the consolation of hope (see pages 167–9).

Blessed are the men of Noah's race that build
their little arks, though frail and poorly filled,
and steer through winds contrary towards a wraith,
a rumour of a harbour guessed by faith.[54]

That's why we still need the great myths of death and return – of Persephone, Osiris, King Arthur, Jesus Christ – that enchant real landscapes and bespeak at the same time the death and return of nature's abundance, the death and return of ourselves. Whether the consolation they offer is 'merely' imagined or the glimmer of a greater reality, we shall not know for sure this side of paradise.

---

[1] Harvey, *The Killing of the Countryside*; Holden & Cleeves, *RSPB Handbook of British Birds*.

[2] Gibbons, *Greece*; Theodossopoulos, *Troubles with Turtles*.

[3] Theodossopoulos, *Troubles with Turtles*.

[4] Ibid.; White, 'The Historical Roots of Our Ecologic Crisis'.

[5] Abram, *The Spell of the Sensuous*.

[6] Schama, *Landscape and Memory*. See also Brody, *The Other Side of Eden*; Heinberg, *Memories and Visions of Paradise*.

[7] Turnbull, *The Forest People*.

[8] Lopez, *Arctic Dreams*, p. 201.

[9] Lee, *Cider with Rosie*, p. 125.

[10] White, 'Historical Roots of Our Ecologic Crisis', p. 10.

[11] Tolkien, 'On Fairy-Stories'.

[12] Anthony Nanson, 2009. Principal sources: Flannery, *The Weather Makers*; Halliday & Adler, *New Encyclopedia of Reptiles & Amphibians*.

[13] It's since come to light that a Tasmanian Aboriginal lineage has survived via a number of women who interbred with colonists.

[14] Lopez, *Of Wolves and Men*.

[15] Alexiou, *After Antiquity*; Harrison, *Forests*.

[16] Garnett, *Greek Wonder Tales*.

[17] Abram, *The Spell of the Sensuous*.

[18] Ward, 'What They Told Buchi Emecheta', p. 88, quoted in Alexiou, *After Antiquity*.

[19] Lupton, *The Dreaming of Place*, p. 22.

[20] An idea introduced to me by Eric Maddern.

[21] Dawkins, *Modern Greek Folktales*; Manning-Sanders, *Damian and the Dragon*.

[22] Kane, *The Wildwood King*; East and Maddern, *Spirit of the Forest*; Tongue, *Forgotten Folk-Tales of the English Counties*.

[23] Jones, *Welsh Legends and Folk-Tales*.

[24] McCaughrean, *100 World Myths & Legends*.

[25] I am indebted to Kirsty Hartsiotis for this observation.

[26] Day, *The World of Tolkien*.

[27] Tolkien, 'On Fairy-Stories' and 'Mythopoeia'.

[28] Abram, *The Spell of the Sensuous*; Chatwin, *The Songlines*; Cowan, *The Aborigine Tradition*.

[29] Anthony Nanson, 'Arthur's Birth and Morgan's Vow', in Fire Springs, *Arthur's Dream* (CD), Abaris Records, Bath, 2001.

[30] Olalla, *Mythological Atlas of Greece*.

[31] Soja, *Thirdspace*.

[32] Parker, 'Arkadian Landscapes'.

[33] Retelling by Anthony Nanson, 2000. Sources: Ovid, *The Metamorphoses*; Hughes, *Tales from Ovid*.

[34] Dotium is believed to have been located at either Ayia or Sykourio, both near Mount Ossa, Thessaly. Vassilis Argyroulis, personal communication, 2007.

[35] Dawkins, *Forty-Five Stories from the Dodekanese*.

[36] An innovation taken from David Metcalfe's telling of the story and independently suggested by some children I told the story to.

[37] Richard Mabey, in conversation with Richard Kerridge, Cheltenham Festival of Literature, Cheltenham, 10 October 2005.

[38] 'σπηλαιόφιλες, που χαίρεστε στα σπήλαια, αεροσύχναστες, / πηγαίες, γοργόδρομες, δροσοντυμένες, ελαφροπάτητες, / φανερές, αόρατες, φαραγγόβιες, πολυανθείς, / που χορεύετε μαζί με τον Πάνα στα όρη, βακχεύτριες'. 'Των Νυμφών', in Papaditsas & Ladia, *Ορφικοί Ύμνοι*. English translation by Kirsty Hartsiotis and Anthony Nanson, 2005.

[39] Larson, *Greek Nymphs*.

[40] Argyroulis, personal communication.

[41] Sebastian, 'The Elucidation'.

[42] Meenee, *Νεοπαγανισμός*.

[43] Lupton, *Dreaming of Place*, pp. 28–9.

[44] Callimachus, *Hymn to Demeter*.

[45] Lopez, *Of Wolves and Men*.

[46] Ben Haggarty, personal communication, 2007.

[47] The name 'Urswick' was taken, Kevan Manwaring recalls, from a wise-man character in the tale of Herne and applied to a British forest goddess correctly called Andraste.

[48] Goodchild, *Capitalism and Religion*.

[49] Revelation 21:1.

[50] Robinson with Neilson, 'Axes of Evil'. Some hardline Christian conservatives, Tracy Radosevic assures me, even welcome environmental meltdown as a sign of the Messiah's impending return.

[51] Alexiou, *After Antiquity*, pp. 165–6.
[52] Tolkien, 'On Fairy Stories'.
[53] Idem, 'Mythopoeia'.
[54] Ibid.

# The Big Picture and the Bigger Picture

Ecological processes take place on a great variety of scales, from the very small to the very large. This essay aims to contextualise sustainability-motivated storytelling within the 'big picture' of science and history – and the 'bigger picture' of metaphysics, which I argue is a crucial but disregarded element of our response to the global ecological crisis.

David Abram, in his book *The Spell of the Sensuous*, draws attention to the way the world is perceived by people in oral cultures (and probably by the earliest humans as they evolved into being): a world in which your consciousness is rooted in the here and now bounded by the ground beneath you, the sky above you, the horizon encircling you. Beyond these boundaries lies uncertainty; whatever is beyond the horizon and beneath the ground can be investigated up to the point you reach an impassable barrier; beyond such barriers and beyond the sky are realms about which you can only make metaphysical speculations.[1] Many ecological processes take place within the 'human scale' of this sensuously perceivable world and the duration of the human lifespan – processes involving animals and plants as well as people and their artefacts. Most of the stories we tell work on this scale. It is vital that we engage with this sensuous reality – and do not keep our minds forever abstracted in text, numbers, screen, phone – so that we be awake to the tangible condition of the environment in which we physically exist.

But ecological processes work on other scales, too, which are more difficult for humans to relate to. They take place on smaller yet visible scales – the epic experience of a snail crossing a garden – and on scales that are invisible without a microscope. Stories of diminutive fairies or charismatic grasshoppers can take us imaginatively into smaller-scale worlds, and science fiction can contrive access to the microscopic, as in *Fantastic Voyage* (1966), a film depicting the voyage of a miniaturised submersible through a sick man's bloodstream.

Ecological processes also take place on the bigger scales – in space and time – of ecological succession, climate change, evolution, erosion, plate tectonics, and astronomical cycles, involving oceans, continents, sometimes the entire globe, and timescales of thousands or millions of years. Such scales require a big leap of the imagination to comprehend. Hence the common device in popular science of contracting the scale to something we can easily understand, such as likening the 4.5-billion-year history of our planet to one calendar year, in which *Homo sapiens* doesn't evolve until twenty minutes before midnight on 31 December and Jesus Christ is born 24 seconds before midnight and dies less than half a second later.

For our ancestors this 'big picture' beyond the reach of our senses was the realm of myth and metaphysics. Science has now largely replaced mythological explanations of natural phenomena with its own stories, which are continually refined by observation and experiment. On this premise of a scientific understanding of the world, I composed the following story – necessarily concise – of humankind's relationship with the global ecosystem:

## THE STORY OF PEOPLE ON THE EARTH

In the beginning, they were hunters of game and gatherers of wild fruit. In those days half the world was covered with ice – and life was tough. Sometimes food was scarce and the weather was harsh. That's when the infants and the old ones would die. That's when the leopards and lions and wolves would come for them. So the people had to apply all their cunning and strength and teamwork to survive. Other times there was plenty and they'd time and energy to sing and dance and make beautiful things to adorn their bodies and their caves.

By and by, the ice withdrew and forests swept like a mantle across the land. The people feared the dark forests. They preferred the open country where there roamed vast herds of mammoth and mastodon, bison and buck. By foot, by boat, they followed the game from land to land. They liked to hunt the biggest kinds of animals. Sometimes they hunted too hard. They killed more than they could eat and the mammoths and mastodons vanished from the earth.

Then someone had the idea of sowing seed from wild grasses – so there'd always be plenty of grain to eat. Someone else had the idea of herding the goat, the sheep, the bull – so there'd always be plenty of meat and milk. With tools of stone, bronze, iron, they cut down swathes of forest to make space for their crops and their livestock. So much food they grew that more of their children could live to have children of their own; and so there came to be far more people than before. So much food they grew that not everyone needed to sweat in toil on the land. The strong men, the clever men, made others do the work for them. They used gold to pay minstrels to entertain them, and craftsmen to make them fine things, and warriors to enforce their will. The more land they possessed, the more gold and power. So they grew greedy for land and all its bounty. They fought their rivals to build cities, nations, empires.

Someone said, 'You should do to others as you'd have them do to you,' but no one really understood what he meant.

And always there were more people to feed than before. In some places the axe, the goat, the plough gnawed the land into a desert, the wind and rain drove away the soil, and the people began to starve. When that happened the warriors and kings would seek out new lands beyond the steppes and seas. But wherever they went, these days, there'd always be other people there before them. There'd always be fighting for the land and many people would die. Yet always before long there'd be more people than ever, killing the game, felling the trees, planting crops, building cities.

Then someone thought of a way to burn coal to drive a wagon along a track or drive a loom to weave cloth or make power to light up a city. And someone else found a way to burn oil to do all that, and yet more, to propel cars freely across the land and shoot aircraft through the sky. With such power, it seemed, they could do anything. They forced the land to produce more food than ever before. Their machines churned out huge quantities of clothes and pots and books and every kind of thing you could imagine. Yet still there was gold and greed. The strong men, the cunning men, always wanted more than they had. They made the people sweat ever harder in the factories and promised them paradise if they spent enough money shopping.

Now there were far more people than there'd ever been before and every year there were seventy-five million more than the year before. And every one of those people needed food, water, fuel, and a home. Every one of them wanted to fulfil their dreams – to fly through the sky and live like a king. They thought that science had conquered nature, that if they tried hard enough, used all their cunning and strength and teamwork, they could have whatever they wanted. But the wild game were gone, the forests were vanishing, the deserts were expanding, the climate was changing, the land was filled with people and there was nowhere left for the children to play.

'We need more land,' someone said. 'Let's make spacecraft and colonise other planets.'

So they built some space rockets, but the problem was they

couldn't carry many people and the planets turned out to be sterile and dead.

Someone else said, 'We can't carry on like this. We don't have enough land for more people.' But no one seemed to understand what she meant.

So the earth itself tried to make them understand. There were storms and floods – fiercer than before – and fires and drought and famine. There wasn't enough food for everyone. There wasn't enough water in the rivers. There wasn't enough oil to last much longer. So the nations sent their warriors to fight for what they needed. The finance markets began to crash under the strain. No one knew who to trust any more.

At last they began to say, 'What are we going to do? How can we stop the climate changing? What will we do when the oil is all gone? Will there be enough food for our children?'

So what happened then?

Well, maybe this is what happened … They said, 'Trust in science. Trust in the market and all will be as well as it can be.' So they blinkered their eyes and bailed out the banks and tried to carry on just the same as before. Because everyone wanted more gold. Everyone wanted more babies. Everyone wanted to do whatever they wanted. So they destroyed the last forests. They burnt all the oil and coal and uranium. They let the climate change and the sea rise over the beaches. They polluted the soil and sea with radioactive waste that would last for thousands of years. And they fought for what they wanted. For oil, for water, for land. Nation against nation. Tribe against tribe. Man against man. It was the strong and cunning who survived. It was the weak who died. There were terrible famines. By the millions they died. There were epidemics and no medicine left to fight them. Terrible it was to be old or an infant in those days.

So nature had her way, and the population fell to a fraction of what it had been: bands of people scavenging in the ruins, struggling day by day to survive, suspicious of every stranger. There was little time for poetry or pretty things. When the wild flowers pushed through the rubble in the spring, no one noticed how lovely they were.

Then again, maybe it wasn't *that* that happened, but this … They said science is all very well, and the market has its place; but we have to change – and, yes, we can! Because there was more knowledge than there'd been before. Where once people had acted blindly, now it was possible to see what was happening. There were some who saw that the way of war and gold was a dead end. They drew together in communities and networks and projects. They became a critical mass – the embryo of a society in which people helped each other instead of fighting and competing, in which people cared about the world around them. Leaders were elected who understood that the system had to change. They made a World Environment Organisation to control the strong men, the cunning men, who were greedy for gold; to make the nations cooperate in peace; to get people to have less children; to get people paid to do work that nurtured things instead of destroying them. There was a battle of words, of course, because people don't like change. Artists and thinkers and even priests and priestesses rose up to speak what needed to be said, to sway people's hearts to care what kind of world they were leaving for their children.

And so, without famine or plague or war, the population fell and the people became attuned to the earth. There weren't so many factories or machines. There weren't so many useless things to buy. People worked more with their hands and helped each other more. They had time for poetry and pretty things and in the spring they watched with delight as the woods and meadows and towns filled with wild flowers.[2]

Different kinds of stories impart different kinds of effect: to amuse, to thrill, to inspire, to educate, to reassure. 'The Story of People on the Earth' is conceived as a 'vatic' story, prophetic in the sense in bardic tradition that one duty of the bard was to speak boldly to the people, and even to the king, of things they might not wish to hear, about the past, present, and future. In the parts of this story which look to the future, both the gloomy and the hopeful scenarios, I've tried to suggest not just a vision of the how the world might be, but also some hint of the *process* of change leading to that future. More important than any vision you might pursue is the quality of relationships characterising the process of change (see page 136). To put it another way, the journey matters as much as the destination, and probably more so.

Process and journey are things that unfold in time. So they lend themselves to representation in story. It's easier to devise a story leading to dystopia than one leading to some improvement in the world. The second law of thermodynamics applies: things tend to become more disordered rather than more ordered; it's easier to smash a cup into pieces than to make one. It requires a lot of brainwork to come up not just with a vision of a better society but a viable process of getting there. Traditional tales do offer useful wisdom (see page 140), but there's a need also for contemporary stories that bring together creative imagination and a knowledge of politics, economics, and science to narrate visions of environmentalist progress (see pages 134–6). One of the few science fiction writers to have made a substantial contribution in this way – as opposed to either depicting a utopia as a fait accompli or narrating a collapse into dystopia – is Kim Stanley Robinson. On the basis of thorough research, his novels depict the rise, against the resistance of capitalism-as-usual, of a green-socialist society on Mars[3] and of a United States government genuinely committed to fighting climate change.[4]

If the journey is going to involve some restraint of our desires, and to unfold over a timescale longer than the human lifespan, then we're up against profound issues of human nature and it becomes clear that the process really does matter as much as any imagined destination. We need utopian conceptions of the process of change more than utopian visions of some distant point in the future. The sceptic will say it's naive even to try: human beings naturally pursue their own interests, one way or another, so the wisest course is to acknowledge this fact, leave us free to do so, and just try to make the best of things. This is the basis of right-wing politics: you take care of yourself and your own people – family, tribe, nation, race, species – using force where need be to defend your interests, and if other people – or creatures – go to the wall, that's tough, they should have made more effort. This attitude makes perfect sense in terms of biological competition but is callous towards the suffering of the losers (see pages 124–5).

That the Nazis' vision of a green utopia was premised on eliminating everyone else who was in the way should drive home the moral dictum that ends cannot justify means. Science fiction is already envisaging oppressive future societies that might result from draconian implementation of green policies.[5] It's one thing to ask people to live lightly on the earth for the sake of future generations, but it would be a puritanical – even Stalinesque – nightmare to expect us to forgo our own fullness of existence for the sake of a future we won't live to see. The aim should instead be to seek a pathway holding a synergy between living lightly on the earth and our own authentic well-being.

The timescale of the processes involved in the ecological crisis – overpopulation, climate change, chemical and radioactive pollution, and the destruction/regeneration of habitats, soil, and stocks of fish, timber, and game – is of the order of hundreds to thousands of years. If we accomplish a mass extinction of a large fraction of the earth's species, as biologists consider possible, we're talking millions of years for the biodiversity to recover.[6] From the perspective of the individual human life, millions of years might as well be eternity, and even a period of hundreds of years into the future takes us beyond that 'horizoned' world we're evolved to deal with. Our natural lifespan of seventy to eighty years is an adaptation to facilitate the transmission of learned knowledge to the third generation.[7] We're wired by evolution to care strongly for our children and grandchildren, to make sacrifices for them, even of our own life if need be; we may even do the same for people we care about who do not carry our genes. But future generations who won't even be born till after we've died don't have the same tangible reality as living people. Evolution has not equipped us to care about them. Moreover, the timescale of economic change and ecological recovery is such that, even if we start making the necessary changes today, the ecosystem may still look in worse shape when you or I die than it is today.

So to ask us to constrain the way we live for the sake of unborn generations, and for the sake of ecological recovery long after we're gone, is to ask a lot of our imagination and empathy. This is something to which environmentalist discourse gives little attention. A reason for that may be that most of this discourse, to be seen as respectable, must operate within the materialist paradigm of science, politics, and economics, whereas the demand that we modify the way we live for the sake of things that will ensue after we ourselves have died is fundamentally eschatological: it has to do with ultimate questions of death, destiny, and states of being beyond this present world. These remain the territory of religion and mythology – out of reach of the investigatory powers of science. They constitute the metaphysical 'bigger picture' which my 'Story of People on the Earth' does not address.

In Christian eschatology, after you die (if all goes well) you find yourself in a restored body inhabiting a restored earth, in which 'There will be no more death or mourning or crying or pain, for the old order of things has passed away.'[8] The secular environmentalist hope is of a future world in which ecological damage is repaired and our descendants live in sustainable harmony with nature. In some Pagan and Oriental belief systems you are reincarnated upon this same earth, which you might perhaps hope to find in improved condition since you were last here. From the existential perspective of a person alive today these scenarios are rather similar: all of them come about after you've died. The secular scenario makes the greatest demand on your selflessness: to make sacrifices for the sake of a post-mortal world in which you, as an individual soul, will no longer exist.

Eschatology is not the only quasi-religious feature of the environmentalist project. Our actions, hopes, dreams, sacrifices must also be premised upon faith in things that cannot be known with certainty. Environmental processes, like political ones, are enormously complex and thus very difficult to predict. Change one parameter in a computer model and everything could pan out differently. The full story of carbon-driven climate change, for example, is very difficult to understand. The one thing we can be sure of is that we won't be able to predict exactly what its effects will be. For most of us, the science has to be taken on faith, from the consensus of experts we trust do understand it, rather as religious beliefs are taken on faith from the pronouncements of priests or scripture. One reason we're failing to respond robustly to the challenge of anthropogenic climate change is that many people, even some scientists, don't believe there's enough evidence it's actually happening to justify the costly measures that would be taken if we were serious about stopping it. The same pattern of reasoning has justified permissive attitudes towards other kinds of environmental impact: a number of species of whales were doggedly hunted close to extinction on the basis there was no persuasive evidence that hunting was seriously threatening their population – until they were so rare that whaling was no longer worth the effort.[9]

Other aspects of the ecological crisis are more tangibly self-evident: habitat destruction, local elimination of wildlife, water shortage, soil erosion, famine, poverty, overcrowding, uglification, the density and speed of road traffic. But faith is also required to sustain hope that the necessary political cooperation will take place to ameliorate any of these problems. Some people I meet are deeply pessimistic that such cooperation is possible; they expect that the world can only get worse. In surrendering hope, they fall into the trap of thereby relinquishing any sense of responsibility to do anything about the problems. Having witnessed two world wars (including the Somme at first hand), Tolkien had pessimistic expectations of the future, and yet it was pivotal to his philosophy – expressed in his myth-making – that, however grim the prognosis, you must not lose hope and cave in to despair (see pages 154–5).[10] The concept of 'hope' here is no mere vague sense that with a bit of luck things won't be too bad, but a value of profound importance, a form of imagination – the ability to 'imagine otherwise'[11] – that's fundamental to the green agenda.

I have in mind both hope within the material world of our senses, and metaphysical hope that extends beyond this world and beyond the exacting parameter of our own death. I do not doubt that some people (the astronomer Carl Sagan, for example, when he was dying of cancer) possess the courage and humility to experience a sense of hope in spite of a sure belief in the inevitability of their own annihilation and, in the long term, that of humankind and the earth itself; but my own hunch is that to sustain hope more generally the acknowledgement of some *possibility* of a greater, metaphysical reality may be vital.

In consequence of the revolution of thought accomplished in the nineteenth century by Darwin, Marx, Freud, and Nietzsche, the twentieth century saw a powerful swing towards a materialist understanding of existence, in which metaphysical considerations are omitted a priori from respectable discourse. This materialist paradigm – the material is the only reality, the spiritual doesn't exist – is, paradoxically, itself a metaphysical proposition, and from future perspectives may prove not to be the end of the story. Could there be a connection between the dominance of materialist doctrine, in our thinking and public discourse, and the present crisis in the way we inhabit the earth?

Modernity's abandonment of baseless superstitions and unprovable dogmas no doubt is an advance in consciousness; but if we throw out the baby with the bath water and deny all metaphysical possibility and if our materialism manifests in a runaway consumption of material goods which is demolishing the ecosystem on which our lives depend, then maybe our consciousness needs to advance further. The ecological crisis and the eschatological questions it raises may be the trigger to revive the currency of metaphysics. Science fiction writer Stephen Baxter suggests that a future spirituality focused on the worship of unborn descendants, instead of the spirits of ancestors, would facilitate more sustainable use of the earth's resources.[12] Nice idea, though I'm not sure it fully answers the questions of motivation I raised above. I think we need other ingredients of spirituality too, involving not a return to the blinkered faith of outmoded religion, or a descent into the cloud cuckoo land of New Age superstition, but an elevation of the imagination as interface with the *possibility* of a metaphysical reality that cannot be known with certainty, that we perceive as through a glass darkly, and which even the (openminded) materialist can engage with in psychoanalytic terms.

Though displaced by science as explanations of natural phenomena, the myths retain their significance in moral and metaphysical territory where science has no competence. In this realm of the imagination, story is supreme. When I was writing *Storytelling and Ecology* my editor Mary Medlicott cautioned me not to make the mistake of thinking that storytelling could by itself save the world. In the big picture, storytelling is but one cultural pressure to set alongside the other arts and media as well as education, politics, economics, and science in working to sustain our ecosystem and civilisation. But when it comes to the 'bigger picture' of metaphysics, accessed via the imagination, story is just about all we have, now that, for many of us, the religions' doctrinal certainties have been swept away. How can we really know, for example, which incidents in the New Testament actually happened, or what words Jesus actually spoke? What we have is the *story* and a powerfully redemptive and transformative story it is. Stories like this one, and the death and resurrection of Osiris, and the underworld descents of Gilgamesh, Inanna, Core, Aphrodite, Dionysus, Heracles, Orpheus, Psyche, Odysseus, Aeneas, Hermod, and the Irish immrama to islands in the west, and the tales in many cultures of visits to otherworld, heaven, or paradise, of golden age or summer kingdom, of the sleeping giant or king waiting to return – these may not be literally true depictions of what awaits us beyond the veil of death, yet they've been a profound source of consolation to people over the millennia and still have the capacity to be so.

That word 'consolation' has acquired a weak connotation – the consolation prize that's little comfort to someone who's lost out on what really matters – so let me spell out that I use it in the more robust sense employed by Tolkien when discussing 'eucatastrophe', the joyous happy ending of a fairy tale:

> The consolation of fairy-stories ... does not deny the existence of ... sorrow and failure ... it denies (in the face of much evidence if you will) universal final defeat ... In such stories when the sudden 'turn' comes we get a piercing glimpse of joy, and heart's desire, that for a moment passes outside the frame, rends indeed the very web of story, and lets a gleam come through.[13]

The secular materialist may warn against the danger that escapist consolation may cause us to turn away from the challenges of the 'real world' and shirk our responsibility to address them. Marx's condemnation of religion as the opium of the masses might apply in our time to any kind of dreamy otherworldliness as the opium of those blind to the abrasive reality of ecology. Following a talk I gave about the Ecobardic Manifesto,[14] one questioner challenged the manifesto's premise – that we live in a time of ecological crisis – on the basis that everything that exists is but a manifestation of one's own consciousness and that in his particular consciousness this crisis doesn't exist and it's therefore needless for him to do anything about it or any other alleged problems in the world. 'The only thing I can do anything about is my own consciousness,' he said, 'and so all I have to do is take care of myself. There's no point me worrying about anything else.' Okay, we do have to take responsibility for ourselves, and to seek to transform ourselves; but this kind of spiritual philosophy, in absolving us of responsibility towards anything other than ourselves, is quite compatible with Thatcherite political economy in which everyone is encouraged to pursue their own interests and any notion of community is discarded. It's as escapist and irresponsible as the advertising industry's invitation to pursue an airbrushed dream of suburban family life, with all mod cons and holidays in the sun, sealed off from the grim lives of the losers in a competitive global economy.

But I would challenge the dualistic thinking that condemns *any* reaching for otherworldly consolation as a bad thing because it might undermine our motivation to address the 'real world's' problems. On one hand, we have a moral responsibility – to ourselves, to other people, to unborn generations, to other creatures on the earth, and perhaps to something bigger, to Gaia or God – to do what we can to ameliorate those problems; which for storytellers means using stories to educate, to warn, to evoke empathy and connectedness (see pages 143–52). On the other hand, we need consolation so that we may live our lives with joy and hope. That hope ought not be an empty hope, a confidence trick played upon the masses by those in the know, as the Bene Gesserit, an order of priestess-courtesans in Frank Herbert's novel *Dune*, consciously deploy the forms of religion to manipulate the currents of history. The possibility of metaphysical hope and meaning can be held in tandem with hard-nosed scientific and political engagement with our ecological problems, just as the faith of those who campaigned against the slave trade helped sustain them in that struggle. For storytellers this means using stories to bestow a quality of enchantment on people, places, actions, epiphanies, eliciting a sense of significance beyond the mundane in what we do and what we are; something that, I would hope, might encourage people to live lives that are creative rather than destructive, to make whatever contribution they feasibly can in their own small way, as Alida Gersie has advocated, instead of simply standing impotent or in denial before an ecological crisis of such overwhelming scale.[15]

It also means mediating those myths and wonder tales about the big issues of life, death, cosmos, exploiting the oral medium's particular strengths of presenting stories in a way that's received collectively, that activates the listener's imagination, that can make a connection with the physical setting.[16] These stories, especially those which follow Joseph Campbell's pattern of quest 'from the world of common day into a region of supernatural wonder' (see pages 13–14),[17] could be seen as metaphors, or symbolic catalysts, of the process we're inviting people to join: a journey whose destination lies beyond the horizon, the hope of a better world; a journey in which each of us imaginatively understands our own life as a thread of significance within something bigger than ourselves, and in which the consolation of metaphysical hope helps to manifest positive change in the material world.

If I may indulge a personal thought to finish, it is my own metaphysical hope that everything of goodness that we do or experience – whether it be thirty years' management of a nature reserve that subsequently gets bulldozed for a new motorway, or a lifetime's experience of learning how to love, or a split second's delight upon seeing the beauty of a snowdrop, or the telling of a story 'that lets a gleam come through' in a lonely man's heart – that all these things that seem ephemeral in the rushing stream of time may in some way that passes mortal understanding endure through all eternity.

[1] Abram, *The Spell of the Sensuous.*

[2] Anthony Nanson, 2008.

[3] Robinson, *Red Mars, Green Mars,* and *Blue Mars.*

[4] Robinson, *Forty Signs of Rain, Fifty Degrees Below, Sixty Days and Counting.*

[5] See Hubble, 'The Flowers of War'.

[6] See Wilson, *The Future of Life;* Leakey and Lewin, *The Sixth Extinction.*

[7] Diamond, *The Rise and Fall of the Third Chimpanzee.*

[8] Revelation 24:4.

[9] Mickleburgh, *Beyond the Frozen Sea.*

[10] Garth, *Tolkien and the Great War;* Shippey, *The Road to Middle-Earth.*

[11] Clarke, *Imagining Otherwise.*

[12] Baxter, 'Faces of God'.

[13] Tolkien, 'On Fairy Stories', pp. 68–9.

[14] Fire Springs, *An Ecobardic Manifesto.*

[15] Alida Gersie, keynote talk, Tales to Sustain, Bishops Wood Centre, Stourport-on-Severn, 21–2 April 2007.

[16] See Nanson, *Storytelling and Ecology.*

[17] Campbell, *The Hero with a Thousand Faces,* p. 30.

# Bibliography

Abram, David. *The Spell of the Sensuous*, Vintage Books, New York, 1997.

Agger, B. *Fast Capitalism: A Critical Theory of Significance*, University of Illinois Press, Urbana, 1989.

Alcock, Leslie, and Geoffrey Ashe. 'Cadbury: Is It Camelot?', in *The Quest for Arthur's Britain*, ed. Geoffrey Ashe, Granada, London, 1971.

Alexiou, Margaret. *After Antiquity: Greek Language, Myth, and Metaphor*, Cornell University Press, Ithaca, NY, 2002.

Ashe, Geoffrey. *Camelot and the Vision of Albion*, Book Club Associates, London, 1975.

Ashe, Geoffrey. *King Arthur: The Dream of a Golden Age*, Thames & Hudson, London, 1990.

Ashe, Geoffrey. *Land to the West: St. Brendan's Voyage to America*, Collins, London, 1962.

Ashe, Geoffrey. *Mythology of the British Isles*, Methuen, London, 1990.

Ashe, Geoffrey. 'Riothamus', in *The Arthurian Encyclopedia*, ed. Norris J. Lacy, Boydell Press, Woodbridge, 1988.

Attenborough, David. *State of the Planet* (DVD), BBC, London, 2004.

Baring-Gould, Sabine. *Curious Myths of the Middle Ages*, Rivingtons, London, 1869.

Bartosik-Vélez, Elise. 'The Three Rhetorical Strategies of Christopher Columbus', *Colonial Latin American Review*, Vol. 11, 2002, pp. 33–46.

Baxter, Stephen. 'Faces of God', *Matrix*, No. 171, 2005, pp. 10–11.

Beckwith, Martha. *Hawaiian Mythology*, University of Hawaii Press, Honolulu, 1976.

Begbie, Jeremy. 'Postmodernism and the Arts: A Christian Perspective', *Articulate*, No. 1, 1998, pp. 16–23.

Bowers, Maggie Ann. *Magic(al) Realism*, Routledge, Abingdon, 2004.

Boyd, Ann S. *The Devil with James Bond!*, John Knox Press, Richmond, VA, 1967.

Bradley, Marion. *Mists of Avalon*, Michael Joseph, London, 1983.

Bradshaw, Gillian. *Down the Long Wind*, Methuen, London, 1988.

Brody, Hugh. *The Other Side of Eden: Hunter-Gatherers, Farmers, and the Shaping of the World*, Faber & Faber, London, 2002.

Bunyan, John. *The Pilgrim's Progress: From This World to That Which Is to Come*, Oxford University Press, Oxford, 2003.

Caldecott, Stratford. *Secret Fire: The Spiritual Vision of J.R.R. Tolkien*, Darton, Longman & Todd, London, 2003.

Callimachus. *Hymn to Demeter*, ed. Neil Hopkinson, Cambridge University Press, Cambridge, 2004.

Campbell, Joseph. *The Hero with a Thousand Faces*, Princeton University Press, Princeton, 1968.

Carey, Jacqueline. *Kushiel's Dart*, Tor, London, 2003.

Carey, John. 'Ireland and the Antipodes: The Heterodoxy of Virgil of Salzburg', in *The Otherworld Voyage in Early Irish Literature: An Anthology of Criticism*, ed. Jonathan M. Wooding, Four Courts Press, Portland, 2000

Carroll, Lewis. *Alice's Adventures in Wonderland*, Penguin, Harmondsworth, 1946.

Carter, Angela. *The Infernal Desire Machines of Doctor Hoffman*, Penguin, London, 1972.

Chatwin, Bruce. *Songlines*, Jonathan Cape, London, 1987.

Clarke, Lindsay. 'Fiction and Mystery: The Journey from Ego to Soul', paper presented to Jung Society, Bristol, 17 April 1999.

Clarke, Lindsay. *Imagining Otherwise*, GreenSpirit Press, London, 2004.

Cohn-Sherbok, Dan, and Dawoud El-Alami, *The Palestine–Israeli Conflict: A Beginner's Guide*, Oneworld, Oxford, 2001.

Connor, Steven. *The English Novel in History 1950–1995*, Routledge, London, 1996.

Cooper, Susan. *The Dark Is Rising*, Chatto & Windus, London, 1973.

Cowan, James G. *The Aborigine Tradition*, Element, Shaftesbury, 1992.

Crossley-Holland, Kevin. *The Norse Myths*, André Deutsch, London, 1980.

Dawkins, R. M. *Forty-Five Stories from the Dodekanese*, Cambridge University Press, Cambridge, 1950.

Dawkins, R. M. *Modern Greek Folktales*, Oxford University Press, Oxford, 1953.

Day, David. *The Doomsday Book of Animals: A Unique Natural History of Three Hundred Vanished Species*, Ebury Press, London, 1981.

Day, David. *The World of Tolkien: Mythological Sources of* The Lord of the Rings, Mitchell Beazley, London, 2003.

De Vries, Jetse. *Shine: An Anthology of Near-Future Optimistic Science Fiction*, Solaris, Oxford, 2010.

Diamond, Jared. *The Rise and Fall of the Third Chimpanzee: How Our Animal Heritage Affects the Way We Live*, Vintage, London, 1992.

East, Helen, and Eric Maddern. *Spirit of the Forest: Tree Tales from Around the World*, Frances Lincoln, London, 2003.

Evans, Sebastian (trans.). 'The Elucidation', in *Sources of the Grail: An Anthology*, ed. John Matthews, Floris, Edinburgh, 1996.

Fire Springs. *An Ecobardic Manifesto: A Vision for the Arts in a Time of Environmental Crisis*, Awen, Bath, 2008.

Fisher, James, Noel Simon & Jack Vincent. *The Red Book: Wildlife in Danger*,

Collins, London, 1969.

Flannery, Tim. *The Weather Makers: The History and Future Impact of Climate Change*, Allen Lane, London, 2005.

Fleming, Ian. *Casino Royale*, Pan Books, London, 1955.

Fleming, Ian. 'Foreword', in Angus Wilson et al., *The Seven Deadly Sins*, William Morrow, New York, 1962.

Fleming, Ian. *On Her Majesty's Secret Service*, Pan Books, London,

Flint, Valerie J. *The Imaginative Landscape of Christopher Columbus*, Princeton University Press, Princeton, 1992.

Friar, Kimon. 'Introduction', in Nikos Kazantzakis, *The Odyssey: A Modern Sequel*, trans. Kimon Friar, Simon & Schuster, New York, 1985.

Frye, Northrop. *Anatomy of Criticism: Four Essays*, Princeton University Press, Princeton, 1957.

Fukuyama, Francis. *The End of History and the Last Man*, Avon, New York, 1993.

Gablik, Suzi. *The Reenchantment of Art*, Thames & Hudson, London, 1991.

Gantz. Jeffrey (trans.). *The Mabinogion*, Penguin, Harmondsworth, 1976.

Garner, Alan. *The Weirdstone of Brisingamen*, William Collins, London, 1960.

Garnett, Lucy. *Greek Wonder Tales*, A. & C. Black, London, 1913.

Garth, John. *Tolkien and the Great War: The Threshold of Middle-Earth*, HarperCollins, London, 2003.

Gibbons, Bob. *Greece: Travellers' Nature Guide*, Oxford University Press, Oxford, 2003.

Goodchild, Philip. *Capitalism and Religion: The Price of Piety*, Routledge, London, 2002

Graves, Robert. *The Golden Fleece*, Hutchinson, London, 1983.

Haggarty, Ben. *Seek out the Voice of the Critic*, Society for Storytelling, Reading, 1996.

Halliday, Tim, & Kraig Adler (eds). *The New Encyclopedia of Reptiles and Amphibians*, Oxford University Press, Oxford, 2004.

Harrison, Robert Pogue. *Forests: The Shadow of Civilization*, University of Chicago Press, 1992.

Harvey, Graham. *The Killing of the Countryside*, Vintage, London, 1998;

Heinberg, Richard. *Memories and Visions of Paradise: Exploring the Universal Myth of a Lost Golden Age*, Jeremy P. Tarcher, Los Angeles, 1989.

Hellig, Jocelyn. *The Holocaust and Antisemitism: A Short History*, Oneworld, Oxford, 2003.

Hemingway, Ernest. *Green Hills of Africa*, Charles Scribner's Sons, New York, 1935.

Henderson, Mary. *Star Wars: The Magic of Myth*, Bantam, New York, 1997.

Herbert, Frank. *Dune*, Victor Gollancz, London, 1966.

Heywood, Simon. *The New Storytelling: A History of the Storytelling Movement in England and Wales*, Society for Storytelling, Reading, 1998.

Holden, Peter, & Tim Cleeves. *RSPB Handbook of British Birds*, Christopher Helm, London, 2002.

Holdstock, Robert. *Mythago Wood*, Victor Gollancz, London, 1984.

Huxley, Aldous. *The Island*, Chatto & Windus, London, 1962.

Hubble, Nick. 'The Flowers of War', *Vector*, No. 258, 2008, pp. 23–8.

Hughes, Ted. 'Myth and Education', in *Winter Pollen: Occasional Prose*, ed. William Scammell, Faber & Faber, London, 1994.

Hughes, Ted. 'The Poetic Self: A Centenary Tribute to T. S. Eliot', in *Winter Pollen: Occasional Prose*, ed. William Scammell, Faber & Faber, London, 1994.

Hughes, Ted. *Shakespeare and the Goddess of Complete Being*, Faber & Faber, London, 1992.

Hughes, Ted. 'Shakespeare and Occult Neoplatonism', in *Winter Pollen: Occasional Prose*, ed. William Scammell, Faber & Faber, London, 1994

Hughes, Ted. *Tales from Ovid*, Faber & Faber, London, 1997.

Hyde, Lewis. *The Gift: How the Creative Spirit Transforms the World*, Canongate, Edinburgh, 2006.

James, Henry. *The Turn of the Screw*, Penguin, Harmondsworth, 1994.

Jefferson, George. *Edward Garnett: A Life in Literature*, Jonathan Cape, London, 1982.

Johnson, Donald S. *Phantom Islands of the Atlantic: The Legends of Seven Lands that Never Were*, Souvenir Press, London, 1997.

Johnson, Susan R. 'Strangers in Our Homes: TV and Our Children's Minds', paper presented at Waldorf School of San Francisco, 1 May 1999, < http://home.datacomm.ch/rezamusic/tv_johnson.html>.

Johnstone, Keith. *Impro: Improvisation and the Theatre*, Eyre Methuen, London, 1981.

Jones, Gwyn. *Welsh Legends and Folk-Tales*, Oxford University Press, London, 1955.

Kane, Philip. *The Wildwood King*, Capall Bann, Chieveley, 1997.

Larson, Jennifer. *Greek Nymphs: Myth, Cult, Lore*, Oxford University Press, New York, 2001.

Lawhead, Stephen. *Arthur*, Lion, Oxford, 1989.

Lawhead, Stephen. *Grail*, Lion, Oxford, 1998.

Lawhead, Stephen. *Merlin*, Lion, Oxford, 1988.

Lawhead, Stephen. *Pendragon*, Lion, Oxford, 1994.

Lawhead, Stephen. *Taliesin*, Lion, Oxford, 1987.

Leakey, Richard, and Roger Lewin. *The Sixth Extinction: Biodiversity and Its Survival*, Phoenix, London, 1993.

Lee, Laurie. *Cider with Rosie*, Hogarth Press, London, 1959.

Le Guin, Ursula. 'The Stalin in the Soul', in *The Language of the Night: Essays on Fantasy and Science Fiction*, ed. Susan Wood, Berkley, New York, 1982.

Le Guin, Ursula. 'Talking about Writing', in *The Language of the Night: Essays on Fantasy and Science Fiction*, ed. Susan Wood, Berkley, New York, 1982.

Le Guin, Ursula. *The Wizard of Earthsea*, Victor Gollancz, London, 1971.

Lewis, C. S. *An Experiment in Criticism*, Cambridge University Press, Cambridge, 1992.

Lewis, C. S. *The Lion, the Witch and the Wardrobe*, Macmillan, London, 1950.

Lewis, C. S. *The Pilgrim's Regress: An Allegorical Apology for Christianity, Reason and Romanticism*, J. M. Dent, London, 1933.

Lewis, C. S. *The Voyage of the Dawn Treader*, William Collins, London, 1980.

Lopez, Barry. 'Apologia', in *About This Life: Journeys on the Threshold of Memory*, Harvill Press, London, 1999

Lopez, Barry. *Arctic Dreams: Imagination and Desire in a Northern Landscape*, Harvill Press, London, 1999

Lopez, Barry. 'The Construction of the *Rachel*, in *Light Action in the Caribbean: Stories*, Vintage Books, New York, 2001.

Lopez, Barry. 'Light Action in the Caribbean', in *Light Action in the Caribbean: Stories*, Vintage Books, New York, 2001.

Lopez, Barry. *Of Wolves and Men*, Simon & Schuster, New York, 1978.

Lorimer, Rowland, and Eleanor O'Donnell, 'Globalization and Internationalization in Publishing', *Canadian Journal of Communication*, Vol. 17, No. 4, 1992, <http://hoshi/cic/sfu.ca/calj/cjc/BackIssues/17.4/lorimer/html>.

Lupton, Hugh. 'Betsy Whyte and the Dreaming', in *Tales, Tellers and Texts*, ed. Gabrielle Hodges, Mary Jane Drummond & Morag Styles, Cassell, London, 2000.

Lupton, Hugh. *The Dreaming of Place: Storytelling and Landscape*, Society for Storytelling, Reading, 2001.

Mac Cana, Proinsias. 'The Sinless Otherworld of *Immram Brain*', in *The Otherworld Voyage in Early Irish Literature: An Anthology of Criticism*, ed. Jonathan M. Wooding, Four Courts Press, Portland, 2000.

MacIver, Robert. *The Ramparts We Guard*, Macmillan, New York, 1950.

Maduro, Otto. 'Globalization and Christianity in the 21st Century', *Catholic Issues*, 1997, <http://www.adelphi.edu/~catissue/postmod.html>.

Malory, Sir Thomas. *Le Morte D'Arthur*, ed. Janet Cowen, 2 vols, Penguin, Harmondsworth, 1969.

Manning-Sanders, Ruth. *Damian and the Dragon: Folk and Fairy Tales from Greece*, Methuen, London, 1973.

Manwaring, Kevan. *The Bardic Handbook: The Complete Manual for the Twenty-First Century Bard*, Gothic Image, Glastonbury, 2006.

Manwaring, Kevan. 'Hill of the Seven Healing Winds: Peace Ceremony', *Storylines*, No. 41, 2007, p. 8.

Manwaring, Kevan. *Lost Islands: Inventing Avalon, Destroying Eden*, Heart of Albion Press, Loughborough, 2008.

Matthews, Caitlín. *Arthur and the Sovereignty of Britain: King and Goddess in the Mabinogion*, Penguin, London, 1989.

Matthews, Caitlín. 'The Circuits of the Soul in Celtic Tradition', in Caitlín & John

Matthews, *The Encyclopedia of Celtic Wisdom: A Celtic Shaman's Sourcebook*, Element, Shaftesbury, 1994.

Matthews, Caitlín. 'The Quest as Shaman Journey in Celtic Tradition', in Caitlín & John Matthews, *The Encyclopedia of Celtic Wisdom: A Celtic Shaman's Sourcebook*, Element, Shaftesbury, 1994.

Mayer, Eric. 'The Post-modern World: The Logic of Late Capitalism', 1997, <http://www.emayzine.com/lectures/postmod.html>.

Mbiti, John S. *African Religions and Mythology*, Heinemann, Oxford, 1989.

McCaughrean, Geraldine. *100 World Myths & Legends*, Orion, London, 2001.

Meenee, Harita. *Νεοπαγανισμοός: η αναγέννηση της αρχαίας θρησκείας*, Archetypo Press, Thessaloniki, 2000.

Mendlesohn, Farah. *Rhetorics of Fantasy*, Wesleyan University Press, Middletown, CT, 2008

Mickleburgh, Edwin. *Beyond the Frozen Sea*, Grafton, London, 1990.

Monmouth, Geoffrey of. *The History of the Kings of Britain*, trans. Lewis Thorpe, Penguin, London, 1966.

Moorcock, Michael. *Wizardry and Wild Romance*, Victor Gollancz, London, 1987.

Morris, William. *The Life and Death of Jason*, Ellis & White, London, 1882.

Murdock, Maureen. *The Heroine's Journey*, Shambhala, Boston, 1990.

Nabhan, Gary Paul. *Cultures of Habitat: On Nature, Culture and Story*, Counterpoint, Washington, 1998.

Nanson, Anthony. *Exotic Excursions*, Awen, Bath, 2008.

Nanson, Anthony. 'For Love of Tam Lin', *Facts and Fiction*, No. 32, 2000, pp. 10–12.

Nanson, Anthony. 'Not Quite Camelot', *Matrix*, No. 169, 2004.

Nanson, Anthony. 'Stories that I Like', *Artyfact*, No. 20, 2000, pp. 4–5.

Nanson, Anthony. *Storytelling and Ecology: Reconnecting Nature and People through Oral Narrative*, Society for Storytelling, Reading, 2005.

O'Connor, Peter. *Beyond the Mist: What Irish Mythology Can Teach Us about Ourselves*, Victor Gollancz, London, 2000.

Okri, Ben. 'Beyond Words', in *A Way of Being Free*, Phoenix, London, 1998.

Okri, Ben. *The Famished Road*, Jonathan Cape, London, 1991.

Olalla, Pedro. *Mythological Atlas of Greece*, Road Editions, Athens, 2002.

Olrik, Axel. 'Epic Laws of Folk Narrative', in *International Folkloristics: Classic Contributions by the Founders of Folklore*, ed. Alan Dundes, Rowman & Littlefield, Lanham, 1999.

O'Meara, J. J. 'In the Wake of the Saint: *The Brendan Voyage*, and Epic Crossing of the Atlantic by Leather Boat', in *The Otherworld Voyage in Early Irish Literature: An Anthology of Criticism*, ed. Jonathan M. Wooding, Four Courts Press, Portland, 2000

Ó Síocháin, P. A. *Ireland: A Journey into Lost Time*, Foilsiúcháin Eireann, Dublin, 1983.

Ovid. *The Metamorphoses*, trans. Mary M. Innes, Penguin, Harmondsworth, 1955.

Padel, O. J. *Arthur in Medieval Welsh Literature*, University of Wales Press, Cardiff, 2000.

Papaditsas, D. P., & H. Ladia (trans). *Ορφικοί Ύμνοι*, Hestia, Athens, 1997.

Parker, Catherine. 'Arkadian Landscapes', *Rosetta*, Vol. 1, 2006, pp. 10–21.

Paul, Gregory S. *Dinosaurs of the Air: The Evolution and Loss of Flight in Dinosaurs and Birds*, Johns Hopkins University Press, Baltimore, 2002.

Peters, Sarah. 'From 2 to 102, Storytelling Is for All Generations!', *Biblical Storyteller*, Vol. 18, No. 5, 2000, pp. 9–10.

Petty, Anne C. *One Ring to Bind Them All: Tolkien's Mythology*. University of Alabama Press, University, AL, 1979.

Pinchen, Heather. 'And Now the Good News', *Artyfact*, No. 10, 1998, p. 11.

Propp, Vladimir. *Morphology of the Folktale*, trans. Laurence Scott, University of Texas Press, Austin, 1968.

Pullman, Philip. *Northern Lights*, Scholastic, London, 1995

Quammen, David. *Monster of God: The Man-Eating Predator in the Jungles of History and the Mind*, W. W. Norton, New York, 2003.

Quatermass, Kat. 'In Praise of Accreditation', *Storylines*, No. 37, 2006, pp. 4–5.

Radcliffe, Ann. *The Mysteries of Udolpho*, Penguin, Harmondsworth, 2001.

Radway, Janice. *Reading the Romance: Women, Patriarchy and Popular Literature*, Verso, London, 1987, p. 29.

Reymers, Kurt. 'Growth and Fast Capitalism', in *Can Capitalism Be Caring?*, State University of New York at Buffalo, 1995.

Riddell, Mike. 'Art for Art's Sake', *Artyfact*, No. 7, 1998, pp. 4–5.

Roberts, Adam. *Science Fiction*, Routledge, London, 2000.

Robinson, Kim Stanley. *Blue Mars*, HarperCollins, London, 1996.

Robinson, Kim Stanley. *Fifty Degrees Below*, HarperCollins, London, 2005.

Robinson, Kim Stanley. *Forty Signs of Rain*, HarperCollins, London, 2004

Robinson, Kim Stanley. *Green Mars*, HarperCollins, London, 1993.

Robinson, Kim Stanley. *Red Mars*, HarperCollins, London, 1992.

Robinson, Kim Stanley. *Sixty Days and Counting*, HarperCollins, London, 2007.

Robinson, Kim Stanley, with Robert Neilson. 'Axes of Evil', *Albedo*, No. 25, 2002, 9–17.

Rushdie, Salman. 'Is Nothing Sacred?', *Granta*, No. 31, 1990, pp. 97–111.

Schama, Simon. *Landscape and Memory*, HarperCollins, London, 1995.

Seltman, Charles. *The Twelve Olympians: Gods and Goddesses of Greece*, Pan, London, 1952.

Shacklock, Geoffrey. 'Fast Capitalist Educational Change: Personally Resisting the Images of School Reform', *Discourse*, Vol. 19, No. 1, 1998, pp. 75–88.

Shippey, Tom. *J. R. R. Tolkien: Author of the Century*, HarperCollins, London, 2001.

Shippey, Tom. *The Road to Middle-Earth*, George Allen & Unwin, London, 1982.

Silverberg, Robert. *The Dodo, the Auk and the Oryx: Vanished and Vanishing Creatures*, Penguin, Harmondsworth, 1973.

Soja, E. W. *Thirdspace: Journeys to Los Angeles and Other Real-and-Imagined Places*, Blackwell, Oxford, 1996.

Soyinka, Wole. *Myth, Literature and the African World*, Cambridge University Press, Cambridge, 1978.

Stearns, Peter N. *Global Outrage: The Impact of World Opinion on Contemporary History*, Oneworld, Oxford, 2005.

Stewart, Annie E. 'Born of This Land', *Facts & Fiction*, No. 41, 2002, pp. 12–14.

Stewart, Mary. *The Crystal Cave*, Hodder & Stoughton, Sevenoaks, 1970.

Stewart, Mary. *The Hollow Hills*, Hodder & Stoughton, Sevenoaks, 1973.

Stewart, Mary. *The Last Enchantment*, Hodder & Stoughton, Sevenoaks, 1979.

Stewart, Mary, *The Wicked Day*, Hodder & Stoughton, Sevenoaks, 1983.

Sutcliffe, Rosemary. *Sword at Sunset*, Hodder & Stoughton, London, 1963.

Strauss, Susan. *The Passionate Fact: Storytelling in Natural History and Cultural Interpretation*, Fulcrum, Golden, CO, 1996.

Svoronou, Eleni. *Ο Τζιτζικο-Περικλής μεγάλος συνθέτης της Ελλάδας!*, Metaichmio, Athens, 2003.

Tessadri, Elena S. *Legends from the South Seas*, trans. Susan Cannata, Rylee, London, 1969.

Theodossopoulos, Dimitrios. *Troubles with Turtles: Cultural Understandings of the Environment on a Greek Island*, Berghahn Books, New York, 2005.

Todorov, Tzvetan. *The Fantastic: A Structural Approach to a Literary Genre*, trans. Richard Howard, Cornell University Press, Ithaca, NY, 1975.

Toelken, Barre. 'The Icebergs of Folktale: Misconception, Misuse, Abuse', in *Who Says? Essays on Pivotal Issues in Contemporary Storytelling*, ed. Carol L. Birch & Melissa A. Heckler.

Tolkien, J. R. R. *The Fellowship of the Ring*, George Allen & Unwin, London, 1979.

Tolkien, J. R. R. 'Imram', in *Sauron Defeated*, ed. Christopher Tolkien, HarperCollins, London, 2002, pp. 296–9.

Tolkien, J. R. R. 'Leaf by Niggle', in *Tree and Leaf*, HarperCollins, London, 1988.

Tolkien, J. R. R. 'Mythopoeia', in *Tree and Leaf*, HarperCollins, London, 1988.

Tolkien, J. R. R. 'On Fairy Stories', in *Tree and Leaf*, HarperCollins, London, 1988.

Tolkien, J. R. R. *The Silmarillion*, George Allen & Unwin, London, 1977.

Tongue, Ruth. *Forgotten Folk-Tales of the English Counties*, Routledge & Kegan Paul, 1970.

Troyes, Chrétien de. 'Perceval', in *Arthurian Romances*, trans. D. D. R. Owen, Dent, London, 1987.

Turnbull, Colin. *The Forest People*, Pan, London, 1976.

Van de Weyer, Robert. *Celtic Fire: An Anthology of Celtic Christian Literature*, Darton, Longman & Todd, London, 1990.

Walker, Roy. *The Golden Feast: A Perennial Theme in Poetry*, Rockliff, London, 1952.

Ward, Cynthia. 'What They Told Buchi Emecheta: Oral Subjectivity and the Joys of "Otherhood"', *Proceedings of the Modern Language Association*, Vol. 105, No. 1, pp. 83–97.

Webb, J. F. (trans.). 'The Voyage of St Brendan', in *The Age of Bede*, ed. D. H. Farmer, Penguin, London, 1983.

Weston, Jessie L. *From Ritual to Romance*, Princeton University Press, Princeton, 1993.

White, Jr, Lynn. 'The Historical Roots of Our Ecologic Crisis', in *The Ecocriticism Reader: Landmarks in Literary Ecology*, ed. Cheryll Glotfelty & Harold Fromm, University of Georgia Press, Athens, GA, 1996.

Whitehead, J. G. O. 'Arwîrac of Glastonbury', *Folklore*, Vol. 73, 1962, pp. 149–59.

Williams, Charles. *War in Heaven*, Faber & Faber, London, 1947.

Wilson, Edward O. *The Future of Life*, Abacus, London, 2003.

Wooding, Jonathan M. 'Monastic Voyaging and the *Navigatio*', in *The Otherworld Voyage in Early Irish Literature: An Anthology of Criticism*, ed. Jonathan M. Wooding, Four Courts Press, Portland, 2000.

Yates, Frances A. *The Art of Memory*, Penguin, Harmondsworth, 1969.

Zipes, *Revisiting the Storyteller: Revising the Past to Move Forwards*, Society for Storytelling, Reading, 1996.

Zipes, Jack. 'Storytelling as a Spectacle in the Globalised World', in *Relentless Progress: The Reconfiguration of Children's Literature, Fairy Tales, and Storytelling*, Routledge, New York, 2009.

# Acknowledgements

The author wishes to thank the editors of the periodicals in which some of these essays were first published and the organisers of the events in which others were first presented. Texts have been revised for this volume.

'Mythscapes of Arcadia' was first published in *Storylines*, No. 32, 2005.

'Mythic Patterns in Popular Entertainment' was first published under the title 'Hobbits, Skywalker and James Bond: Mythic Power in Popular Entertainment' in *Articulate*, No. 1, 1998.

'The Metaphysics of Imaginary Worlds' was presented in various forms in a module on Writing Fantasy and Science Fiction which I taught at Bath Spa University from 2001 to 2009.

'Lost Islands: Myth and Reality' was presented at the launch of Kevan Manwaring's book *Lost Islands*, Chapel Arts Centre, Bath, 18 May 2008.

'Wonder Voyages' was presented at the Exotic Excursions workshop, Othona Community, Burton Bradstock, 24–7 September 2009.

'The Myth of King Arthur: A Creative Tradition' was presented at the King Arthur at Candlemas workshop, Othona Community, Burton Bradstock, 1–4 February 2008.

'The Promise and Pitfalls of Christian Agenda in Stephen Lawhead's Pendragon Cycle' is to be published in *Vector*, No. 266, 2011.

'Telling Merlin' was first published in *Storylines*, No. 16, 2001.

A version of 'Writing It and Telling It' was written for Bath Spa University's *Creative Writing Centre Newsletter* but never published because the newsletter ceased publication.

The reviews of *The Iliad* and *On Common Ground* were first published in, respectively, *Facts & Fiction*, No. 38, 2001, and *Storylines*, No. 39, 2007.

'The Meeting of Sacred and Secular' was first published in *Biblical Storyteller*, Vol. 19, No. 2, 2001.

'The Telling Place at Greenbelt' was first published in *Facts & Fiction*, No. 37, 2001.

The review of *Mark* was first published in *Storylines*, No. 25, 2003.

'The Benefits of Amateur Storytelling' was first published in *Storylines*, No. 50, 2010.

'What Does "Accreditation" Mean?' was first published in *Storylines*, No. 38, 2007.

'Telling Other Peoples' Stories' was first published in *Storylines*, No. 40, 2007.

'The Storytelling Imagination as Catalyst of Tolerance and Transformation' was presented at the 4th Olympus Storytelling Festival, Tempe, 3–4 July 2009.

'Tales to Sustain' was first published in *Storylines*, No. 33, 2005.

'What Do You Mean, "Ecobardic"?' was first presented at the Ecobardic Mini-Fest, Cae Mabon, Llanberis, 30 April to 3 May 2009.

'Age of Enchantment' was first published in *Resurgence*, No. 258, 2010.

'Mapping the Ecobardic Territory' was first published in *Storylines*, No. 51, 2010.

'Faith, Freedom, and the Fast-Capitalist Commodification of Story' was first published (in bowdlerised form) under the title 'A Free Vision and the Shadow of Fast Capitalism' in *Articulate*, No. 3, 2000.

'Telling Stories from the Big Picture of Ecological History' was presented at Tales to Sustain, Bishops Wood Centre, Stourport-on-Severn, 21–2 April 2007.

'Two Sides to a Story: Storytelling as a Tool of the Imagination in Conflicts over Environmental Resources' was presented at a workshop hosted by A Bit Crack, Rising Sun Country Park, Newcastle, 8 March 2008.

'How Can Storytelling Re-enchant the Natural World in an Electronic Age?' was presented as the keynote lecture at the Storytelling and Environmental Education conference, Environmental Education Centre of Eastern Olympus, Palios Panteleimonas, 11–12 May 2007, and published in *Αφήγηση και περιβαλλοντικη εκπαιδευση: Κείμενα από την ομότιτλη διημερίδα που πραγματοποιήθηκε στο Κ.Π.Ε. Ανατολικού Ολύμπου στις 12 &13 Μαίου 2007*, ed. Tasoula Tsilimeni and Nikolaos Graikos, Environmental Education Centre of Eastern Olympus, Palios Panteleimonas, 2007

'The Big Picture and the Bigger Picture' was presented in preliminary form at Tales to Sustain, Cae Mabon, Llanberis, 9–12 October 2008.


Many thanks, for help of diverse kinds, to: Simon Airey, Vassilis Argyroulis, Tina Bilbé, Chris Bostock, Pete Castle, Jon Cree, Amy Douglas, Hamish Fyfe, Alida Gersie, Nikos Graikos, Dudley Green, Malcolm Green, Philip Gross, Ben Haggarty, Tony Jacques, Satish Kumar, Dan Keding, Angela Knowles, Vivis Ksagara, Hugh Lupton, Mary Medlicott, David Metcalfe, Martin Palmer, Simon and Cynthia Nanson, Jo Oland, Jay Ramsay, Eleni Samara, Viky Sarivasili, Glenn Smith, Chris Sunderland, Marika Trekli, Tasoula Tsilimeni, Stella Wiseman, Shana Worthen, Jack Zipes, and especially to Kirsty Hartsiotis, Eric Maddern, Kevan Manwaring, and Tracy Radosevic.


The author and publisher are most grateful to the late Mary Palmer, whose generosity facilitated the publication of this book.

# Index

www.awenpublications.co.uk

*Also available from Awen Publications:*

# An Ecobardic Manifesto
## Fire Springs

What is the raison d'être of the arts in an age of global ecological crisis? In this auda-cious document, Fire Springs present a new vision for the arts, one that holds together commitment to artistic integrity and craftsmanship with responsiveness to the peculiar challenges of our time. Foremost among those challenges are the strained relationship between human beings and the ecosystem we inhabit and the vital need to sustain em-pathy for that which is other than ourselves. Fundamental to the arts' task in such an age is a willingness to embrace contradiction, not least the deepening polarisation be-tween scientific and economic materialism and metaphysical sources of meaning and hope. This pamphlet is a clarion call to everyone working in the arts today who wants their efforts to make a difference.

Art Theory/Literary Criticism ISBN 978-1-906900-07-6 £2.50

# Exotic Excursions
## Anthony Nanson

In these stories Anthony Nanson charts the territory between travel writing and magic realism to confront the exotic and the enigmatic. Here are epiphanies of solitude, twi-light and initiation. A lover's true self unveiled by a mountain mist … a memory of the lost land in the western sea … a traveller's surrender to the allure of ancient gods … a quest for primeval beings on the edge of extinction. In transcending the line between the written and the spoken word, between the familiar and the unfamiliar, between the actual and the imagined, these tales send sparks across the gap of desire.

'He is a masterful storyteller and his prose is delightful to read … His sheer technical ability makes my bones rattle with joy.' *Mimi Thebo*

Fiction/Travel ISBN 987-0-9546137-8-5 £7.99

# Soul of the Earth: the Awen anthology of eco-spiritual poetry
## edited by Jay Ramsay

Beautifully crafted, yet challenging received wisdom and pushing boundaries, these are cutting-edge poems from a new generation of writers who share a love of the Earth and haven't given up on humans either. In poems as light as a butterfly and as wild as a storm you'll find vivid, contemporary voices that dare to explore a spiritual dimension to life on Earth and, in doing so, imply that a way out of our global crisis of ecological catastrophe, financial meltdown, and bankruptcy of the spirit is to look beyond the impasse of materialism. With contributions from poets in the USA, Canada, UK, Australia and New Zealand, this anthology reaches out across the planet to embrace the challenges and blessings of being alive on the Earth in the twenty-first century.

'All real poetry seeks to "renew the face of the earth" – and so to resist the exploiting, banalization or defacing of what lies around us. I hope this collection will serve the renewal of vision we so badly need.' *Most Revd Dr Rowan Williams*

Poetry ISBN 978-1-906900-17-5 £11.99

# The Angel in the Forest
## Niamh Clune

In the lush forest of Vancouver Island, Dr Niamh Clune has an encounter with an angelic vision that will change her life – a timely warning to a world on the brink of ecocide. Based upon her research into psychology and spirituality, this is a lucid and topical overview of the soul-wound of the world and how it can be healed.

Psychology/Spirituality ISBN 978-1906900113 £9.99

# The Fifth Quarter
## Richard Selby

The Fifth Quarter is Romney Marsh, as defined by the Revd Richard Harris Barham in *The Ingoldsby Legends*: 'The World, according to the best geographers, is divided into Europe, Asia, Africa, America and Romney Marsh.' It is a place apart, almost another world, and this collection of stories and poems explores its ancient and modern landscapes, wonders at its past, reflects upon its present. Richard Selby has known Romney Marsh all his life. His writing reflects the uniqueness of The Marsh through prose, poetry, and written versions of stories he performs as a storyteller.

Fiction/Poetry ISBN 978-0-9546137-9-2 £7.99 Spirit of Place Volume 2

# Tidal Shift: selected poems
## Mary Palmer

Knowing her end was near, Mary Palmer worked on her poems – compiling her very best and writing new ones with a feverish intensity. This is the result, published here with her full cooperation and consent. These are poems from the extreme edge and very centre of life – words of light that defy death's shadow with a startling intensity, clarity and honesty. Containing poems from across Mary's career, selected by Jay Ramsay, *Tidal Shift* is an impressive legacy from a poet of soul and insight.

'She has the courage to confront struggles and sickness, the world's and her own. Unpious but radically spiritual, she stays faithfully questioning right to the end.' *Philip Gross*

Poetry  ISBN 978-1-906900-09-0  £9.99  Profits to Dorothy House Hospice

# Iona
## Mary Palmer

What do you do when you are torn apart by your 'selves'? The pilgrim poet, rebel Mordec and tweedy Aelia set sail for Iona – a thin place, an island on the edge. It's a journey between worlds, back to the roots of their culture. On the Height of Storm they relive a Viking massacre, at Port of the Coracle encounter vipers. They meet Morrighan, a bloodthirsty goddess, and Abbot Dominic with his concubine nuns. There are omens, chants, curses … During her stay Mordec learns that words can heal or destroy, and the poet writes her way out of darkness. A powerful story, celebrating a journey to wholeness, from an accomplished poet.

'Always truthful, this poetry confronts both beauty and ugliness and makes space for light to slip between the two.' *Rose Flint*

Poetry  ISBN 978-0-9546137-8-5  £6.99  Spirit of Place Volume 1

# Thirteen Treasures
## Kevan Manwaring

Thirteen years, thirteen poems, thirteen treasures … This latest collection of poetry from the Winner of the Bardic Chair of Caer Badon, and author of *The Bardic Handbook* and *Lost Islands*, features poems about personal soul-places: Bath, Northampton, Bardsey Island, Isle of Man, Isle of Purbeck, Cardigan Bay, Gower, the Malvern Hills, and Venice.

Poetry  ISBN 978-1-906900-03-8  £4.99  Spirit of Place Volume 3

# The Firekeeper's Daughter
## Karola Renard

The tales in this collection reclaim myth as a way of relating to the Now, to our individual and collective story, that is often lost to the conscious mind. From the vastness of Stone Age Siberia to a minefield in today's Angola, from the black beaches of Iceland to the African savannah and a Jewish-German cemetery, Karola Renard tells thirteen mythic stories of initiation, featuring twenty-first-century kelpies, sirens, and holy fools, a river of tears and a girl who dances on fire, a maiden shaman of ice, a witch in a secret garden, Queen Guinevere's magic mirror, and a woman who swallows the moon. The red thread running through them all is a deep faith in life and the need to find truth and meaning even in the greatest of ordeals.

Fiction  ISBN 978-1-906900-18-2  £9.99

# The Immanent Moment: poems for now
## Kevan Manwaring

The sound of snow falling on a Somerset hillside, the evanescence of a waterspout on a remote Scottish island, the invisible view from a Welsh mountain, the light on the Grand Canal in Venice, chasing the sunset on a motor-bike … *The Immanent Moment* looks at the little epiphanies of life, moments of lucid awareness and personal revelation. Each poem captures these fleeting pulses of consciousness in sinuous, euphonic language. A meditation on time, mortality, transience, and place, this collection celebrates the beauty of both the natural and the man-made, the familiar and the exotic, and the interstices and intimacy of love. With humour and humanity, these poems encourage one to be fully alive in the miracle of each waking moment.

Poetry  ISBN 978-1-906900-13-7  £9.99

# The Winged Unicorn
## Marko Gallaidhe

This collection brings together Marko Gallaidhe's articles from *The Green Book*, Bath's legendary arts journal published throughout the 1970s: the mysteries of Gawain and the Green Knight, Mary Magdalene, St John the Baptist, the Sidhe, the Holy Grail … all are explored in original ways by this peer of R.J. Stewart and Caitlín Matthews. Also included: a fairy story, the long-lost song-cycle 'The Birth of Merlin', illustrations by the author (a trained artist and stone-sculptor) and a full profile of this extraordinary man.

Folklore/Mythology  ISBN 978-1-906900-02-1  £6.99

# Places of Truth: journeys into sacred wilderness
## Jay Ramsay

Poet and psychotherapist Jay Ramsay has been drawn to wild places all his writing life, in search of a particular deep listening experience. Here he shares his soundings. 'Trwyn Meditations', a sequence set in Snowdonia, begins this twenty-three-year odyssey. 'By the Shores of Loch Awe' takes us to the fecund wilds of Scotland. 'The Oak' celebrates an ancient tree in the heart of the Cotswolds. 'The Sacred Way' is an evocation of Pilgrim Britain. 'Culbone' records the hidden history of the smallest parish church in England in a steep North Somerset valley near where Coleridge wrote 'Kubla Khan'. The final poem, 'The Mountain', takes us beyond, in all senses, touching the places where we find I and Self. A timely and timeless reflection about our place on the planet.

'Ramsay speaks of the sacred and enduring in a world lost in the secular and transient … and of the currents of joy that offer a constantly renewed faith in the power of love as an agent of change.' *Roselle Angwin*

Poetry ISBN 978-1-906900-08-3 £9.95 Spirit of Place Volume 4

# Dancing with Dark Goddesses: movements in poetry
## Irina Kuzminsky

The dance is life – life is the dance – in all its manifestations, in all its sorrow and joy, cruelty and beauty. And the faces of the Dark Goddesses are many – some are dark with veiling and unknowing, some are dark with sorrow, some are dark with mystery and a light so great that it paradoxically shades them from sight. The poems in this collection are an encounter with many of these faces, in words marked with feminine energy and a belief in the transformative power of the poetic word. Both spiritual and sexual, earthy and refined, a woman's voice speaks to women and to the feminine in women and men, often with the rawness of pain and betrayal, but also with a resurgent strength, or with the calm consciousness of simply being. The book charts a journey from the abysses of pain and separation from the divine, of sorrow, of centuries of suppression and the memories of it, but then reaches back to transcendence and love. The shock of pain is counterpoised by the joy of living and by the pure and ultimately triumphant dance of life. The poems speak of an openness to life, a surrender to the workings of love, and a trust in the Dark Goddesses and their ways of leading us through the dance.

Poetry/Dance ISBN 978-1906900120 £9.99

# The Signature of Kisses
## Simon Miles

Simon's poetry explores the distant intimacies of lovers, the negative spaces of our lives, and life's divine comedy, as he searches for his Muse through the layers of his own Hades and Elysium. In 'Close Encounters of the Furry Kind' he plays the clownish ringmaster. There are moments of stunning lucidity and Blakean memorability in lines such as 'Every past of pain lends my songs more living flame.' Often the poetry is Hughesean in its depiction of primal sexuality and painful passion. There are touches of Ginsberg in 'The Clues Are All There' and a touch of Dylan Thomas's boozy bawdiness in 'Folk-club'. And in the 'The Earth Is Four Theatres' he accomplishes a daring tight-rope walk – an eco-paean for our time.

Poetry  ISBN 978-1-906900-05-2  £6.99

# The Long Woman
## Kevan Manwaring

An antiquarian's widow discovers her husband's lost journals and sets out on a journey of remembrance across 1920s England and France, retracing his steps in search of healing and independence. Along alignments of place and memory she meets mystic Dion Fortune, ley-line pioneer Alfred Watkins and a Sir Arthur Conan Doyle obsessed with the Cottingley Fairies. From Glastonbury to Carnac, she visits the ancient sites that obsessed her husband and, tested by both earthly and unearthly forces, she discovers a power within herself. *The Long Woman* is an exploration of the sacred landscapes of the past and the secret landscapes of the soul.

'A love letter to the English landscape.' *Bath Chronicle*

Fiction  ISBN 978-0-9546137-5-4  £6.99  The Windsmith Elegy Volume I

# Windsmith
## Kevan Manwaring

A man of peace in a time of war, Isambard Kerne must choose between the power of words or swords. The fate of both Earth and its Shadow hangs in the balance. Will he be able to master the Way of the Windsmith in time to save the valley of his ancestors? Or will the terror of war change Kerne into what he fears the most?

Fantasy  ISBN  978-0-9546137-6-1  £9.99  The Windsmith Elegy Volume II

# The Well under the Sea
## Kevan Manwaring

Imagine an island at the crossroads of time where lost souls find each other ... Isambard Kerne, Edwardian antiquarian, missing in action at the Battle of Mons, finds himself in the Afterlands of his Celtic ancestors and has begun the Way of the Windsmith, the path he must take to come home from the world of the dead. Having learnt the secrets of the East Wind, he must sail to beyond the West Wind, to the fabled Island of the Blessed, Ashalantë, where the visions of Plato, Da Vinci, and Brunel have come to life. Here he meets the legendary aviatrix Amelia Earhart, who is assigned to instruct him in the art of flying, but they find themselves falling in forbidden love. Torn between duty and desire, the two become embroiled in a tragic chain of events that threatens to bring about the destruction of not only this otherworldly paradise, but its shadow: Earth.

Fiction ISBN: 978-1-906900-10-6 £9.99 The Windsmith Elegy Volume III

# The Burning Path
## Kevan Manwaring

Three strangers meet in a nameless desert and must come to terms with their past before they can escape it: a First World War airman; an American aviatrix of the thirties; and a French poet of the skies from the Second World War. They are the lost of history and must go into the desert to find themselves. To find peace they must walk the burning path. Each is forced to confront the question: 'What are you prepared to sacrifice for the one you love?'

Fiction £9.95 ISBN 978-1-906900-19-9 The Windsmith Elegy Volume IV

# Writing the Land: an anthology of natural words
## edited by Kevan Manwaring

In these pages, lovers of nature will find poems and prose about wildlife, trees, water, earth, light, places, travel, memory and time. Contributions range from the funny to the profound, the down-to-earth to the spiritual. Informative, but never preachy, these words are to be enjoyed. Dip into this anthology for relaxation, companionship and inspiration.

Environment/Poetry ISBN 0-9546137-0-8 £5.00 Profits to Friends of the Earth